Education in Computer Generated Environments

This book examines the implications of computer-generated learning for curriculum design, epistemology, and pedagogy, exploring the ways these technologies transform the relationship between knowledge and learning, and between teachers and students. It argues that these technologies and practices have the potential to refocus on the human factors that are at the center of the learning process.

Sara de Freitas is Director of Research and Professor of Virtual Environments at Coventry University. Sara was responsible for setting up the Serious Games Institute, a hybrid model of research, business and study, the first institute of its kind. She publishes widely in the areas of game-based learning, e-learning and education policy.

Routledge Research in Education

For a full list of titles in this series, please visit www.routledge.com.

Education in Computer Generated Environments

Sara de Freitas

Routledge
Taylor & Francis Group
NEW YORK   LONDON

First published 2014
by Routledge
711 Third Avenue, New York, NY 10017

Simultaneously published in the UK
by Routledge
2 Park Square, Milton Park, Abingdon, Oxon OX14 4RN

*Routledge is an imprint of the Taylor & Francis Group,
an informa business*

Library of Congress Cataloging-in-Publication Data
Freitas, Sara de.
  Education in computer generated environments / Sara de Freitas. —
First edition.
      pages cm. — (Routledge research in education ; 104)
   Includes bibliographical references and index.
  1. Computer-assisted instruction.   2. Curriculum planning—Data
processing.   I. Title.
   LB1028.5.F754 2013
   371.33'4—dc23
   2013015126

ISBN13: 978-0-415-63402-1 (hbk)
ISBN13: 978-0-203-09470-9 (ebk)

Typeset in Sabon
by IBT Global.

SUSTAINABLE FORESTRY INITIATIVE   Certified Sourcing   www.sfiprogram.org   SFI-01234
SFI label applies to the text stock

Printed and bound in the United States of America
by IBT Global.

For Guy

Contents

Figures

Tables

Boxes

Foreword

We are witnessing a genuine revolution in education. Some of us are already immersed in it. Some of us are standing nervously on the poolside unsure whether or how to plunge in. Others are denying that any such revolution is anything other than make-believe. The last group in earlier centuries would have been members of the Flat Earth Society.

What is the revolution? The evolution of computers over the last seventy years to the position today where they now offer computer generated environments in learning and forms of communication with almost anyone in the world instantaneously. In the vanguard of this revolution are the young people themselves, including those of school age, who are deriving intense levels of intellectual stimulation (verified by brain research) from playing games on computers with others or on their own, which exceed in levels of enjoyment, stimulus and depth of learning anything that they encounter in the traditional classroom, which they tolerate more or less passively as their daily lot at school.

A long way behind them are the teachers, the parents and educationalists. They understand something of the revolution, and many are excited about it. But very few of them really 'get it'. They will be carried forward, more or less willingly, by the young people in the vanguard. They may even get to enjoy the revolution, and to improve their own learning immeasurably. At the back are the politicians, the civil servants, the union leaders and the university professors. They are the people, above all the politicians, who are determining the shape and purpose of the school system. Yet, as Sara de Freitas points out in this book, there is a danger 'where the political need of the education system to demonstrate its success by its own measures, outweighs or ignores the needs of the learner for a rich, unlimited and enjoyable learning experience'.

The world over, governments are using computer technology, not to liberate schools but to enslave them. They do so in a ferocious drive to improve exam performance, the like of which has never been seen before in the history of the world. They say they are motivated by a concern to improve educational attainment, above all for the least advantaged, and many are sincere in that wish. But they are equally motivated by their own needs to boast of year-on-year improvement in exam performance, and improvement in world league tables against competitor nations. The needs of the teacher, still more the student, can be squeezed out, depersonalised in a mechanised national factory education system. de Freitas points out that evidence of things going awry are when 'a nation's official school grades [are] steadily improving across the board (that is a government's mission is accomplished) but universities and employers—when testing individuals independently from the state system—[are] noting a decline in or deficit of key skills'. Ever more precise curriculum specifications, and ever more rigorous inspection regimes, might work for the politicians and administrators. They might work less well for the school, the teacher and the student.

Digital technology is transforming higher education in the second decade of the 21st century. The four core activities that universities exist to provide can all be done better or as well with the new technology. Why would any student want to go to a lecture at their university which is a passive experience when they could listen to the world authority on the same subject give a lecture on their own screen, freezing the frame to take notes or cross reference? Why would any student go to a university library when the books and articles are available on their own screen, and they can use multiple references far more readily? Why go to seminars when MOOCs (Massive Open Online Courses) provided by Coursera and others can connect them with fellow students across the world? Why even sit tests and exams in universities, the final 'hard' attribute of higher education, when computers provide far more personalised and valuable learn-and-test opportunities to learn deeply where they are going wrong and how to improve?

Computers will revolutionize schools in the same way in the third decade of this century that they are revolutionising universities in the second decade. As this book so clearly shows, the education system has to change, because the methods of teaching and the methods of learning will never be the same again. We cannot 'un-invent' the computer, nor can we wish computer generated environments would go away. What is really exciting given Moore's Law (i.e. computing power is doubling roughly every eighteen months) is that we are in the mere foothills of seeing how computers will transform learning and teaching. Not the least of their benefits is individualised as well as social learning, active rather than passive learning, and the experience akin to that of a memorable field trip rather than of an inert classroom.

None of us knows where this journey will end; there are plenty of pitfalls along the way, not the least the need to develop our young people ethically and physically, as well as intellectually. But this book provides as good a map to the future as one can wish for in this rapidly evolving world.

Dr Anthony Seldon, Master of Wellington College

Preface

The inspiration for this book first came to me about ten years ago when I was working at Birkbeck College in London, in the early years of the new century. At that time, it seemed to me that there was a tantalising sense of convergence between some of the cross-disciplinary research that I was both conducting and reviewing as part of my work for the College. My work and research at Birkbeck involved numerous studies which looked at the first attempts to create computer based learning models (e-learning) and computer based educational games. As a result, I found myself looking ever more closely at the role of play in education, at the early studies of computer generated training simulations and at a raft of work advocating new approaches to the ways in which people learn.

Firstly, what seemed to be emerging from the research into play at that time was a step change in our understanding of the role of play in education. For most of the twentieth century, firm and somewhat Victorian attitudes to play—what play is, what play is for and when we can or should play—prevailed in most formal education systems. These attitudes to play rested on notions of purely recreational pursuits or leisurely diversions, with a very clear situational and functional demarcation between playground and classroom and a formal differentiation of games and studies. However, the contemporary cross-disciplinary research at the turn of the new century seemed to be confirming that play is, behaviourally speaking, primarily a form of learning. That is, play is a way of learning how to do something by rehearsing or simulating behaviours, tactics or actions, in a way that does not have adverse or lethal real-life consequences.

At that time, new computer based training simulators were increasingly being used by the military and industrial sectors for exactly this type of learning, that is, training individuals and groups without the risk of harm to the trainees or their equipment. And notably, some of these training simulators—think combat or flight simulators—began to be marketed as recreational computer games and were proving themselves to be both highly popular and highly profitable. However, these simulator games that were being produced and played for recreational and leisure purposes were still clearly effective training tools, with which the player was learning how to do something while also being entertained.

Hence, it struck me that the practical and conceptual demarcations between play and training or learning seemed, in these sectors at least, to be dissolving. And just as we might consider a television science documentary as both entertainment and education, it seemed to me that these computer generated simulators should be reconsidered and properly regarded as both entertainment and learning tools. What's more, with these sectors demonstrating that the development of learning and training tools could be not only cost effective but actually highly profitable, the prospect of an increasing commercialisation of education and learning in the widest sense seemed imminent.

At the same time, many educators and indeed many learners were looking again at pedagogic strategies—that is, they were considering the merits of creating and implementing a greater diversity of systemic approaches to learning. Here then, the seeming convergence of a wider willingness to adopt new and diverse approaches to learning, complemented by the emergence of new tools with which to learn, seemed to be signalling the potential for a new era in education.

In this book I refer to 'new learning', and this is simply a shorthand way of referring to the consideration, creation and implementation of new approaches to learning or new tools for learning.

To that end I have tried to set out some of the new approaches to learning that have emerged in recent years. At the same time, using cross-disciplinary research, I have tried to set out for educational content developers the basic parameters and some of the issues that need to be considered in the design of more effective computer generated learning environments, training simulations and learning games.

It is however also important to emphasise that new learning is just that —new. If what we have now is a clear idea about the potential of new strategies and tools, then what lies ahead of us is the hard work of creating, trying and testing new approaches, in pursuit of the evolution of a diversity of routinely effective educational systems, that offer each and every learner the best and most appropriate way for them to learn.

It is often the case with academic books that, even where a sudden momentary insight is the inspiration, the finished work can take years or even decades to come to fruition. Even where the concepts in play might seem simple or straight forward to the author at the outset, it is nonetheless often the case that setting out new concepts or indeed new academic approaches in a disciplined way can be a considerable challenge that involves not only the testing of concepts over time but the contributions of colleagues, the support of research sponsors and the patience of publishers.

This book certainly falls into that category and so I need to thank everyone who has given me their time or help, over the last few years, and especially all those colleagues who have helped me to formulate and refine my thoughts, with their incisive and insightful feedback.

Working at Birkbeck College, University of London, with its history as a Mechanics Institute in the nineteenth century and its links with the father of Utilitarianism, Jeremy Bentham, was an inspiring experience and I can only thank colleagues there including Professors Mark Levene, Alexandra Poulovassilis and George Magoulas, as well as Professor Sir Timothy O'Shea for their patient and timely support. For their insights into learning theory and practice I owe a debt of gratitude to many colleagues at the Institute of Education, University of London, including the whole London Knowledge Lab family especially Professor Diana Laurillard, Professor Richard Noss and Dr. Martin Oliver.

This book brings together the consolidated work from several reports, papers and books undertaken since 2001, including two reports for the Joint Information Systems Committee (JISC) and numerous articles on game-based approaches, e-learning models and virtual world learning. The book therefore covers the period of my Learning and Skills Research Centre Fellowship at Birkbeck College London, funded through the Centre, so many thanks to the support of Dr. Ursula Howard, Jill Attewell and Dr. Carol Savill-Smith. Supporting the development of the e-Learning Programme at the JISC, I also worked as a consultant for the e-Learning Programme, and for their support during this period I thank Paul Bailey, Sarah Davies, Sarah Knight and Sarah Porter.

I left Birkbeck a little over five years ago to set up a new institute in the Midlands, where I am fortunate to have a truly industrious and inspiring team around me at the Serious Games Institute (SGI), Coventry University. The SGI family includes many colleagues: Drs. Sylvester Arnab, Yung-Fang Chen, Ian Dunwell, Maurice Hendrix, Petros Lameras, Fotis Liarokapis, David Panzoli, Panagiotis Petridis, Genaro Rebolledo-Mendez and Craig Stewart. Doctoral students include: Vanessa Camillieri, Samantha Clarke, John Denholm, Kyriaki Hadjicosta, Suriati Jali, Tom Matko, Charn Pisithpunth, Kam Star, Li Ping Thong and Tom Willans. Administration includes: John Zhao, Jay Panesar and Corinne Edwards. Also, for inspiring my work and for their patience, I also owe a significant debt of thanks to my close colleagues and allies: Professor Madeleine Atkins, John Latham, Professor Ian Marshall, Frank Mills and Tim Luft.

In a way, the unsung heroes of academic research are the agencies and funding organizations that painstakingly organize our research and development into a framework for practical application, so I must thank our many external funders for their support, including: Advantage West Midlands, British Council (Prime Ministers Initiative Fund), Department for Transport, British High Commission Singapore, Department for Education and Skills, European Commission, European Regional Development Fund, Engineering and Physical Sciences Research Council, Higher Education Funding Council for England, Hildebrand Ltd, Jaguar LandRover, Joint Information Systems Committee, Technology Strategy Board, Royal Society and the West Midlands Strategic Health Authority Health and Innovations Education Cluster.

Dialogue and reflection are the well springs of creativity and innovation, and for finding time in their busy schedules to discuss ideas that intrigued or fascinated me, I offer particular thanks also to my long term intellectual friendships with co-authors and colleagues including: Professor Paul Maharg, Professor Jill Jameson, Dr. Pamela Kato, Professor Terry Mayes, Dr. Diane Jass Ketelhut, Dr. Igor Mayer, Professor Piet Hut, Professor Stephen Heppell, Dr. Chris Yapp, Dr. Rick Ferdig, Dr. Michela Ott, Helen Beetham, Dr. Rhona Sharpe, Professor Grainne Conole, Dr. Kristian Kiili, Professor Mike Zyda. Without our conversations and interactions I would not have been able to formulate such a clear understanding of the links and development between learning theory and practice, the concepts behind the learners experience and the effective design of learning experiences.

A number of case studies have also been critical for realizing the vision of 'new learning' so thanks to Richard Gerver, Professor Katie Salen, Professor Paul Maharg, Dr. Ian Dunwell, Dr. Katherine Brown and Dr. Sylvester Arnab for their inputs with these case subjects.

Routledge have long been committed to the plight of educationalists and education science, so I must of course thank them for continuing to support academic authors such as myself. So I thank Routledge and in particular Alex Masulis, Stacy Noto and Lauren Verity, as well as Michael Watters at Integrated Book Technology, Inc., who have given this book a chance to reach a wider audience.

Lastly, I must thank my husband who always inspires me with insightful arguments and his deep wealth of understanding about all subjects. I dedicate this work to him and all those who believe in the power of education to bring out the best in the human spirit.

Birmingham, England, June 2013

Introduction
Learning in Computer Generated Environments

Imagine how inspiring it would be if a history teacher could take her pupils on a guided tour of the Court Rooms of the Pharaohs, through the Temple of Solomon or the streets and the Forum of ancient Rome. Imagine how engaging it would be for those children to step into the world of our ancestors, to be able to meet them and to see for themselves how they lived. Consider how useful it would be if all the events, people and places in the period of history that pupils were studying could be realistically simulated in the classroom and explored with their teacher; *and how much more useful* if that simulation and tour or lesson could, if necessary, be accessed and joined or even re-played from the pupil's own home.

In the second decade of the 21st century, we already have most of the techniques and technologies we would need to deliver this notional history lesson of the future, but if these technologies or methods *are* to be trusted and incorporated into the processes of education there has to be an informed societal debate about the merits of such an innovation, about the known challenges for socially engineered transitions in education and ultimately, if we are to see the wider use of simulated computer generated environments and experiences in education, about the validation of strategies that can ensure tangible gains from any systemic uptake of these new tools.

Over the last decade or so, an increasing number of people working in the education sector, both in the United Kingdom and abroad and from pre-primary learning through post-doctoral education, have become aware of the growing potential for new technologies and teaching theories to deliver better and more effective methods of teaching. However, whilst the potential is clearly there, the task of converting that potential into effective new teaching tools (and quantifying the benefits) still remains a challenge. That challenge necessarily begins with an articulation of the qualities that characterize effective teaching and learning, and this book sets out to examine current practice and whether computer generated environments, which include immersive and virtual learning environments, like our notional history lesson, above, can offer teachers and students strategies and tools which result in a more effective learning process.

There is, of course, no such thing as 'the perfect lesson' any more than there is a perfect teacher—each individual student, after all, has differing preferences and needs. But if we were to consider the pre-requisites of an effective teaching session or lesson, certainly one of the first qualities that must spring to mind as being vital is that the contents of a lesson—that is, what is being imparted and studied in the lesson—should be memorable to the student, both in the short term and the long term.

Whilst this might sound obvious, it is well worth stopping to think about the memorization of information and the part that this aspect of learning plays in our education. For instance, how many of us can remember *any* individual and specific lessons from school—that is, particular lessons that stand out as truly memorable?

We all have a generalized memory of sitting at a desk listening to a teacher or reading—an amalgam of all our classroom memories. But try to remember a specific lesson on a specific day: what did you learn in that half-hour or one-hour lesson and what else did you learn in that subject, that year, specifically? Then try and remember all the lessons you had at school, each one individually. In other words, just how much information of any sort—what percentage, say, of all the information presented, imparted and studied—can any of us recall from the hundreds and sometimes thousands of hours of input for each disciplinary subject area at school or university?

Obviously we do learn a lot through our education, but the point here is that we are not simply recording machines and our natural capacity to absorb and retain information is neither unlimited nor flawless. In educative systems which use the memorization of information as a key methodology, it is then important to realize just how much information we as human beings are capable of *forgetting*. This human factor is one of the greater challenges that educators and educative methodologies have to and have always had to contend with. How do we make the contents of individual lessons or studies as memorable as possible for the student?

There are, of course, some obvious clues evident within the traditional educational approaches that most of us will have grown up with. For example, it's easy enough for most people, when asked, to recall the few field trips and out of school activities that they went on when they were at school. Moreover, it's fair to say that most people can remember a great deal of what they saw and experienced on these trips, to an extent that they simply can't bring to mind for most other school days or lessons. In other words, these types of lessons or *learning experiences* were particularly memorable.

There is, of course, a good reason why this should tend to be the case and that is that such *multisensory experiences* play to the strengths of the human memory and particularly to its highly developed capacity for storing visio-spatial information (Brewer et al., 1998). The human memory has necessarily evolved to be very good at retaining a substantial volume of information about the three dimensional world around us, storing all of the locations we have visited and all of the separate journeys that we have made, along with all the different directions to and from all these different places, so that they all fit effortlessly into an organized mental map of our environment.

This observation about the modern *human* memory was, of course, already true of our most distant arboreal ancestors; the ability to navigate through their three dimensional habitat of a jungle or forest using complex pathways of branches and routes that had to be remembered was in our ancestors aided by a capacity to conceptualize a mental map of their environment *and* a capacity to memorize and recall that map.

Thereafter (around four million years ago), our ancestors traded life in the tangle of the forest for a less complex habitat—the flat and relatively easily navigated plains of Africa. The extra or surplus mental capacity that our ancestors possessed did not atrophy, however; in fact, quite the opposite happened—their memory and conceptual capacities actually increased. These hard-wired mental capabilities would be co-opted—by our ancestors and their close relatives—to support an ever more sophisticated progression of tool-making, hunter-gatherer cultures. Throughout this long period, we evolved an increasing capacity for experience-based learning, which became essential to the transmission, preservation and refinement of skills such as tool-making and behaviours such as tracking or hunting. Therefore, just as a highly evolved visio-spatial and logistical memory capacity served hunter and gatherer alike when navigating their environment and locating food or water, so the re-allocation of memory capacity to an increasing range and volume of experiential learning served cultures where vital tool-making technologies and survival skills *had to be* refined, learnt and passed on. Over this same period (between 4 million years ago and 125,000 years ago), our ancestors also gradually acquired the capacity for complex phonetic language, thus demonstrating an increasing development for their capacity for conceptualization. However, it does need to be emphasized that throughout this period, instruction and experiential learning would for the most part have been *augmented* by the growing capacity for language, not replaced by it.

What we would call traditional teaching strategies—involving the abstract representation, recital and communication of information or knowledge through language alone—must have evolved within the linguistic cultures that first enquired about and speculated on, the nature of the world beyond their immediate physiological needs. The power of language is that you can describe to others, things that cannot be or have not been directly experienced, by them. And there can be no doubt that our ancestors took full advantage of that power, to develop their conceptual and intellectual capacity. The result was the creation of an oral tradition within human cultures, in which the transmission and learning of knowledge, skills, language and tribal customs or beliefs, was central.

The oral tradition was both an education system and a repository for the preservation and accumulation of culturally valuable information and was likely in place, in some form or another, when the first modern human left Africa over 70,000 years ago. Thereafter, the species-wide development of tribal knowledge and customs continued over the ensuing millennia, all the way down to and into the historical period (around 4000 BCE), where methodological and disciplinary forms of education, were first documented.

The Greeks and Romans of classical antiquity, living in the period just after the half-way point between the invention of writing and our own times (i.e., 3000–2000 BCE), give us some of our first articulate descriptions of formal education. They had access to a substantial and growing volume of texts, representing the intellectual output of dozens of cultures accumulated over millennia. The division, organization and compilation of these tracts and texts into different subject categories formed the basis of and content for an education system that involved the teaching of different subjects. Crucially, the subjects that the ancient Greek education system was interested in were the fields of disciplined or methodological intellectual enquiry, and these 'disciplines'—the approved subjects of the ancient curriculum—increasingly required the teaching of abstract concepts, principles and methodologies. To achieve this our ancestors considered, developed and refined the *methods of teaching*, and described the methods—such as the didactic, Socratic and dialectic approaches—that could be used to inculcate mental skills and abstract concepts in the same way that demonstration and instruction are used: to teach physical skills and actions. But these ancient educators also had a consideration of, and approach to, *the methods of learning*—most particularly in their description and utilization of a memorization technique called 'the loci method', or 'memory palace'. This entailed the visualization by the student of an imagined three-dimensional space or place—such as a house or a palace—in which items of knowledge could, in the student's imagination, be 'placed' or stored in various locations so that sequences or chains of information could be visualized in and linked to a progress through the mental mapping of the imagined space. Thus, abstract facts, concepts and long chains of information—a disciplinary narrative—could be more effectively memorized and recalled.

From the first documentary articulations of our traditional formal education system in these ancient yet familiar descriptions, we do find a coherent consideration and synthesis of *system* and *method*—*that is, between the education system, the methodologies of teaching (didactics) and the methodologies of learning (mathetics)*. That consideration clearly reflects an awareness of the particular nature of human memory processes and an understanding of the benefits of working in sympathy with them using strategic methodologies.

Crucially, it still remains the case today that the human memory copes best with retaining bits of abstract information when they are related in the memory with different visio-spatial cues (i.e., visual or location-based cues) *and*, whenever it is possible, with *experience-based* learning. That is why it is still so much easier to remember lessons or field trips that capitalize on this characteristic of the human memory and, indeed, that is why this kind of visio-spatial and experience-based memorization or learning is still used whenever possible in educational settings. It is then widely understood that these tools can augment and bolster the more static and predominantly aural-linguistic approaches of traditional didactic approaches to teaching, in which the information to be learnt—including the disciplinary narrative—is recited and explained orally by the teacher or is communicated in an abstract way using two-dimensional tools such as white boards, books or text.

There is however, nothing new in the observation that visio-spatial strategies for memorization or experience-based learning—seeing, doing or experiencing something for one's self—are usually more memorable than just being told about something; this, of course, is why educational field trips or outings have traditionally played some role in education, albeit until now they have usually had to be limited to the occasional treat due to the cost and effort that such outings incur. What *is* new, however, is the potential to simulate and model these types of learning experiences in the classroom using immersive three-dimensional computer generated environments (CGEs).

Most people will, of course, associate CGEs and simulations with playing computer games, but it is important to remember that 'play' is itself part of the broad spectrum of experiential educational approaches. Like other animals, human infants, children and adolescents use play and playful behaviour to explore and understand how to navigate the environment around them, to support social interactions and exchanges, and through the simulation or mimicry of adult behaviours to practice and learn adult skills.

Crucially, play allows us to imitate and practice these skills in a non-threatening and non-consequential way from the youngest age possible. It allows us to replicate what we observe and learn and to test our skills—both physical and intellectual—so that we can repeat and refine our actions until the point at which they become effective, effortless and instinctive. Crucially, play also allows the possibility of innovation.

What play capitalizes on, then, and this is relevant to effective learning, is the educational power of experience—learning through doing—and the fact that most of us learn to walk, run, throw, catch and play hide-and-seek or football in this way, illustrates just how effective play can be as a learning tool. Here, then, there may be another point in respect of remembering what we learn, since most of us can remember perfectly well as adults what we learnt through play as children, such as football, netball or any number of a host of fairly complex games. The rules of most of these childhood games don't really contain so much less information than, for example, a recital of a dozen or so of the basic laws of physics, but it's not hard to guess which sets of rules most people will remember in more detail in the long term. Part of this, of course, may be that play is almost by definition entertaining and therefore it may well be—as many would argue—that where learning is entertaining it is also more memorable.

In our schools today, however, the systemic emphasis is more on *approaches to teaching* than the experience of learning. Learning in the classroom generally entails memorizing individual bits of information, which we then assimilate and organize into 'chains' of related information. Out of these chains of information we try to create a mental 'picture', 'map' or 'narrative' of a given subject area from which it is then possible for us to retrieve the specific facts that we need, and that we have memorized, at a given time. It is, of course, generally this element of learning—the retrieval of 'facts' and 'narratives'—which is tested. Here, then, each subject consists of components which need to be organized into a consistent, cohesive and holistic whole. In other words, the disparate bits of information all need to be memorized, organized and re-articulated in a way that is accurate and consistent and makes sense both to ourselves and to others. However, this in turn depends upon the amount of information that can be assimilated in any given lesson or course of lessons and that will be influenced by the over-all efficacy of the learning experience. Or, put another way, it will depend on how memorable individual lessons and modules are to the student, and this brings us back to the question of whether CGEs can deliver more effective teaching and learning tools in this regard.

CGEs—virtual worlds and immersive learning environments—certainly do allow us to practice academic skills and the application of knowledge. But they do this in a way that looks and feels much more like playing than learning. This is so because they allow us to 'experience' situations, interactions and exchanges in an environment that simulates the real world and real-world conditions—just as with most play the experience is a three-dimensional simulacrum of the experience for which we are trying to hone and perfect our skills. Through role playing, scenario creation and e-mentoring, virtual and immersive worlds would seem to offer tools which can provide unlimited situational experience and an economical system by which to practice and improve performance. Additionally, computer generated learning environments (CGLEs) clearly can provide a visual and kinaesthetic experience which is potentially more entertaining and more memorable for the student.

Crucially, CGLEs do play to our visio-spatial strengths when it comes to memorizing information, since they are navigable three-dimensional environments of the type that the human memory is so well adapted to memorize. Consequently, it should be possible to make use of the assets noted above, both for situational or experiential learning *and* for memorizing disciplinary narratives and facts.

Such systems are, of course, also inherently suited to testing. For example, computer games allow the user to progress through set levels of increasingly difficult challenges (tests of skill or knowledge) with the gradual accumulation and improvement of skills. This type of learn-and-test model is analogous to the test-and-advancement pattern through the various levels of education. CGEs therefore have huge potential—when allied with traditional tools and methods—for supporting a substantively new approach to learning and testing.

For the first time in a very long time we have a growing number of new learning tools, a growing number of new teaching methods and a growing amount of new learning content all available to the front line of education, and this provides us with a historic opportunity to re-think and re-organize how we learn, what we learn and where we learn.

In some respects we are, of course, already beginning to use immersive media technologies to provide an alternative scope for how we learn and train. This book will therefore also look at the current pioneering of immersive learning in order to examine and quantify the impact of the 'first generation' of these new teaching tools on education as a whole.

This in turn requires an examination of various epistemological considerations which describe the relationships between knowledge and learning and between teachers and students. Here, then, it is much easier to understand and assess the disparate theories of learning (pedagogy) which are currently in use if one has at least a basic understanding of the theories of knowledge (epistemology), which underpin these pedagogic approaches (de Freitas & Jameson, 2012).

Epistemological as well as pedagogic considerations are hugely important for the development of effective learning in immersive worlds because, in order to design (or 'choreograph') the most effective learning *experiences*, we need to be able to minimize the gap between *what* we are aiming to teach in terms of the knowledge to be acquired (e.g., statements, concepts, ideas, information, skills or processes), *how we teach* (e.g., through demonstration, instruction, explanation or exploration) *and how we learn* (e.g., by instruction, experience, practice or collaboration).

Here, then, is another reason why field trips or experience-based methods of learning are generally so effective, as the gap between the learner and the subject studied is minimized. Similarly, learning in immersive worlds has the potential to be highly effective, as long as the gap between the immersive world and the physical world, where the skills will be used, is kept suitably close or the learning transfer between contexts is straightforward and easily understood.

It is perhaps worth emphasizing the last point. The replication of the activities, processes and interactions needs to result in learning that can easily be transferred between contexts. If the replicated environment is suitably close to the physical environment in terms of activities, processes and interactions, then the learner is, of course, much more likely to make an easy transfer between the two.

Where this is not the case, the transfer of what is learnt between contexts must be straightforward and easily understood. A good example here is basic human ethics. The vast majority of us will have learnt our first lessons on this subject through play or games, at a very early age. Sharing, playing to the rules, taking turns and not cheating are ethical elements to childhood play and lots of different games but crucially, our learnt concepts—conditioned by social interaction—are transferable between different games and into the wider context of life itself.

Between the design of real or virtually enacted learning activities, processes and social interactions and the learner there are, however, a number of key conditional elements or filters which need to be taken into account. Here, the infrastructure for learning (e.g., the institutions), the prioritization of educational content (e.g., a standard curriculum) and the standardization of educational practices (e.g., target- and policy-driven delivery) are all relevant. These can be considered as the 'system of education' as a whole, and this system is culturally and historically situated and nuanced.

The danger however, is that as a result of cumulative developments in these areas over time, the educational 'system' becomes over-emphasized, to the detriment of the processes of teaching and learning. At best, such an over-emphasis upon the education system can lead to an obfuscation of the central motivations which underpin the individual's needs. At its worst, however, the misdirection of focus can lead to a neglect of the quality of the learning processes and an indifference to the development of methodology. A simple test can be applied here by contrasting the number of examination boards and schools inspectors in an administrative jurisdiction with the number of educational content developers and pedagogic researchers.

Informational modes of learning, rigid curricula and constant assessment are useful for any system that needs to produce measures of the success of the system within its own terms. However, unless alternative experiences are offered for comparison, the efficacy of the actual learning experiences can't really be quantified beyond the terms of the system. Here the danger is an imbalance in which the political need of the education system to demonstrate its success, by its own measures, outweighs or ignores the needs of the learner for a rich, unlimited and enjoyable learning experience, which results in transferable 'real-world' skills. The hallmark of such an imbalance would be a situation where for example, a nation's official school grades were steadily improving across the board (that is, a government's mission is accomplished) but universities and employers—when testing individuals independently of the state system—were noting a decline in or deficit of key skills.

If, then, the leaders of education in our societies do find that there is a *perception* of a fundamental skills deficit (e.g., for literacy, numeracy or foreign languages), that surely is just the sort of cue that should prompt us to re-focus our understanding of learning back onto the human factors, which are at the centre of the learning processes.

This book therefore aims to re-examine the key relationships of learning in order to explore how we might utilize the new immersive tools to offer teachers and tutors new opportunities for creating learning experiences, which provide learners with more empowering and engaging approaches to learning and, consequently, with more effective and memorable learning.

The emergence of CGEs has added to the need for complexity and sophistication in our understanding of physical and non-physical or 'ethereal/abstract' spaces, which in turn provides a an opportunity for innovation in the ways we consider and use these virtual spaces and the physical spaces that they may at times be associated with. The exploration of the relationship between abstract and physical spaces is not new, but the advent of CGEs is a significant development which has a clear potential in the education sector and thus an exploration of the themes specific to education seems timely.

Whether we use virtual and hybrid spaces for learning, role playing, communications, collaboration or research, the inescapable feeling is that we are utilizing a new media form in a familiar way. When we read a book, to a certain extent our imaginations create the mental picture of the world or the events we are reading about and so to a certain extent we experience the subject matter. When we watch a film we are watching simulations of events and settings and again, although to a greater extent, we witness and experience the subject matter. In films, since the visualization of the subject matter is presented to us, we have less work to do mentally to remember what we have seen and therefore most people can recount the narrative of a film more easily than they can with a book.

When we enter a CGE, however, we can interact with the content and the setting in a way that mimics direct experience even more effectively than a film does, but this, of course, represents a development from existing media forms rather than a distinct or separate break. In fact, in many ways, we can see the media of constructed non-physical spaces evolve from the imagined ritual spaces of our ancestors, through story tellers, books and theatre and on through to television and recently virtual worlds.

One point here, though, is that virtual spaces and environments tend to be more communal immersive experiences than we have been used to with books or television. Fortunately, the perception that computers in general and virtual worlds in particular preclude social interactions has now been comprehensively debunked. Computer generated environments, it has now been realized, are very sociable places—hence the emergence of digital social media—and this is one of the key factors that makes the exploration of virtual spaces so engaging: exploration and socializing are, it seems, constants in terms of human entertainment.

It seems obvious, then, that virtual worlds have enormous potential when it comes to providing the infrastructure for individuals to collaborate across sectors, across national boundaries and between disciplines and institutions (de Freitas et al., 2010). The use of virtual worlds to assist collaboration does not, however, replace the use of face-to-face interaction but supports and augments other forms of social contact. Any discussions about the use of computer generated environments or virtual worlds thus needs to consider the social communities that are using these immersive CGEs and understand that the growth of online communities and the ongoing development path of CGEs are inextricably linked.

At the intersection of the social and immersive forms of communications there lies an incredibly powerful set of discourses that may be used to support learning. When combining social and immersive technologies we get at a 'sweet spot' where learners can be engaged, motivated, improve their performance and 'lose themselves' in the flow of the learning experience—or, in other words, *become immersed*. Here, the immersive approach can emulate our physical experiences whilst supporting designed learning activities, learner control and collaborative social interactions. However, in order to get to this point or 'sweet spot' we need to adopt a more process-centred approach to learning, one in which the learner is truly placed at the centre of the processes of learning.

This book therefore offers readers the opportunity to consider alternatives to the current approaches to education with the proposal of more process-based approaches. To do this, though, we need to model learning in terms that can bridge the conceptual gap between the systemic and process-based approaches. In addition, we need to understand how immersive learning environments support process-based approaches. The practical answers to these questions are drawn from user groups, and from developing participatory approaches, in which users and developers work together iteratively to present solutions and process models.

Recently, and significantly, brain scans of learners learning in conventional ways and those of learners playing games have revealed that learners playing games used their whole brain, whilst those using traditional learning approaches were only using a proportion of the frontal lobe. This timely work has revealed the powerful capabilities of learning through play; in one functional magnetic resonance imaging study of a computer game, for example, 'the activation pattern reflect[ed] brain-environment interactions rather than stimulus responses' (Mathiak & Weber, 2006: 948). In parallel, work on mirror neurones (premotor neurones), which fire both when an animal acts and when an animal *observes* the action performed by another animal, reveals that simulated activity is an extremely powerful form of learning. Although this type of research is only just now starting to come to public attention, the potential for learning through simulations and games is already clear, and impressively, early empirical results arising from at least one randomized control study on serious games seem to indicate that this type of learning has the capacity to present 'significant differences' when compared with traditional forms of learning (Kato et al., 2008; Knight et al., 2010). If these early results can be replicated in other studies, we may see the beginning of a major transition in the way that learning in immersive worlds will be perceived by traditional learning institutions in the years to come.

At present, however, based upon studies with users across all levels of education, it has been noted that many tutors. are unable to judge when to use games and simulations, which tools to use and how effective they would be (de Freitas & Oliver, 2006). It is thus, at this time, imperative that we begin the difficult process of evaluating which methodologies have the most potential and in which areas they can be effectively implemented. To this end, it is important to have some method for modelling the learning experiences in order to help quantify the relative merits of different approaches.

The model used for this book, *the Four Dimensional Framework* (de Freitas & Oliver, 2006), was based upon research with learners and was developed to address this type of challenge. It has since been used to develop, analyze and evaluate games for learning (Brown et al., 2013; Jarvis & de Freitas, 2009). In this model, the four dimensions or points of reference are *the context, the learner, the representation of the game world and the learning theory and practices.* The framework itself was specifically designed to support more effective selection, design, development and use of game-based and immersive learning tools, software and platforms. Overall, this type of model aims to make clear the connection between theoretical considerations and practical interactions (theory and practice), and for this reason it is a useful way of connecting processes and modelling them.

The *context* of learning plays a central role in the process of learning, and is hugely important in respect to making learning relevant to the real-life processes at work in our everyday activities. Context, however, is not just about the institutional and disciplinary setting but includes the social and political framework within which relationships occur. Following this premise, the Chapter 1 seeks to outline and explore the changing contexts for learning, tracing how the core relationships at the heart of learning are being re-organized to better fit with global aspirations, shifting power balances and changing social networks. The chapter also explores the educational system itself, presenting some of the key recent changes in education and exploring how the gap between educational practice and policy development could be narrowed to support enriched learning experiences.

Understanding these key contextual changes, I believe, helps us to understand the wider changes taking place in education *and* the pressures to adapt to these changes that are being felt in all our educational institutions. In this respect, the tensions between micro- and macroforces lead to some difficult questions about the relationship between systems, institutions and learners. In particular, we need to ask if that set of relationships should be, as it now is, eclipsing the central relationship between the teacher, the learner and the subject studied.

How the learner's experiences will be formed in the face of these tensions is still a matter of debate since purely learner-centred approaches have not really been integrated into educational systems at present. Nonetheless, the swiftness of social and technological change, in particular with the development of social software and immersive learning environments, does offer the opportunity to reshape future strategies for learning and for the learner. Such changes, though, link through to other social tensions such as the drive towards a greater democratization of social networks on the one hand, as evidenced on the web and through social media communities, and the increasingly hierarchical structures of societal governance and control on the other. These types of contradiction lead to a need to reconsider the contextual drivers involved in any societal change, and we therefore need to debate not just the political motivations but also the prevailing social developments—particularly amongst those of an age to be in education—where 'self-organization' and a desire for more democratic systems provides the touchstone for future developments and new applications.

It is, however, in terms of context impossible to ignore the political pressures on our systems. The need for governments to persuade electorates that they are managing education directly and effectively across the board results in an element of assessment and additional administrative output for institutions and teachers that is not naturally a part of the educative process. It is in this light that we need to debate whether a proscribed curriculum, ongoing tests for students and performance tables for institutions serve the interests of the learner to the same degree that they serve the aims of government. In other words, we need to understand education policies in terms of how they are intended to meet the needs of a government in its desire to show parents and voters that it is doing a good job.

Obviously, despite protests to the contrary, the more simple a given exam is the more people can pass it, and this is good for any government's education statistics with which it would want to promote *its* performance. A simpler exam does not, however, help the student who would otherwise be motivated by a more challenging level of testing. That student must be content with competence rather than excellence. It needs to be emphasized, therefore, that a government's needs are not always necessarily the same thing as the needs of the individual learner—whose main concern may be for a flexible, responsive and engaging provision of the most effective and ambitious education possible.

In fact, the actual needs and preferences of the learner as an individual have not really been properly foregrounded in the current set up. The accommodation of the perspectives of ministers, departments, parents and voters is front and centre, but the learners and teachers have been somewhat sidelined and this, to an extent, is exacerbating the decoupling of policy and effective learning practices. This is a crucial problem, which involves the need to *re-align* the relationship between policy makers, institutions and individual learners. The aim here is thus to support teachers, promote a more creative curriculum and provide more diversity for learning in general *and* to aid more effective and focused policy making in the future.

Greater democracy of provision and longer durations of learning do serve to highlight the growing importance of learning in our culture. However, the drivers or policy makers for the personalization of learning have not, as yet, really started to unlock the potential that open educational resources and learner generated content will increasingly offer in formulating educational provision and quality over the next ten years. Therefore, whilst the move of education towards lifelong learning strategies, learning pathways and a greater empowerment of the learner is ringing in some of the changes, the need to address any control strategies and policy issues that are impeding more effective education is both compelling and pressing.

Here, perhaps an old maxim—*non scholae, sed vitae*—may be appropriate. That is, education should be 'not for school but for life' or, put another way, we do not learn just to take tests and sit exams to satisfy the school or the state but instead to comprehend our world and develop skills that enrich the human experience of life. My husband's school used this Latin maxim as their motto and they explained it to parents thus: Our main aim is not just to teach children what they should know—today's fact may be tomorrow's fallacy—so instead we aim to teach children how to master the art of learning.

Many of the recent changes that influence our consideration of context thus centre upon relationships that lie at the heart of education and learning. Most particularly we need to re-examine the relationship between the learner and the tutor, the learner and the subject studied and, indeed, between different learners. Today, along with the increasing importance of education for knowledge economies and a changing educational epistemology, new approaches to education—which take into account the effectiveness of learning through play, the contribution of social interactions and the human predisposition for learning through the active exploration of new environments—are emerging.

Ultimately, this trend is leading to a revision of tutorial support and practices and an exploration of the scope for tutors to adopt 'choreographic' approaches to teaching in which they can use a range of pedagogic approaches tailored to the task at hand. At the same time, teachers can start to explore the new educational tools that have the potential to do for education now what the Industrial Revolution did for manufacturing in the 19th century.

For teachers and learners, these tools can *re-create* ancient worlds from the past for learners to experience, new locations from the poles to the pyramids to visit and study, new ways to rehearse and to support skills and new pathways with which to link cross-disciplinary communities.

Today's educators now have more tools for the demonstration and explication of subject matter than at any time in history, and the preliminary studies of game-based learning are indicating particular strengths with regard to accelerated learning and longer durations (permanence) of learning recall. This is evidenced in Chapter 2, where the role of *the learner* is highlighted and explored. Learning as play, as social interaction and as exploration characterizes this dimension of learning. The approach presents both unique possibilities and challenges for tutors and their development of learning experiences and activities in the future (de Freitas & Maharg, 2011).

The emerging tools create an imperative to contemplate how we might 'choreograph' experiences for the learner with the involvement of role play, exploration and discovery rather than solely through overtly directed learning with purely informational mechanisms. What cannot be avoided, though, is the idea that any major innovations will necessarily have implications for accreditation, assessment, evaluation, verification and validation of learning content—and, of course, content production. Consequently, these considerations need to be addressed in any debate about the scope for any 'new' era of learning.

Ultimately, it will be the demonstration and acceptance of theories and practices associated with learning, rather than the specifically technological components, that will drive any far-reaching changes in education. Crucially, teachers already have many of the necessary skills to explore and test the potential of these new learning opportunities, and ultimately it is individual teachers who will have to refine the best practical strategies for their use. Similarly, it may well be that the social and informative practices of learners in *their* day-to-day lives will have an increasing influence on the uptake of new tools and new approaches in education, as these learners gain greater control over their own learning strategies, outcomes and outputs.

The ability to create computer generated representations of physical world spaces with simulated experiences, characters and demonstrations allows us to be fully immersed into a virtual space designed for learning. In this space learners can be guided through experiences, challenges, quests and missions: to rehearse skills, increase their knowledge and develop their understanding of a subject area. The levels of fidelity allow us to cross personal, societal, geographical and historical boundaries and to explore the full gamut of human understanding; the interactive and connective nature of such spaces allows for creativity and construction through scaffolding and collaborative support.

Learning through exploration allows for increased learner control and plays to the greatest strengths of learning in a real or simulated environment. Our highly developed capacity to remember the scene around us, to be immersed within that scene and to play an active role in it, means that we can readily capitalize on the experience of immersive learning environments. Here we cannot only replicate the field trip model of learning but can create the field trips of teachers' and students' *dreams*, where the learner can 'go to' and 'experience' any event, in any location, in any time. Role play and the use of narrative extends that reach and can help to produce virtual learning experiences that easily convert to real-world knowledge or skills. Learning as *exploration* allows for further possibilities, such as e-mentoring and collaborative learning within distributed groups, which can extend out the communally lived virtual experiences into truly new realms of enquiry (de Freitas & Neumann, 2009).

Here, then, the world represented inside an educational game (*diegesis*) and its limits and boundaries are worth examining, and Chapter 3 closes with a consideration of these issues. Within the game or virtual world there is a distinctive need to create a coherent and consistent experience for supporting learning. This is achieved through appropriate levels of fidelity, the capacity to cross between different spaces and identities, effective flows of processes and experiences, the use of narrative or quests and the levels of interactivity supporting learner control and feedback.

Part of understanding *how we learn* entails the need for the creation of a usable map of the relationships between physical, conceptual and virtual interchanges with others, and of our production of outputs and content for sharing with others. This aspect of the pedagogic enquiry can then be referred to as the 'cartography of learning'. The cartography of learning—that is, the mapping of the learning environment in both conceptual and physical terms—is examined in Chapter 4, which presents a model for learning that supports *exploration* within immersive, real and hybrid spaces, helping us to promote reflection and social interaction as primary components.

The consideration of context, representation and the needs of the learner, feed, of course, into a wider and more theoretical debate about the pedagogic approaches used to support teaching practices. In Chapter 4 we will consider how play and playful learning is re-organizing the way we think about the smallest unit of 'new learning': the *learning experience*. This new form of learning emerges to a certain degree out of a pattern of changing societal power structures in which, in general, individuals are seen as being far more central to a given social process than has previously been the case. From the point of view of learners, the notion of lifelong play has re-organized our understanding of learning considerably. In the modern era of skills-based digital media games, adults have been re-acquainted with a more memorable and entertaining form of learning. And while the systems of education were once antipathetic to—or at last unaware of—the processes of game-based learning, many are now adapting to these. The first compelling signs of a *systematic re-alignment of educative practices and forms with the requirements and preferences of learners* gives notice that playful learning will increasingly have a place in formal as well as informal education.

So on the one hand there is a need and an opportunity to radically rethink our formal educational systems; on the other we can see the move to a 'new learning' already taking place. Together the learner, the representation, the context and learning theories and practices can be realigned to a vision of learning more focused upon the *learning experience* than on information and facts. The move towards a process-centred learning approach has already started to help us to build up much more complex learning sequences and design patterns than was previously practical. These experiences, built up by discovery missions and challenges (tests), capitalize on and nurture 21st century skills and place an equal emphasis upon both transferable soft and hard skills. *Crucially*, learning is not one process but a series of processes that can be mapped, replicated, simulated and analyzed using different methods and approaches, and therefore it seems self-evident that the future of learning with CGLEs will be more informatively considered and designed with a focus on these processes of learning rather than on national systems of education.

Together, when properly balanced, these key elements can result in an enriched learning process (via sets of processes), matching the experience of the lived world, but in a safe and unthreatening play arena. As long as learning is crafted into these experiences and as long as there is meta-reflection permitted, this learning in immersive worlds can be rewarding and advantageous. While there are differences between learning in traditional contexts and learning in virtual contexts, there is no reason why these cannot be mixed to provide benefits for learners to support new areas of learning through play, emulation, simulation, socializing, rehearsal and e-mentoring.

The potential for us to step through the frame and become active and interactive participants in a historical event, as a particular character from history, or as a chemist undertaking a chemical experiment, or even as a philosopher giving examples of a difficult concept clearly lays open the potential for more imaginative approaches to learning, allowing tutors the potential to extend their ways of *demonstrating* difficult ideas. Just as we can go on a field trip in the lived world, we can also play in the sandbox worlds that we have developed, extending our understanding, supporting distributed communities or simply meeting other learners' in the virtual world to undertake assignments.

The 'Conclusions' section of this book sets out the potential that social and immersive strategies could have upon our culture and society. However, the power of immersive education to transform learning experiences in qualitative ways is not seen as an either/or alternative to traditional learning. In particular, face-to-face learning still represents the 'gold standard' of education, but new tools are emerging that force us to consider the direction of change in society, and hence in education. As education continues, arguably as the central organizing aspect of society, the temptation to control it increases too, and the resisting of social strategies such as 'self-organizing communities' may provide a central tension that influences education over the next hundred years.

While a solution to many of the frustrations and under-achievements of the current system may be here, it is important that we do not squander our chances of improving education by stepping backwards—or worse, over-controlling our educational institutions. Just as for the vividly remembered field trip from youth, learning in immersive worlds presents us with the ability to remember learning experiences for longer, engaging and motivating us as learners and capturing the images and sounds more intimately than in merely informational modes, thus helping us to foster the greatest possible creativity, enthusiasm and appreciation of learning in all our students.

DEFINITIONS AND A NOTE ON THE FORMAT OF THIS BOOK

The book uses terminology that some readers may not be familiar with, so Appendix A provides a glossary of terms. But it is probably worth noting two definitions here in the main text.

The term *computer generated environments* is used here as a 'catchall' term to include interactive games, simulations, virtual worlds and some interactive digital content (such as interactive learning materials). However, this book has its focus firmly upon education and learning, and therefore the term *computer generated learning environment* is also used. The book also includes use of the terms *immersive worlds* and *virtual worlds* to bring together terms that are often used separately. In this book we are looking at both games that include rule systems and virtual worlds for exploration which are unstructured and more open and socially focused. In addition, the use of the term *simulation* is in general (but not always) used in this book to mean an interactive environment as well, but in general, the term refers to any tool that replicates real-world activities and tasks. So to conclude, in this book the term *computer generated environments* is used to mean interactive and often 3D environments; the terms *virtual worlds*, *immersive worlds* and *simulations* are used to refer to virtual worlds and game environments; and the term *computer generated learning environments* is used to mean indicate computer generated learning environments that are interactive.

The book refers to *immersive worlds* in a quite general way to include games and simulations used for non-entertainment applications, although this definition is problematic in the sense that the line between entertainment and non-entertainment is itself slightly arbitrary in the light of more entertaining learning games being used quite widely. However, it does give an emphasis to the Platonic distinction between playing for fun and playing for learning. This is an important distinction as it brings the 'serious' applications of games and virtual worlds into the centre of the discussion about learning and also because it places the notion of play at the heart of learning.

Immersive worlds here thus include games and simulations within serious applications, the use of virtual world applications and some interactive digital media, while *immersive worlds* extend beyond Flash and Java games to virtual world applications; the use of games for mixed reality, with augmented reality and for 'lifelogging' are some of the convergent forms emerging with educational applications. Additionally, the use of 'mash-ups' in which a combination of applications can be used—for example, global positioning systems and sensor technologies in the physical world alongside games and virtual applications in the virtual world—are creating new hybrid spaces and are also educationally interesting.

The book also makes use of call-out boxes, which are interspersed throughout the book providing additional information and case studies to help the reader to visualize the kinds of applications available and to provide additional detail to guide understanding where concepts are in need of greater clarification. The appendices provide a glossary of selected terms used in the book (Appendix A), a list of educational games discussed in this book (Appendix B), a list of virtual world categories (Appendix C) and a list of virtual worlds currently available online (Appendix D).

1 The Context of Learning

The *context* of learning plays an extremely important role in the *processes* of learning (Dewey, 1997; Laurillard, 2002; Vygotsky, 1962). When we talk about context of learning, what we are referring to are the socio-political, institutional and disciplinary contexts within which the central relationships of learning are formed and operate. We can describe these relationships as being between *the educational systems*, the *institutions* (including teachers) and the *learners*.

The educational system provides the national or regional education legislation and strategies, along with the learning management systems—including curricula and accreditation—that will be used by teachers and learners. Schools and colleges are also part of this system within which their role is the *organization and delivery of the accredited processes of learning.* They achieve these systematic aims through the placement and arrangement of the learners into classes with class timetables—which order and organize learners in time and place—and through the application of an instructional curriculum that orders understanding into information to be remembered, recited and tested.

Within the wider context, the school or college has a position of socio-political importance as part of the education system, but also it is an *institution* in its own right. These *places of learning* have their own traditions and internal systems, their own internal politics and often their own scholastic traditions and preferences. Moreover, although each institution may be part of the wider system, each will also have a unique identity as an organization. That identity, along with the institutional traditions and setup, is an important factor that helps us to understand the institution's relationship with the teachers or tutors and with the learners. These relationships are important because schools use a system of organization (Scott, 2001) that incorporates 'embodied' roles. According to the *Stanford Encyclopedia of Philosophy*,

> an institution that is an organization or system of organizations consists of an embodied (occupied by human persons) structure of differentiated roles. These roles are defined in terms of tasks, and rules

regulating the performance of those tasks. . . . Further, these roles are often related to one another hierarchically, and hence involve different levels of status and degrees of authority.[1]

In a sense, in an educational institution such as a school or college, the teacher occupies a differentiated role which is interdependent with other roles in the organization.

The learner, too, has an integral role as recipient of 'knowledge' in the more traditional formulations of learning or as an active learner in the modern models. The consideration of the learner in our post-modern position at the beginning of the 21st century represents a unique challenge for the contextual understanding of learning in that the learner is supposedly the main focus for all the processes in the school or college. At the same time, however, the learner's role is still rather hazily defined, in terms of our definition and understanding of an *institution* as an organization with embodied roles. The learner should in all probability be defined as a differentiated role, subject to tasks and rules and to the authority of the school teacher and board. The learner is both within the system—the purpose of the system—and yet strangely in some ways outside the system. We will focus more upon the learner and learning processes in the following two chapters but it is important to note here that we cannot, in a Deweyian sense, consider the learner in splendid isolation from the wider context of learning.

The separation of the school as an institution with its hierarchical ordering of tasks and roles from the human processes of learning epitomizes perhaps another great challenge for any potential re-organization of our educational systems—that is, that many of our institutions today are undergoing rapid evolutionary change to adapt to a different ordering and new understanding of information that has more widely resulted from the emergence of the information age (including new technologies). This theme is discussed elsewhere in greater detail (de Freitas, forthcoming), but it is crucial to consider it, as the impact of our changing and evolving understanding of information has given rise to new challenges that will ultimately affect education such as the rapid proliferation of information, both validated and invalidated, as a result of computerization and digitization (Negroponte, 1995). Moreover, in the modern era the new centrality of the concept of information over more archaic notions of 'knowledge' illustrates both a general transition away from the hierarchical and unified concepts of the past towards more multiordinal and subjective notions of informational utility. This shift in terms of the consideration of information is, however, just one instance of how the old formalizations of order and arrangement are changing. The old notions of hierarchies and unities generally have little favour in the modern world, and in the 'post-information society' these notions seem to be breaking down altogether, leaving us to consider what the role of our educational institutions will actually become over the next ten years.

So while our understanding of educational systems has been quite aligned with the institutions and organizations that deliver education to learners, today this assumption of educational systems and institutions being the same thing seems to have unravelled. In particular, the methods of educational delivery of content have themselves become more diversified with the emergence, for example, of e-learning and online learning, distance education and lifelong learning (de Freitas & Jameson, 2012).

Understanding the context for learning today therefore involves understanding the contexts, processes and strategies used to support learning and learning experiences. In fact, the idea of structuring learning processes according to social and political contexts, roles and rules, which may have sat well in the 19th century, seems to be slightly anachronistic in the modern information society, which is governed more by the tendency to open and free access to all content, such as is delivered via the World Wide Web (Berners Lee, 2000).

Today the emphasis is rightly upon the learner or the learning experience and processes rather than governed by the organization and systems of education—at least in conceptual terms. However, at least in respect to computer generated environments (CGEs), a re-organization of the system, tasks and rules needs to be considered just in order to deliver this type of content and approach to learning because the specifics of the organization, such as class size and duration, seem to be impeding the flow of information and the open structures that we are becoming familiar with in our non-disciplinary and out-of-school lives.

To get a picture of the differences between school and home, it is worth considering a few statistics: according to a recent European survey by the International Software Federation of Europe (2010), researchers have found that 74% of those between 16 and 19 years of age (n = 3000), 60% of those ages 20 to 24, 56% of those 25 to 29, and 38% of those 30 to 44 consider themselves to be gamers. In a national survey undertaken for the UK Department for Transport, which focused upon game play in 9 to 13-year-olds (n = 1,108), we found that a large proportion (53%) of children regularly play games intended for adults; in fact, we found that *Call of Duty* (rated PEGI-18) was the most played game in that age range—by 53% of boys and 12% of girls (Dunwell, Christmas & de Freitas, 2012). In our national survey, girls were more likely to spend time on social networking (70%), as opposed to boys (57%). The same survey found that children were using the Internet on average 5.4 times per week, and they were playing console games on average 3.1 times per week and online games 2.4 times per week. They were playing games with other children online for on average 61 minutes per day, with 30% responding that they play games for up to an hour, 21% playing for three hours per day and 13% playing more than three hours per day (Dunwell et al., 2012).

In this way, how children are learning and what they are doing in their spare time has changed considerably over the last twenty years. Online entertainment and social networking have to a great extent re-organized how children are *playing* when they are at home, and is even having an impact upon how children are *learning* at home. The impact of game culture and social networking upon school education has to date been minimal, however. In most educational systems, the drive towards making content available online, tracking learners through learning management systems and introducing computers into classrooms has prompted the main changes wrought by new information and communications technologies (ICTs) and e-learning projects to introduce more digital systems into education have in some senses at least been seen to have stalled, not least because of a *technology push* that has in general emphasized technology over content and monitoring and tracking over any tangible pedagogic gains for learners (de Freitas & Jameson, 2012).

While the use of games and social networking online has become a major component of children's lives, formal education however have been limited, and relatively unsuccessful by most accounts, despite studies comparing online learning and traditional learning finding no significant difference. But despite the latter having significant benefits of scalability, the main task of selling blended learning to tutors has been difficult and slow. However, in the United States it is fair to say that these efforts have been quicker to take hold, probably due to a certain pragmatism in the favouring of financial savings and benefits. For example, in 2010, over four million K–12 (primary education and high school) students participated in a formal online learning program in the United States, with 'online learning enrolments growing by 46% per year'.[2] Moreover, a recent United States research report that focused on students leaving school courses found that '47% said a major reason for dropping out was that "classes were not interesting" and they were "bored", and notably, 88% of dropouts had passing grades'.[3] In the United States, 29% of higher education students took an online course in 2009. The reasons for this move towards online and distance learning are complex, but they do reveal that in the battle between what children are doing at school and what they are doing in their own time, leisure time seems to be engaging and motivating them in ways that in formal education we are only beginning to become aware of and adopt into practice.

The major impediment to making all formal education as engaging and motivating as learners' leisure activities at home is seemingly the school *system* itself and the mechanisms—including the roles, rules and tasks—for keeping that system in place: classrooms, age and stage ordering of learners, class duration, classes, disciplinary silos and the instructional mode itself. While these seem set and static in the current formulation of schooling, things could not be more different in social gaming environments, where communications are multiordinal and unfettered, structures and rules are discrete, and learning is tested not through the linguistic (oral or written) repetition of information but by the undertaking of cumulatively more difficult missions and challenges. Crucially, the acquisition of skills is *rapid* because the challenges and missions can be attempted as many times as the players need to and whenever they want to; if they fail they can, as it were, re-take the test straight away, as many times as is necessary, making the requisite adjustments and corrections to their approach, until the mission is accomplished or the skill achieved. In these environments testing is automated and is used subliminally as a feature of the entertainment. That is not to say that all learning should be as it is in a game–this is, of course, too simplistic. But in order to keep children and adults engaged in education and learning, we need to look at what works in such games and CGEs, and try to distil how this could inform us in developing a new set of rules and structures and a new system of education that more closely follows the human preferences and capacities for learning and scaffolds the formation of skills needed for a digital age.

In relation to their potential role in a fully functioning educational system, this book aims to explore what makes games and virtual worlds so engaging and considers how we can utilize aspects of these qualities to re-engage students in formal education and, importantly, to deliver adults who have both the skills they value and need and those that support a successful and dynamic intellectual, technological and post-industrial economy. But this means considering all the elements of the four dimensions of learning—context, learning theory, learning representation and the learners themselves—and working out how we might best deploy our understanding of a *new learning* to re-create a system that matches the needs of society and the individual.

Of course, education was ever in flux, and the pressure of change is a fact of life for any developing and growing system (Dewey, 1997). However, in order to understand that change we must first consider the *context of change* for education. There is a need to understand the current context of learning and to examine how educational processes, institutions and practices work within this current context. For example, while there have been assumptions about pushing technologies into schools, colleges and universities, there has not always been the conceptual or pragmatic scaffolding around this deployment—and that has often had the opposite impact from the one intended. While the tools of new technologies and online content repositories constitute the first steps into the *digitization of learning*, the most important aspects—the system of education, including the tutors, the structures and the disciplinary ordering—have remained in place, enforcing a lock on any real change in our classrooms and seminar rooms. In order to consider this issue, then, the way we consider learning itself comes under the microscope.

As a 'cultural construct', *learning* has become less something that we gain (e.g., an objective understanding of knowledge), and more something that is experienced (e.g., a subjective learning experience), as John Dewey and others have noted. This subtle but significant conceptual shift implies a re-ordering of the educational system that has only just begun with technology-enhanced learning and various new national e-learning projects. Moving away from the traditional understanding of learning as *objectively gaining from a significant other an understanding of 'knowledge'*, today learning is being re-considered as *a set of subjective and contextualized processes used to inform, socialize and upskill learners*. But just as books were considered the basic units of our 19th century ordering of school and the disciplines, today it is *the learning experience itself that is the unit of learning processes*. As in the field study trip, the experience of learning *in situ* and through defined problems, missions and challenges promises the potential to remember the experience for longer and thus aids the aim of more fluently contextualized learning within that remembered activity.

　·　*Context* is thus used here to mean the context of learning as a whole, including the educational system itself, the cultural context within which that system is located and the context of the learner—that is, how individuals are placed, their background and other specifics. In a sense, every learner is unique and has different sets of experiences to draw from, has different perspectives about learning and different preferences for how he or she learns. This being the case, the way that learning evolves over time must take into account the need to deliver subjective, unique, personalized and adaptive learning that in turn delivers an immersive and involving experience.

FROM THE CRADLE TO THE GRAVE

Since the 19th century and earlier, a trend towards legislating for increasing the age of children participating in formal education has continued to gain ground, and is part of a wider democratization in society which includes widening access to education, welfare and public health services and the advent of universal suffrage, equality and human rights.

In the United Kingdom, for example, the introduction of the universal provision of state elementary education for all was part of the 1870 Education Act, which also incidentally brought with it voting rights for women (although regrettably, only on school boards). The continued widening of provision of education for more people for longer in their lifetimes—for example, from ages 14 to 16 in 1972, and from ages 16 to 18 (as is planned)—has continued to bring formal education to wider communities of learners. As early as the 16th century, Comenius envisaged universal education for girls and boys up to 18 years of age—with an additional six years for the best students at universities (Hill, 1991). This project has found its apotheosis in the provision for lifelong learning—that is, learning for adults throughout life, through continuing professional development and re-training—and has ultimately prompted a new consideration of education as being a constant 'from the cradle to the grave'.

Somehow, however, over the period from the 19th century to today, the division between education and learning has deepened, leading to an enforced kind of disconnect between the design and delivery of learning 'at the frontline'—in the classrooms and seminar rooms to learners—and the *system* of education, which includes the infrastructure of learning (institutions), the prioritization of educational practices (curriculum) and the standardization of educational practices (target and policy-driven delivery). The reason for this, I would argue, is conceptual; earlier in my career, I was working with one national education department and was shocked to learn that there was no pedagogy group in the whole department, despite its maintenance of all of that country's school, college and university funding and policy advice.

At that time, even as the grasp on the theories of learning was absent from policy making, the disconnect between learning processes and educational systems was deepening because if you have no idea about the competing strategies and how they deliver effective learning, how can you make any effective educational policies?

This disconnect prompts and leads to what I term the *alignment principle*. In simple terms, those making policies must have some informed guide as to what impact their policies will make at the 'coal face', or in this instance the 'chalk face', because if they do not have a full and proper understanding of *how* students learn, well-intentioned efforts can still result in stagnation—or worse, decline. The greatest danger perhaps is that of making policies that are really about an education system and *its* overall results for the public—in terms of voting—and which are not about the learner's experience. Ironically, it is this emphasis on the system's results that may well be the greatest impediment to better societal results in education. In many cases, the systems that have evolved are now far too disconnected from the inherent processes of learning, and this has led directly to a misalignment of educational policies, practices and strategies.

For example, over time, the macro-politico-economic factors, such as trends towards longer periods of learning over an individual's lives, were considered rather uncritically as a good thing, without much reflection or analysis of why or how that trend fits with the modern learner, the modern educational system and the rules and roles that they support. A notion of 'utility' or public good—happiness for the maximum number of individuals underpins this approach; the idea was developed by Jeremy Bentham, John Stuart Mill, and others in the 19th century (Bentham, 1987; Mill, 1998; Sandel, 2009). In this sense, there is a perceived social benefit for the society when more of its population are well educated, or educated to the highest level possible.

In this utilitarian sense, then, education is seen more and more as a social tool for growing national wealth whilst improving benefits for individuals in terms of, for example, increasing employability and individual wealth. While utility is regarded as a central guiding educational policy component, the deeper cultural and social purpose of education has detached from learning and its centrality not just as utility but as part of a wider movement towards a more process-based (and user-centred) understanding of information—that is, as part of the subjective processes of the individual.

In this way, the educational system on the one hand is serving the macropolitical objectives of ideas formulated and developed in the 19th century, and on the other, more pragmatic side, learning is being re-organized to reflect a *set of processes* and as a *learning experience*. Predictably, perhaps, the historical disconnection between the two has seemed to deepen recently, making education and learning very different terms, imbued with very different meanings in the 21st century context, from their meanings in the 19th century. Just as the systems and systematization characterized the 19th century, so today the understanding of *process* dominates our theoretical thinking and approaches. Furthermore, some of the notional certainties of education seem to have changed quite radically from the 19th century, when notions of knowledge, unified meanings, the disciplines and set roles and rules were highly influential. Today, in a pedagogic sense, new notions about learning have emerged, where the trope of unified objective meaning—and its acquisition—has given way to the consideration of subjective truths; and where changing and diversified roles predominate and cross-disciplinary and flexible learning are quite commonplace.

Whether it is our perception of the meanings of education and learning that have changed or whether they have qualitatively transformed in the period that Manuel Castells and others have termed the *information society* is debatable (Castells, 1996, 1997, 1998). However, the changes in our *understanding* of education and the institutions that educate, in light of the capacity for the digitization of information, *is* notable (de Freitas, forthcoming). With information rather than knowledge as the key currency in our understanding of learning, the unit of learning has literally become information, and with the advent of the modern computer, the Internet and as a result the 'rise of the network society' (Castells, 1996), this unit can be reduced to even smaller data *bits*.

At least to some extent, then, the 'information society' has wrought a new social ordering, and the hierarchical structures that were integral in the 19th century and that maintained institutions, at least in terms of the roles and rules of the learning institution, had begun to unravel. But the concepts of the 19th century, of social democracy, utility and latterly *open access*, have become the key words of the 'network society'. It is *open access* in particular that has such a natural affinity with the democratization of all our social structures and, perhaps ironically, it is *open access* which presents the greater confrontation to the *system* of the school, the college and the university, as 'open access to information for all' opens out the experience of learning beyond the confines of formal education. For example, it is notable in this respect that the home schooling movement in the United States is growing.

However, open access to content and resources is just one of the issues around changing contexts for learning. While the Internet and open access resources have provided an impetus for the OpenCourseWare movement, online learning and open educational resources (Johansen, 2011; Walsh, 2011), the repository idea of learning doesn't seem to have gained any real ground. Early ambitious projects to digitize learning content, such as Jorum and others that focus upon pure digitization of information, where the end purpose is merely open access, have signalled specific challenges. For example, the idea of learning objects without pedagogic or even institutionally situated context has not broadly gained favour with teachers; this is largely because they are not convinced by the use of 'acontextual' or 'decontextualized' information and resources. There is, then, in some quarters a discernable disinclination towards open access to educational resources *or* any major movement away from situating learning, in an institutional location-based context. This once again highlights the importance of context to the consideration of learning processes.

The differentiation between open educational resources *per se* and our own human processes of learning presents the possibility for a conceptual transition, which has significant implications for learning and teaching, not least for the role of the tutor. Traditionally, the tutor prepared the materials of teaching and delivered them; today, however, the idea of teaching using resources developed by others is a very familiar practice and has become far less extraordinary in formal educational contexts than it once was. This trend has been advanced by e-learning materials, such as off-the-shelf videos, games and interactive puzzles and activities, which are often expensive to produce but which are easily made available for sharing with others over websites and within learning management systems. However, by separating learning materials and resources from the teacher, some issues of pedagogic context do emerge, although in a slightly different sense. While teachers have always utilized a range of available resources—be they books, diagrams or television programmes—learning and teaching, in a sense, is about imbuing these resources with context and subjective meaning and making them 'come alive' for learners.

A newer trend is the production of content produced by learners themselves. This is becoming more prevalent in areas where learners have access to the tools of production—for example, in film and animation studies, music production and new media courses. However, the potential for this trend to continue is significant as more access to tool kits and cheaper access to development tools become available. For example, in games courses, learners can develop their own games and these can be used by others for learning and training purposes. Past projects, such as the Making Games project at the London Knowledge Lab, gave children access to software with which they could make their own games (Pelletier, 2005, 2009). The *Game Maker* software similarly allows teachers and learners to develop their own games and share resources (Overmars, 2004). The real long-term impact of this trend in the wider context of learning is unclear at present, however any increase in the general decoupling of content production from teachers' control will have a definite impact in the future, as the traditional nineteenth- and twentieth-century role of teachers in the preparation and delivery of learning materials falls away.

Learning without teachers is an emerging trend, which includes pure online learning and forms that emphasize group learning. Moreover, as surveys undertaken by this author attest, while learners have strong preferences for learning with tutors, other strong preferences included both learning on the job and learning with peers (de Freitas & Jarvis, 2009). Further research in the health area has demonstrated how learning in groups *can* be more effective than teacher-based learning (Woltering et al., 2009). While research on learning *styles* has been comprehensively debunked in a number of studies (among them Coffield et al., 2004), clearly there are many factors involved in preferred learning modes, including the learner's expectations and past experiences. However, it is apparent that the new modes of content production play less well to the hierarchical, teacher-centred model and are a better fit with flexible learning, the meditational role of the tutor and peer or social learning models which focus upon 'problems', challenges and activity-based learning (Vygotsky, 1962).

These 'new' models for learning are not really *so* new, but their implications for how the wider context of learning could best be adapted does in turn have implications for the institutional arrangement, including durations of lessons, roles of the teachers and tutors, a focus upon discovery or 'exploratory learning' (de Freitas & Neumann, 2009), and an increasing emphasis upon social learning or social interactive learning. The term *social interactive learning* simply refers to learning based upon dialogue and social interactions (de Freitas & Liarokapis, 2011). However, it should be noted that in previous work around learning theories, it was notable that theories in the social interactive area were fairly sparse when compared with those in associative and cognitive groups (see, e.g., de Freitas & Jameson, 2012; and Mayes & de Freitas, 2004, 2007; an exception is Wenger, 1998).

With the shift described above, the set up of the place of learning—that is, the institution—within the wider context of learning may need to be re-organized for more social learning modes, just as the need for learners to interact with one another has already resulted in minor re-organizations of *physical* class spaces. Notably, many projects looking at physical learning spaces have moved towards more flexible multipurpose arrangements of learners through seating and computer positioning—less in straight rows and more in clusters and circles. For example, a qualitative study of arcade spaces by Kathryn Whitmore and Lindsay Laurich found three principles for learning that describe this transition well: 'clustering and collaborating, inverting traditional structures of power, and reconstituting access and ownership' (Whitmore & Laurich, 2010: 21). Thus, in the case of education spaces today, social interactive learning is driven more by the preferences of learners and less by institutional architecture or systemic precedents. Notably, this affects not just the spaces of learning but also the content of learning, the method of learning and teaching and the roles of learning (e.g., content maker/teacher/learner).

The commitment to the democratization or universality of education means more than just open access to resources; it entails the notions of lifelong learning to reach larger numbers of learners at all stages of their lives and also, crucially, it means renewed consideration and development of pedagogy—that is, of the learning and teaching methods that are to be employed to support new learning processes. It is interesting to note that a contradictory set of trends in higher education is emerging: alongside the trend and push on the one hand towards more democratization, there seems to be a contradictory counter-position, pushing for the tightening of systematic and institutional controls. For example, the recent introduction in the United Kingdom of *more* top-down controls and micro-management of frontline teachers and academics is hard to explain, particularly as one would have expected flatter hierarchies to be more sympathetic with and more complementary to a wider democratization of education and where one might have expected *more* devolved power and control to teachers and tutors, not less.

To my mind, this is a difficult contradiction to explain. It could be explained as a reaction to the reality of the learner's needs or more pragmatically as a re-assertion of the control of the education system over its institutions and individual teachers. Some commentators have considered this as symptomatic of a general socio-economic trend which, amongst other effects, has seen financial pressures put on universities to make profits. In a certain sense, then, the education sector is fragmenting, with some parts being run according to business imperatives rather than according to broader altruistic educational principles. I have commented on this in other works and concluded that there is a persistent contradictory dialectic between the concepts of freedom and information (de Freitas, forthcoming). Alongside the trend towards democratic civil systems, open access to education and freedom of information, the intrinsic needs of governments, multinational organizations and institutions vying for power and control re-assert themselves. For the time being, from the point of view of governments and large institutions, the powers that society gains from more democratized systems is largely done so begrudgingly. It seems, therefore, that the more that open access and freedom of information is claimed by the public, the more the hierarchical reaction against this will be evident (de Freitas, forthcoming).

However, the lack of a conceptual basis for *new learning* forms could also explain the reactionary positions taken—at least in educational circles. Within 19th century paradigms, micro management and hierarchical control strategies make a lot of sense, as societal 'change' was not a really popular notion when the modern school system was devised by our Victorian cousins. Societal improvement was aspired to, but the notion of change, *in the social order or the structures of power,* was an unwelcome guest in their general social philosophy and in the institutions they established. Their systems were characterized by prescriptive and culturally defined roles and rules, generic utilitarian architecture and practices and regrettably limited ambitions in terms of any social mobility that might or should result from education. In some ways, then, it is unsurprising that systems and institutional models that were created in a time when the aim was to support and preserve a set social structure are not culturally inclined towards the consideration of revolutionary changes.

Ironically, however, in our own age the reaction against change probably worsens the situation. For example, and to stay with the open educational resources debate, while universities in the United States such as the Massachusetts Institute of Technology have promoted this approach with enthusiasm, in the United Kingdom I have noticed how many universities do not entertain or follow this approach. In fact, the reverse has happened: in general, learners who are not enrolled in courses cannot gain access to any university content. While admittedly, this is changing—with massive open online courses—it is notable that the rigid access controls universities have on their teaching materials and content emphasizes the deeper survival reaction *against* decoupling teaching practices and teaching materials.

The current 'lock down' on higher education assets and materials will inevitably change as open resources become the order of the day, but it is likely to be the learners, and not the institutions, that will force this re-organization—and this is because the structures of universities have inherently evolved to be impervious to social change and are therefore very resistant to any such reorganization. The culture of many universities is generally very risk averse, conservative and highly influenced by 19th century practices. But without the conceptual basis for change the position is completely logical and understandable.

This characteristic also explains why universities have been slow to adopt computer generated environments and simulations as a new model for learning. CGEs offer a new mode of learning and teaching which is outside of the comfort zone of many teachers and tutors. But they also offer a level of immersion into a subject area that is quite unique. (See Call-Out Box 1: Immersion.) As well as being closer to real world experiences, tasks, activities and problems, CGEs such as game environments, virtual worlds and computer modelling *immerse* the learner and at the same time give more control for teachers to monitor and adapt to learners.

Box 1.1   Immersion

The notion of immersion and immersive learning is worthy of deeper consideration. There are a number of studies centring upon the effectiveness of game-based learning that I have been involved with, and it is interesting to look back and see how the debates commenced in the learning simulation literature—in particular, how the debates around *levels of fidelity* have informed our understanding of games and virtual worlds.

Immersion can perhaps be considered as being total or partial, but a more subtle consideration of the various levels of immersion can be helpful. Arguably, immersion—as it relates to the learning experience—is supported through different layers and components. These components include:

- *The levels of realism of the activities and closeness of activities to familiar actions experienced.* This factor connects with the fidelity of the environment (below) and how it is navigated and explored by the player in the game or world.
- *Familiarity and consistency of the interface (visual and audio) to the user.* Any jarring of experience in this regard can lead to dissociation or cognitive overload of the learner. The normal rules of usability apply here, but the level of difficulty of the learning experience and the level of engagement of the learner are also important factors.
- *The use of narrative.* Narrative can help with immersion as well, and some studies (e.g. Dickey, 2011) highlight narrative as playing a central role in effective learning design for serious games. Flow is critical to this process of being in the game or world, and therefore the level of difficulty and engagement of the game/world needs to be correct.
- *The levels of fidelity.* Levels of fidelity should equate with the learning need, for example certain learning does not need to be realistic to be effective. How levels of fidelity are selected is dependent upon the requirements and ICT capability of the learner or learner group. However, people who play entertainment games regularly are accustomed to a high level of verisimilitude. But to what level fidelity is affected by expectation, and whether negative transfer is connected with fidelity, are still subjects for research within CGEs. An internal logic of the world is required—and a consistency of quests and pathways will reinforce immersion.
- *The levels of interactivity.* These include how much control learners have, how intuitive the design and functionality are, what changes learners can make, and how far can they affect the system as a whole.

Learning in CGEs is both inherently immersive and social, opening up new ways to present, produce, share and reflect upon interactions and activities. The power of CGEs is thus considerable, but fitting their use into formal education has proved difficult and challenging, not least because of the contextual issues outlined above—that is, the rules, structures and roles of the educational institution seem to be at odds with social immersive learning and in particular the attempts to create and adopt really effective game-based learning (Egenfeldt-Nielsen, 2005). The wider question for us then is, do we want to adopt CGE learning approaches? Alternatively, we can ask if we can afford *not* to exploit these new tools?

This book does not set out to try to make an adversarial argument for the deployment of CGEs in education, but aims to outline a new vision for learning in which CGEs can be productively fitted. That vision encompasses a system that is defined more by learning experiences than curricula and set texts, one in which CGEs can play a central role that can enrich and enliven these experiences. One way to think of this is in the sense of an overview that considers how games and simulations are currently being used in other non-education-focused sectors. For example, these simulation- or game-based approaches have been used in military training (Smith, 2010) and business training (Faria, 2001). Medical training has also been successfully using simulations for a quite a while now. Of course, it is true in some cases that school education games are used as a central learning tool (Gee, 2003). In fact, in infant education, play is a significant and major aspect of learning. But the further up the ladder we ascend in the formal education sector, the greater the resistance grows and the more ideas about games and play being childish, non-serious and without value come to the fore.

While philosophers since the ancient Greek period have been concerned with play as a form of learning, even Plato created a distinction between playing for fun and playing for learning. We will consider play in a little more detail in the next chapters, but it worth noting that the context of learning and training does have a direct bearing upon whether CGEs will be deployed, and interestingly it is the *sectoral* context rather than the *disciplinary* context that has a greater influence over uptake. Perhaps having a historical link to certain teaching tools makes some sectors more open and prepared for using these tools. Notably, in contexts where training involves 'life or death' skills, there has been a much more ready, efficient and effective take-up of these tools. Why, then, in formal education contexts have we been so resistant to utilizing these exciting and potentially unlimited environments?

I think it is also worth observing that formal distinctions between training and education are also becoming more blurred, which opens up more possibilities for adopting training tools, materials and approaches in formal education contexts, and vice versa. As noted in our work around learning theories, while in the past training generally deployed associationist theories, such as task-centred learning approaches (Gagné, 1970), today more cognitive approaches have been adopted. Likewise, in education, more associative (task-centred) approaches are also more in evidence, as the lines of division between different learning theories have become more blurred. The erosion of general distinctions within education and training is most clearly seen in the learning models deployed and the uptake of tools that were once used in only one part of the sector but which have proved transferable. For example, most education and training organizations use some form of learning management system for tracking student/trainee performance and for storing teaching materials (e.g., proprietary software such as *Blackboard* or open source tools like *Moodle*).

Another instance of transferable tools and approaches that are employed in different sectors is the use of games. 'Gamification', as it is beginning to be known, is the introduction of game mechanics and game elements, such as competition or leader boards applied in general work, education and entertainment activities (Deterding et al., 2011). It builds on the strengths of games to motivate and engage users and to test their knowledge and skills. Games also build upon social learning capabilities. Theoretically, if we can learn to harness the capabilities of games, we can re-engage a new generation of learners and appeal to hard-to-reach groups of learners in new ways. Building on the strengths of game-based approaches (e.g., engagement, motivation and immersion), teachers and tutors in different sectors now have new tools and cultural forms in common.

Yet however we look at this area of *potential* for learning, it is hard to escape the contradiction which remains before us—that is, between the potentials of the open access and flexible tools and forms at our disposal and, conversely, the control structures and strategies of the institutions. How can we bring in any changes when our institutions are so imbued with 19th century rules, regulations and roles? Somehow we must comprehend that if we continue to try to impose control strategies it will be a counterproductive impediment to the systemic change that is required if we are at least to keep the bare bones of our systems in place for the future. In all probability, the greater our resistance to change, the more absolute the demise of our institutions could be.

There are plenty of cautionary tales to be told here. One by one, industries and sectors—many of which had Victorian origins themselves—have been caught cold by the implications of new trends and technologies, which allow universal access to information and digital products and which demanded new institutional approaches. Many established high street shops and chains which had once thrived disappeared within a decade of the new economic realities of the information age. Media content providers–songwriters and filmmakers—have watched the value of their products plummet as national and international distributions fell and copyright systems collapsed. Television companies and newspapers, which once distained any concern about online competition, have since seen advertising revenues and sales plummet as new media forms have competed for and won an ever increasing share of their market. The post offices, those great Victorian institutions which once seemed a reliably permanent landmark in every local community, have started to disappear as whole swathes of their business have been lost to digital communication systems. The obvious lesson of the age, then, is that *we need to adapt a lot of our systems to change.*

In all these examples there were benefits that affected the user of the service or consumer of products that were not fully acknowledged or appreciated by the organizations or institutions that faced the pressures of change that resulted from a wider societal take-up of digital forms and technologies. In education, the possibility of remote access to classes from the home—using digital technologies—has obvious benefits. For example, in a virtual classroom—*accessed remotely*—absenteeism can be ameliorated, physical bullying is impossible, harassment of pupils *or* teachers is recorded and can be checked and disruptive behaviours can be filtered out of the experience of enthusiastic learners. There are, of course, many very compelling arguments against remote learning for children and particularly for very young children. However, it is worth remembering that there are arguments on *both* sides that take into account different individual needs in a child's developmental health and welfare *and* the challenges to any system's efficiency. And these kinds of factors do have an impact on cultural change.

However, the democratization of education—that is, the trend to broaden the reach of education and towards opening up access to learning materials—is still confronted by a cultural tendency to rely on control strategies such as those advocated by the more risk-averse and anti-change lobbies that would generally aim to keep the traditional learning models in place. It is not altogether surprising that, as the reach of education has broadened, systemic and institutional controls have started to tighten. This is likely a reflex systemic reaction to the *real politik*—the more the loss of control and power is felt by those who assume an entitlement to control, the more the requirement and effort to preserve control grows.

The notion of the *learning experience,* which fits in well with a new pedagogy that emphasizes activity-based, problem-based and situated learning, seems to fit less well with the practices designed for the spaces of the conventional educational systems since it assumes an unbounded and dislocated conceptualization of space and learning. Such an experience is three-dimensional, unbounded in space and time, limitless and essentially subjective. Therefore, learning can take place anywhere, at any time and in any context. The power of the learning experience is that it does not need an institutional framework or organization to take place. The *new learning* is so challenging to institutions because it sets out this comparatively new unit of learning—that is, the *learning experience.* I would argue that such a unit is more comprehensive and better reflects the processes of thinking, such as memorization. However, working with the concept does involve an understanding of the likely reorganizations that might need to occur in terms of deployment, assessment and verification within the education system.

The problem is thus how institutions deal with this challenge; should they embrace these *new learning* approaches? This book does not seek to provide any definitive answers to this question but to consider the options available to policy makers and institution managers. It seems generally that most learners, tutors and teachers are in favour of changes. However, a cultural resistance to change in the educational institutions promotes a more reactive stance: *If it's worked so far, why can't we just keep the system going as is?* This argument however, is a highly subjective and somewhat predictable institutional response that fails to address the fact that various commentaries in the United Kingdom in recent years have *suggested* to the government and parents alike that *our* system is *not* working. Of course, it's much easier to blame individual teachers and institutions for 'failing' than it is to consider that something about the nature or political administration of the education system might be responsible for the failure to deliver the universally high standards of education that society hopes for. However, at the level of individual institutions there are pressing frontline issues such as the level of disengagement of the learners, the frustration of the teachers and the attraction of the new technological forms to children in the home that are driving the debates for change. And with most Western governments pulling out of any further pushes towards universal university education when most are barely half way to 100% participation, there are societal and economic arguments for exploring these potentially cheaper but still highly effective new learning forms. These arguments—economics and effectiveness—are the same arguments that drove uptake of the new forms of training and learning in other sectors, most notably at first in the military and industrial sectors.

Context is really a dividing category. Educational environments are places where information acquisition–centred learning models are prevalent. Traditional learning focuses on information collection, synthesis and analysis, and on textual or aural modes of communication; it is characterized by asymmetrical ratios of tutors to pupils and closed spaces (e.g., the seminar room or lecture theatre). On the other side of the equation, social interactive learning with an emphasis upon learning experiences and activities, collaborative learning and the use of exploratory spaces (virtual, real and hybrid) offers a new terrain where learners can explore information according to subjective and personalized frames of reference and changing identities and roles.

If this trend is set to continue, the implications for education *are* significant not least because of the efforts that will be involved in the re-organization of our physical and virtual spaces, the development of interest-led online communities and the shift towards more exploratory modes of learning. (See Call-Out Box 2: Online Learning Communities.) Clearly, we *are* seeing the emergence of new learning forms that centre on process and learner-centred endeavours. However, what specific implications this holds for the future of learning, assessment and accreditation are still debatable. For change to be paradigmatic we would need to see shifts in all these key areas and in the structure of the institutions themselves, affecting how universities and schools are organized on *all* levels.

Box 1.2   Online Learning Communities

Online learning communities are relatively recent, but are notable because of the large numbers of engaged community members. In communities such as *America's Army*, game play engages players for many hours. In particular, the level of engagement with multiplayer games is notable, as studies of the longevity of players on these games have indicated. For example Yee (2003) found that participants were playing on the entertainment online multi-player game *Ultima Online* for as long as 28.1 months; *Everquest* was played for as long as 22.7 months, indicating the power of this form for engaging large groups of players for significant periods of time.

In the future, games for learning, for health and for business may be developed using similar models that focus upon facilitating activities. A popular example is the *America's Army* game, originally released in 2002 and now up to version 3.3. It was developed on the Unreal engine by the U.S. Army's Moves Institute, and has a huge player base, with nine million downloads to date. The game has quite a significant training component as players go from relatively simple shooting practice and levelling up to team-based exercises. Notably, alongside these gold label games are very large numbers of community members, with numerous fanzine sites where users can chat and share strategy and game 'cheats'.

Multiplayer games have captured the popular imagination with their realistic graphic capability and tie-ins to social software and communications tools. The area has unsurprisingly become the subject of anthropological study and cultural investigation within the learning context, not least because of the complex levels of social interactions that have emerged (Herz, 2001; Paraskeva, Mysirlaki & Papagianni, 2010). For example, the emergence of multiplayer games have promoted the development of 'self-organized' combat clans, resulting from the beta version of *Quake*; these clans have persisted for years, and

> [t]here are thousands of them. The smallest have five members; the largest have hundreds and have developed their own politics, hierarchies, and systems of governance. They are essentially tribal—each has a name. . . . Although the clan network may seem anarchic because it is fiercely competitive and has no centralized authority . . . it is a highly cooperative system . . . largely because the players that comprise them, have a clear sense of shared goals (Herz, 2001: 183–184).

It is unsurprising, perhaps, that these clans and guilds follow some of the patterns Van Gennep (1960) and others have noted in relation to rites of passage. One similarity is the process of initiation into the game and community, and onto different levels—for example, from warrior to orc in *World of Warcraft*. The use of these formats for supporting learning is in its infancy, but it clear that links between levelling up, crossing boundaries, playing roles and following narrative development are powerful learning tools. If we could replicate these approaches in a CGE specifically designed for school education, for example, we could harness social interactive learning and playful learning together.

Non-game social communities today are pervasive, and in particular the growth of Facebook to 845 million active monthly users is a most notable example. But while the community is more focused upon sharing personal content such as photos, games from Zynga accounted for 12% of the 1 billion net income generated in 2012, a significant and growing contribution. So the link between games and online communities continues, and could be adapted and adopted more in a new learning platform aimed at children and adult.

It is evident that the process of empowering the learner is just a part of the formal learning journey from primary to tertiary to lifelong education as well as the informal pathway at work and in the home. Furthermore, the process of innovating learning requires *active participation* on the part of learners, tutors and content producers. But the trend of wrapping learning services around the individual learner is set to deepen as more tools, services and approaches evolve and become widely (and freely) available.

To achieve their own learning objectives and become active and critical citizens, lifelong learners certainly need to be more empowered by the educational system and in the current web-enabled global and competitive market. If they are not well served they may go elsewhere—or learn online. To support this more active engagement, 'personalized' learning content (de Freitas, 2005) may be produced and delivered by and for learners in a relationship where learners are both the producers and consumers of learning materials, services, activities and, increasingly, *experiences*.

Learning communities that exist independent of the location of the school may help promote new opportunities for collaborative learning practices— across discipline, institution, age and stage—but new web technologies, social software and games applications in particular are facilitating these creative and varied opportunities for team and collaborative learning— 'from the cradle to the grave'.

THE ALIGNMENT PRINCIPLE

There are of course, as we have discussed, some significant impediments to changes taking place in our schools, colleges and universities. We have explored some of these in the previous section and in particular, the 'disconnect' of the *system* of education from the learner. Part of the reason for this *disconnect* is the way that macro level education policies can encroach on the internal systems of educational institution and the practices of teachers. The result is often felt as an attempt to micro-manage the entire learning process with the monitoring of staff performance, school performance tables, excessive testing, politically influenced changes to the curriculum and a restriction of individualistic or creative teaching. These developments have created an environment in which change is not promoted or received with as much enthusiasm as it might be. It's one thing to say that a bad workman blames his tools; it's another thing altogether to make a good workman use bad tools—that is, old, broken, ineffective or inappropriate tools. The issue here perhaps centres on what I would term the 'problem' of educational policy, and that problem arises from what can be described as a *misalignment*—between the policy makers on the one hand and the learners receiving services on the other.

In some senses, this is part of the general articulation of control and power structures we are all so familiar with, from the work of commentators such as Michel Foucault (1980) and others in the critical theory tradition. Our governments control and direct the public education sector—through educational policies—in order to raise standards, to improve skills for the knowledge economy, to maximize public investment and to ensure quality of education provision for the maximum good (utility). The issue here for governments is thus how to develop policies that are effective in a political sense—that is, in relation to opinions of the electorate.

It is difficult to pinpoint why the development of education policy—globally—has been so problematic over the last 20 to 30 years. In the context of the United Kingdom, one possible explanation that surfaces from a consideration of higher education in 19th century England could help us to understand the problem—at least in the British or Anglophone context. Robert Young, as part of his chapter on the 'chrestomathic university', describes the emergence of two models from the 19th century: 'the ecclesiastical, conservative model and the vocational, radical model, corresponding, as the opponents themselves often specified, to the politics and religion of the upper and middle classes' (Young, 1996: 192). Briefly then, the radical educationalists, including the utilitarians and non-conformists, argued against the ecclesiastical notion of *truth,* believing that 'knowledge should be up to date, useful, practical, changed according to the results of theoretical investigation and scientific research, and taught in a democratized secular form' (Young, 1996: 192). As Young argues, this position remained firmly in place, to the extent that it left little room for the Socialist Left. Young argues that

> the position of the British Left with regard to education was one of profound ambivalence. From Robert Owen onwards, the socialist movement did regard access to knowledge as a means to political power and social transformation. But following Marx's critique of [Adam] Smith and later utilitarians, socialists were hostile to an ethics of knowledge

in which education is designed to be useful, and amounts to the learning of skills necessary for efficient capitalist production . . . one effect of this was the striking absence of a politics of higher education identifiable with the aspirations of the working class (Young, 1996: 192).

Young attributes this to 'the extent to which the issues of "truth" versus "use" and arts versus sciences continue to dominate the politics of education' (Young, 1996: 194). These persistent tensions help to explain how the development of policy can become divorced from the ongoing development of learning theories and practices. Crucially, our conceptualizations of knowledge and information have become far more sophisticated and have, at any rate, changed over the last century and a half. Young also points out how central the question of access to educational services was in the 19th century, noting that 'political agitation moved through a succession of excluded groups, from Dissenters, to women, to the working class' (Young, 1996: 195).

Moving between these utilitarian and humanist positions, the focus in policy making is around supporting truth, knowledge and utility, but any emphasis upon the learning processes, learning theory and learner behaviour is completely left out of the equation. The political discourse here has distorted the very purpose of the educational systems because it has unwittingly created this disconnect between the institution and its learners. I broadly refer to this as a *misalignment* between the policy makers and the learners, and it also explains why so much educational policy does not achieve the intended impact. Perhaps a third missing approach to educational policy is at the lower, 'granular' level: that of learners and their requirements, which entails a process-driven and focused understanding of education more rooted in pragmatism and practices than in control or tribal or cultural heterodoxies and imperatives. *Utility* is not, however, a dirty word, and I believe that a sense of utility must still frame the development of *new learning*. Equally, *access* is still a central consideration in the politics of learning, but the emphasis must now extend to the learner's *access to educational resources* rather than just the learner's *access to the system of education*.

To gain a re-alignment of policy and practice therefore, it is essential to re-consider the education theories that learning is based upon today *and* to gain a better understanding of how we might be able to perfect the techniques of learning rather than spending our efforts on an endless re-organization or re-prioritization of what is learnt. To do this we need to step back and assess learning theory, learning contexts, the role of the learner and how learning content and material might be delivered in the future.

Worryingly, the situation at present seems to be accelerating the disconnect between the institutions and their learners and is exacerbated by very old and at times anachronistic yet persistent discourses. These discourses prevent education institutions from modernizing themselves or from re-invigorating the debates around the introduction of effective new approaches and technologies to support more engaging learning experiences. The micro-management or managerial approaches of leadership in the academy, in particular, have also presented problems for affecting change management with technological and pedagogical advances. Leadership is, of course, a factor here, as is the need for clear and simple visions for education of the future.

So, what can be done to try to modernize our systems and institutions? Well, when in doubt, it is always useful to consider what the key objectives and purposes are or will be. In this case, learners want an enriched and stimulating learning experience; for them it is less about technology and more about social engagement and immersion in learning. So the question that relates to the context of learning and to the future of learning must be, *how do we develop a new learning whilst offering the learner—at all ages and stages—a stimulating and exciting learning experience?*

The *misalignment* of policy and practice in education that I have alluded to means we need desperately to revisit our learning theory, evaluate the quality of the current learning experience and re-connect policy with practices—ideally, through participatory policy design strategies, which include the active involvement of tutors *and* learners. Such a process entails a re-consideration of the roles, rules and curriculum of formal education and presents new opportunities for re-moulding those roles, rules and curricula objectives. We also need to consider how new tools can actually support and enhance learning rather than offering them as part of a 'technology push' for its own sake. Tools like e-learning, online learning and game-based learning *should* be *part of* the toolset of the teaching practitioners and should be used to 'choreograph' *engaging immersive learning experiences.*

Much lip service has been paid to support *learner centred approaches*, but until at the macro policy level and the meso-institutional levels we start to integrate these approaches into routine strategies, we will continue on with the 'lock down' of learning resources, rigid micro-management of teaching staff and the peripheralization of the learner. The issue here is that the 'revolving door profession' (Smithers & Robinson, 2004) is losing well-qualified and committed teachers who cannot take the increasing micro-management of their practices, and risks losing others who want to re-gain *some* creativity in their chosen profession. This is thus one way to really drive up quality standards; to give back more power and control to the frontline rather than try to shift the control of practice and standards up the line to those, who in some cases, have no substantial or recent experience of frontline theory, delivery and practice.

The idea that public institutions can be run like businesses presents a major culture shift for schools and universities. But with many university boards now containing some or even a majority of business leaders, this trend to run public universities as businesses looks set to deepen. The days of running courses for any reason other than to make financial gain or sustain commercial industrial sectors are gone, and this understanding of education as a *service* is now part of a wider transformation of the public sector, which has been encouraged to be more like the business sector. While this emphasis is arguably quite utilitarian, it signifies how classic economics, rather than politics, has become the overriding concern of the early 21st century. This was probably inevitable as part of the general post-industrial move towards service industries, and the transformations can also be seen part of the *real politik* of our age, which is characterized by globalization, population growth and pressures on natural and national resources amid a global economic downturn. Population growth, a sense of entitlement to universal access to higher education and the negative effects of the economic downturn have put pressures on most countries' economic capability to provide wholly tax funded university services beyond school (and certainly in the British and American contexts). Hence, the opportunities for 'free' access to higher education, with total costs covered by taxpayers, are being phased out and will not likely return, making even greater the imperative to re-align our systems and institutions and to use new means to provide educational services and benefits for the greatest number of learners. Indeed, many universities have attempted to widen the scope for attracting fee-paying students by, for example, supporting more industrial attachments for students, which in turn offers them the benefit of improved post-education employment opportunities.

In the 19th century aspiration to extend the access to education to ever wider classes of under-represented groups, and in the 20th century drive to focus upon a comprehensive system of schooling—which advocated the 'one-size-fits-all' approach—planning most often centred upon a notional learner. To correct this, and thereby achieve a better and more individualistic understanding of the learner in respect to policy development, terms such as *personalization* have been put forward (de Freitas & Yapp, 2005). The term, although admittedly problematic in some ways, at least suggests the possibility of building services around the individual, thereby recognizing the individuality of the individual's needs and his or her preferences in the processes of learning. And it does reflect some of the recent advances in how we conceptualize lifelong learning. The notion, if not the exact term, is then useful since it serves to correct the abstract, often undifferentiated and generic consideration of the learner that we once had. The capability of information-based systems, such as learning management systems, game environments and content management systems, to adapt to the personal requirements of each user is then relevant to the consideration of personalized or tailored education services. The notion—*personalization*—does also provide an emphasis on the fact that educational systems will be there to support the educational needs of individual learners and their specific requirements rather than the needs of a societally posited education *system*.

This situation is exacerbated by the need for quick adaptation to new trends, such as the provision of ICTs. However, the educational institutions we have grown up with were designed for slower-moving changes, and they often find that existing organizational processes do not fit well with rapid and continual change. As a result, the institutions do not always adapt well and cannot always easily find solutions that benefit all parties. While this is often evidenced at the strategic level, the issue is clearly one of the adaptability of *institutional* processes and structures. The net result of the mismatch between established organizational processes and the rapid change of learner expectation can in extreme situations lead to over-stretched resources, strains on infrastructure, pressure on staff and the reduced performance of learners. The solution is surely to re-couple policies with the learner's experience, and this can only really be addressed with the re-alignment of the relationships between the main actors in the learning process and through a wider understanding of learning theory as it is applied in practice.

The need to adapt to a more learner-driven educational system is placing a greater emphasis on the *quality of the learning experience* and the supporting organizational processes. A combination of drivers that are both learner-led/bottom-up and policy-driven/top-down may well be needed in order to support better alignment and to deliver better systems and support (de Freitas & Oliver, 2005), but might also help to provide opportunities for transitioning to new approaches of learning—for example, those that are experience-based. However, social interactive learning, the wider use of computer generated environments and the growth of social media communities should be acknowledged as likely and key agents of change in the processes of learning.

THE LEVELS OF EDUCATION

To understand the context of learning, then, it helps to understand how different levels of the institution and organization relate to the wider macro-political context and how they relate to the micro level context of the learning processes taking place. To do this requires understanding systems and *systemic change*. Our ability to understand change in organizations and institutions is vital to any efforts to adapt our systems. Systemic change can however, be difficult to predict and hard to assess or measure at the outset. For the ease of understanding change and its impact upon systems (e.g., the school or university system), the distinction between *external* and *internal* pressures of change is made here. By way of illustration, the education system currently has external (*exogenous*) pressures of change such as educational policies and governmental inspections, and internal (*endogenous*) pressures of change such as high staff turnover. These pressures, for example, may affect the optimal performance of the system, change the rate of development or have a positive or negative impact upon the effective mediation of learning processes and experiences.

Because there is a limited impact of policy on learning processes *per se*, the impact of any external form of pressure for change is more likely to affect the institution and the politics of the sector, thereby affecting only two levels of the education system: the meso and macro levels. On the micro level, in a present-day school or university learning processes taking place in the system are influenced more by *internal* pressures, such as the changing pedagogic strategies used by learning practitioners. This disparity of influence explains perhaps why policy changes can often be minimal in terms of the practices of learning and how they how are actually undertaken at the 'chalk face'. Again we can see the disconnect between the levels quite clearly.

Breaking down an understanding of the context for learning into different levels may make it easier to consider and apply. For example:

- The *micro level* incorporates the learning *processes* at work, involving the learner, the learning experience and social learning interactions with others.
- The *meso level* involves a consideration of the educational institutions or organizations. Together, they collectively provide the infrastructure for the learning experience, providing a kind of container for social interactions and a facilitator of learning.
- The *macro level* includes the policy and strategic developments affecting education—for example, the government of education, how the institution interacts with the national education policy and practices and the role of the ministry of education to develop and deploy governmental policy development in line with regional, national and international priorities.

At the *micro level* of the actual learning processes, the most important interaction is that between the system and the individual learner. This interface traditionally takes the form of the relationship between the tutor and the learner, but we are beginning to understand the roles that more complex interconnected social relationships (e.g., peer groups, family) are playing in learning and this needs to be *fully* understood. Here we also need to consider the prevailing learning theories and practices.

At the *meso level* lies the educational institution (e.g., the school, college, university). It is perhaps harder to explain in purely social terms, as the organization includes a more complex inter-arrangement of communities of individuals, roles and rules. The meso level reflects the intersection between the learner and the institution, which is bounded and controlled by the roles and rules.

The *macro level* is the layer of contacts between the institution and everything external to the institution and is most in flux, as it is buffered by many of the contextual factors guiding the overall system: social, politico-economic and techno-cultural changes. However, the links with the system, which are external to the processes of teaching and learning, in fact make it harder to align with the processes occurring on the ground. The role of government, as it relates to this macro level, is to structure policy and strategic priorities at regional, national and international levels and to ensure that policies are deployed effectively and economically.

Understanding change in this stratified way is as much about seeing how we affect systems and about changing our behaviour accordingly, as it is about affecting policy changes that control our systems. Importantly, such an understanding recognizes the complex relationships that underpin institutions and education in a simplified way that aids comprehension. Table 1.1 provides an overview of the three levels used here, to simplify our

Table 1.1   The Micro, Meso and Macro Levels of Learning

Level	Component of learning	Factors for consideration	Relationship to system
Micro level: learning processes (e.g., learning and teaching strategies)	Learning: the learner	•The links between virtual and physical contexts for learning •Exploring different learning experiences •Choreographing learning (e.g., pedagogic strategies, models and frameworks used by practitioners—and learners).	Diegetic: Link between virtual and real spaces > convergent forms (e.g., mobile, Augmented Reality, Alternate Reality Games, etc.)
Meso level: institutional (e.g., delivery and support of learning)	Institutions: organizational culture, management and change	•The blur between formal learning and informal learning (e.g., lifelong learning, 24/7 access to learning) •Disciplinal context •Tutor support (e.g., continuing professional development) •Leadership strategies (e.g., distributed, transformational) •Technical support (on-site and remote)	Inter-/intra-diegetic: between and in both spaces
Macro level: educational and social policy (e.g., policies for education)	Policy: national, global trends and policies	•Context of use •Socio-technical policy •Alignment principle—policy institutions, learning	Non-diegetic

understanding of the complexity of the education system, in the context of schools, colleges and universities. To understand the education system—and in this case the *context of learning*—we need to engage with the *micro*, *meso* and *macro level* changes all at once, even though they are not necessarily happening all at the same rate or in the same way.

I have noted that the learning processes of the education system are not always well aligned with the policy development strategies. This is a systemic issue leading to the disconnect that affects the meso level of education. However, to solve the problem is not so straightforward either, since that disconnect is widening as global priorities increasingly begin to shape policy and as institutions adapt to these and other macro factors such as economics. As education systems become more developed they become more complicated as well, so it becomes harder and harder to control institutions. So, when considering developments in the education system as a whole, we need to remember that continual re-positioning, re-organization and additions can: (1) make the systems more complicated; (2) make the institutions harder to control via changing policies; and, (3) create a wider disconnect between frontline services and policy level developments. This is unfortunately a self-perpetuating and self-reinforcing situation. For example, it is the hierarchical formation of the relationships in the mediation of power—held by the school board, for instance—that works as an unconscious barrier between the policy objectives of the government and the frontline learning processes.

For a resolution of this conundrum then, either (1) greater interaction needs to take place between the levels or (2) the meso level needs to be charged with a more permeable role for communicating with and formulating governmental policy and learning theory. But both these approaches require quite radical organizational shifts. However, the alternative is poorly deployed and developed policy and strategy with a *growing* disconnect between policy development and learning practices. To achieve this re-alignment, either the hierarchies (control structures) need to be removed at every level—which would be difficult to achieve unless a concerted new system of control was put into place—or the meso level needs to be removed entirely, which seems unlikely due to the historical formation of the education system. Alternatively, a greater degree of engagement with learners in policy development needs to be effected. Overall this author would advocate the latter, less cataclysmic and more participatory approach to the development of education policy, genuinely involving more of the actors throughout in the control and organization of the process.

Crucially, a debate is needed as to whether it is desirable or useful for policy to make changes to core micro level learning processes at all. The real permeability seems to be at the meso level, and it is here that debate around whether and to what extent the hierarchies, roles and rules should be kept in place. If we assume that the role of educational policy *is* to effect qualitative changes in learning processes, then it is certain that some sort of re-alignment does need to take place. In fact, for all policies (*macro level*), institutions (*Meso level*) and learners (*micro level*), the re-alignment needs to be effected. So, while the ambition for policy to control and drive all and any changes in the other levels is problematic for the reasons stated above, it is still a necessary component of governmental thinking and approaches. If policy thinking could be more sensitive to the realities of the frontline delivery constraints and challenges, and if it could integrate a greater degree of participation from learners and tutors, it could be strengthened even in terms of its impact and efficacy. Similarly, the requirement for *institutions* to align with learner requirements, to improve the engagement of learners and to better support employment and industrial interconnections means that a more collaborative approach by them would help them to be more resilient against the rapid changes of the 'information society' (Webster, 1995). Here a need for strong leadership is required not for the oversight of micro management strategies that simply support new government directives but for the application of real transformational *and* distributed leadership. The need to avoid strictly managerial approaches in favour of a mix of top-down and bottom-up approaches is critical (de Freitas & Routledge, 2013; Young, 1996; Yukl, 1989).

It is notable that the growth of the use of digital formats to support learning is mostly taking place at the micro level—and this is new. I say it is new because, traditionally, systemic and institutional innovations have been the main mechanisms available to make change at the 'chalk face'. When it comes to the exploitation of new theory and technology in recent years, however, top-down policies have either not been forthcoming or have involved an element of poorly thought through introductions of technological approaches or a 'technology push'. This type of problematical technological push was evident in the area of e-learning, where there was a limited understanding about the new formats in government departments and it was hard to predict what shape these formats would evolve into *and* because of the misalignment problem I have outlined.

What the international debates and practices around e-learning and online learning have now revealed are the capabilities to *personalize the learning experience* through the process of innovating learning practice— for example, by adopting the use of e-tools, authoring software and web services (de Freitas & Jameson, 2012; Sharpe & Beetham, 2007; Sharpe, Beetham & de Freitas, 2010). While new services require teacher training and continuing professional development—to help tutors acquire new technical and pedagogical skills to exploit the new tools—it is fair to say that many of the new software and services that are emerging are becoming easier to use and require less tutorial input. As usability advances and interoperable standards become embedded, tutors will become more adept at using e-learning materials and services.

On the micro level of education between the teacher and student, access to online materials gives us more potential for teaching to evolve in new ways, to adapt to learner needs. On the institutional meso level, we need to promote more creative strategies for supporting personalized learning experiences—for example, through teacher training and continuing professional development. Technical support also needs to be provided to facilitate the introduction of innovative learning practices. Importantly, new models that better ensure a closer fit to learner requirements are needed—models that start with user requirements, take on board pedagogic drivers and are sensitive to the pragmatic issues of learning in formal contexts, such as access to technology and infrastructure, team teaching, disciplinary differences and cross-disciplinary challenges, quality assurance, assessment and accreditation, and computer generated learning spaces and facilities. Moreover, with increasing informal learning opportunities, better links with the way that ICT is currently being used in the home needs to be envisaged as part of the contextual issues that drive institutional curriculum development and support strategies.

Content development is, as we have seen, a major area of controversy in the changing educational paradigm. In the future, the idea of co-development of content, for example, would be a useful approach for bringing together the best interests of industry and academia. Policy development in areas such as intellectual property rights could support the development of open access to new content, and Creative Commons licensing offers a new useful model. Greater user engagement and feedback in the key areas—curriculum design, content production and delivery, assessment and accreditation—can help academic, educational, industrial and media-based stakeholders to work together more effectively to provide enriched learner experiences and to support more seamless learning journeys—with fewer 'transitions' (Sharpe & Beetham, 2007).

While there is a need for a fresh alignment of policy development, institutional processes and the requirements of the learner at the centre of this debate, there is a significant tension between control strategies of national governments on the one hand and changing learner expectations on the other. Governments still aim to control national, regional and local education policy in its entirety through a hierarchical regime, but the tendencies and horizons of the learner take into consideration the emergence of online communities which have flatter hierarchies or none at all. These communities promote interdependence and mobile identities, with an emphasis upon *sharing* control, content and data. With greater empowerment, learners may have increased scope to choose to learn in different—and for some, more effective—ways. Conversely, if educational control is reinforced with further homogenous and top-down strategies that focus upon control over learners and a desire for conformity to socio-political expectations or 'norms', this could—and, I believe, *will*—jeopardize the long-term development of creative teaching and the quality of the learning experience. In the language of evolutionary mechanics, the development of more successful forms is linked to diversity and the opportunities for diversification within the eco-system—in this case, the wider education system.

What is at stake here, along with the results for individual learners, is the future of our educational institutions. If we are to retain them we will need to debate and resolve some difficult questions. We will need to have a clear understanding of our expectations in the 21st century about what education is and what it does, and we will need to work out the best strategies to organize schools, colleges and universities so that they can still have a place in the social and geographical landscape of the future. This book aims to contribute to this debate and to give shape to some of the questions we need to address going forward. Having a vision for education is one aspect of this process, but engaging the learning communities is really the most important aspect, as we need to bring all the parties on board to shape what our education systems will look like in the future; and we need to get it right.

As an aside, we might recall the cautionary lesson observed earlier, that in the United Kingdom the Post Office (or General Post Office) was intimately involved in the development of the national telecommunications system *and* the modern computer that would in combination deliver the Internet and electronic mail services that ironically have so eroded the agency's institutional rationale today. Tommy Flowers, who worked on the Bletchley Park development of the first modern computer, was a Post Office engineer and, moreover, the agency was briefly the guardian of the new technology in the post-war period. Regrettably for the Post Office though, top-down controls—and a stated need for national priorities, secrecy and security—resulted in the directed loss of the technology and the opportunities: the machines were smashed and the technicians were sworn to secrecy. The denationalization drive that followed in the 1970s, '80s and '90s saw telecommunications services and Post Office mail services separated and sold off to raise government revenues. The result is that an institution that was central in the development of the technologies of the age and that was well placed to be an international provider of ICT services has atrophied and shrunk to a shadow of what it was and of what it could have been.

The 'revolution' in learning, if it can be called that, reveals how shifts in the content, methods and location of learning are bringing with them the opportunity to re-evaluate many of the central processes underpinning learning. This transition to *social interactive learning* carries with it the potential for re-casting learning in terms that further broaden the *duration*, *reach* and *place* of learning. So any new vision of learning would need to take account of this tendency and aim to find a way to incorporate an understanding of learning predicated upon social interactions, flexible spaces, multimodal learning and exploratory learning approaches. In terms of the context of learning, the locus of new technology enhanced learning approaches is sometimes messy and difficult to completely comprehend and design for, but the role of different spaces—online spaces, virtual 3D spaces and in particular, physical learning spaces—seems to offer a new mode for the organization of learning in specific contexts and places.

The bridges between virtual, online and physical spaces provide real potential for social interactive learning by connecting the spaces of learning together and placing more emphasis upon individuals and their interactions. However, this also creates difficulties with respect to how (and whether?) the context of learning can be controlled and how policy can have a direct impact upon its usage. Multi-layered spaces in this way present a potential mechanism for changing the ordering of learners and learning content, social interactive learning and the processes of learning. This is so because they allow learners to interact in online, physical and virtual spaces, either simultaneously or asynchronously.

It is notable that learning technologies such as mobile, games and social software are considered in some literature as *'disruptive* technologies' (Conole et al., 2008). The capability of these mechanisms that deliver learning content to confront and disrupt normal learning spaces and approaches is considered in pejorative terms. But what is really 'disruptive' here is the fact that these approaches both liberate the learner from a formal learning context in the traditional sense (e.g., learning in a classroom) *and* take learning out of a controlled and mediated space that can be presided over by institutional rules and policy development models. In this way, 'disruptive technologies' can be seen to result in a decoupling of learning *delivery* from a specific educational context, and we have seen that this approach is generally resisted and so is usually unsuccessful in practice. But in a purely pragmatic sense, these unique modes for accessing learning content place a greater focus upon the individualized and personalized learning processes, and that is a desirable influence.

Disruption then lies in the decoupling of the institutional (meso) and policy (macro) levels from the micro level of the learner and the learning processes. This is not to say that learning can ever be *acontextual*, as all learning is contextual and interrelated within the learner's experience and understanding. Rather, the structures around the educational system are becoming interdependent with the learning experience. This is dangerous from a governmental point of view, as it would effectively remove any control over access to learning content and potentially any control over content production. Disruption in this case means disruption of the *system of education*—not disruption of the processes of learning.

While learning cannot be acontextual, taking learning into multiple contexts and spaces is becoming far more prevalent with the emergence and wider use of games and social software communities. For example, alternate reality (or mixed reality) games blend real spaces with overlays of virtual content and imagery; mobile games allow content to be delivered directly to smart phones; and online games allow social communities to form around in-game activities. Virtual worlds also offer new spaces for remote and distributed communities of learners to coalesce around practices and interest areas (Wenger, 1998). The emergence of these opportunities for social interactions in non-formal contexts, perhaps arguably, has two main benefits: firstly, that learning can become more pervasive and lifelong; and secondly, that 'learning as experience' is offering more potential for learning and teaching practices. However, as discussed above, on the negative side they are considered disruptive and decoupled from institutions and policy making. But certainly, the re-arrangement of 'learning as experience' is re-casting and re-ordering the realities and possibilities of learning today, and this has implications for future and new learning.

Game-based learning, learning in virtual worlds and learning with online resources together offer a new set of instruments to facilitate experience-based learning. At the same time, they also imply a new empowerment not just for learners but potentially for teachers, too, as they deliver into the hands of teachers unique capabilities to craft learning experiences. However disruptive this may be to the existing power structures, the liberation for teachers and learners and the paradigm shift for 'learning as experience' is undeniable. But it is important to be wary of purely technologically driven change and instead to focus upon learning and the learner and really take on board the importance of understanding what constitutes learning and what best supports that learning experience.

Previous work undertaken by this author and Jill Jameson found the importance of re-considering learning theory (*pedagogy*) in the light of e-learning practices and technology enhanced learning discourses (de Freitas & Jameson, 2012). If the new learning paradigm means that there is a greater emphasis placed upon the learning experience, then we need to consider how learning theory wraps around that experience in pragmatic and applied ways. Theory for theory's sake is not the answer here—any more than technology for technology's sake is; but understanding what is really happening in social interactive learning, for example, will assist us with designing and developing effective learning environments of the future.

It would be foolhardy to not consider the role of globalization in the changes to educational systems. Clearly, the need and the capacity to reach out to international communities have an impact not just upon research but upon learning and teaching practices. While new computer generated environments open up data sets and access to digital learning resources, it is the access to individuals and their understanding which really offers a new learning strategy. The emphasis upon social interactions in globally facilitated communications networks has potential for group learning, team teaching, peer assessment and group work (de Freitas et al., 2010).

While the debates on e-learning have often centred upon research findings that have invariably found 'no significant difference' when comparing e-learning or technology enhanced learning with traditional approaches (Russell, 1999), this has generally been interpreted as evidence that there should be no wider uptake of the form or change in direction. However, macro level factors such as falling national budgets and increasing student numbers are not merely incidental factors; they are some of the key drivers of systemic change that are, of course, concerned with the implications of the 'no significant difference' finding. If there is no significant difference in results, the logic goes, the affordability and reach of any competing options come to the fore in any assessment of their comparative merits.

Interestingly, though, two recent studies have found evidence of a *significant* difference in the results of game-based learning approaches over traditional approaches (Kato et al., 2008; Knight et al., 2010). Statistically speaking, we would need to undertake more studies that replicate these results to fully validate the observation. However, if the indications *are* substantiated, it would be a very significant finding, as the assumed gold standard for education has always been face-to-face learning. Whether or not the consideration of what constitutes the 'gold standard' changes, the potential of *blended* game-based and CGE approaches to have a greater role in education is increasingly apparent in terms of *results,* as well as in terms of economics or reach. And either way, the learning and teaching communities will need to consider scientific evidence that pertains to the micro, meso and macro levels of the education system, teaching practices and learning processes.

To unravel or disrupt the central relationship between teacher and student would be unthinkable in any time in the past, but today, with growing student numbers and reducing funding for education, it is becoming clear already that the relationship *is* being 'disrupted' by the emergence of immersive environments—and computer generated environments, in particular. Evidence for the effectiveness of team-based and peer-based learning methods over tutor-led learning is attested to in recent medical scientific research (Buljac-Samardzic et al., 2010; Deardorff et al., 2010). Early indications, at least in medical contexts, are that tutor-led learning may not always be the best delivery mechanism. In one study with nurses that this author has been involved with—to assess the use of a first-generation game simulator, *Triage Trainer*—we found that tutor-led learning only ranked second in the nurses' preferred methods of learning—after 'on the job' or experiential training (de Freitas & Jarvis, 2009). This is what we are referring to when we say that other modes of learning can be used to support the learner's experience and aid efficiency of training; forms that are sympathetic to the learner's preferences will in most cases start from a better pedagogic footing.

Computer-based game play is increasingly pervasive today, and students in schools are playing games most days, according another of the studies I've been involved in (Dunwell et al., 2012). *Call of Duty* was the most popular game we found in our study and the reasons for that game's popularity—multiplayer capacity, high fidelity graphics, compulsive game play with team missions, challenges and a competitive element—derived from the level of budget that was allocated to the game. This game and others like it deliver highly immersive experiences, with social player communities that are engaged and motivated in a way that they aren't currently in schools. It is hard to overstate the challenge for educators and policy makers that this evidence-based research presents, but to bury our heads in the sand over the issue could be lethal for the survival and longevity of our educational systems–at least as we currently know them.

It is this author's belief that understanding how and why learning in computer generated environments is so effective—and even more effective than traditional learning when part of a blended solution (Knight et al., 2010)—would allow us to better design purpose-built environments that may be used as learning tools and critical teaching resources in the infrastructure of formal institutions. This is not to say that this will be an easy or painless undertaking, but it is necessary for our formal institutions to adapt if they are to triumph over other growing global brands of increasingly commercialized education services such as unguided online learning, open access and distance/remote learning, home schooling and lifelong or post-educational learning.

THE CONTEXT OF LEARNING PLACES AND SPACES

We cannot fully consider the contexts of learning without an understanding of the context of *the places and spaces within which learning is undertaken*. Traditionally, the *place* of learning was considered in strict terms—for example, the lecture hall or the classroom–but today, with digital technologies and communications dominating our social interactions, the idea of learning in a single physical space seems strangely antiquated.

It may be hard to envisage now, but in the days before television and modern digital communications, teaching was far more like a performance; the audience—the students—were analogous to theatregoers who were to be entertained with an intellectual recital or spectacle rather than a literary theatrical diversion. As Thomas Markus expresses it,

> The essence of teaching space is that the audience catches a small fragment of a *corpus* of knowledge at a time, a *corpus* to which the performer has access. And the fragment is presented as a dramatic spectacle. . . . The teaching space is closer to the theatre, where the full story is not revealed to the audience till the end. The ancient actor-audience relation indeed gave its name to the first teaching space—the *anatomy* theatre (1993: 229; emphasis added).

I would perhaps prefer to speak of the anatomy theatres as the first teaching spaces *dedicated to a single discipline*. Lecture theatres in general, however, do maximize the spectacle of the lecture and the authority and centrality of the lecturer, to engage the learner and to differentiate the social hierarchical relationship between the teacher and the student through their respective location or situation, in the space; as Markus notes, 'In the [19th century] anatomy theatres and university lecture rooms there was a lecturer-audience relationship which required a segregation based on temporary status and not class—for in due course the taught would become the teachers' equals' (1993: 239).

While the lecture theatres conferred power upon the lecturer through spatial ordering, the classroom also revealed the spectacular or theatrical nature of learning. Again, in these *teaching* spaces, the desks were in general ordered in rows of benches where the viewers' attention was centred towards the position of the teacher, though, as Markus notes, 'In America greater and wider recognition was given to individuals and small groups' and a plan from 1831 reveals 'individual desks for simultaneous teaching' (1993: 91). Just as with lecture theatres, classrooms were subject to changing designs over the years, but the 19th century focus upon spatial arrangement and functional design has had a big impact upon the *learning* spaces of today. However, while the Victorian architects aimed to organize and contain students in their spaces, in the 21st century our designs for learning spaces are beginning to diversify; notably, some computer generated learning spaces are not now bound to any one place and, similarly, many different learning spaces can be accessed from one or any place.

In the past, a set logistical organization of tutors and students figured in the classroom in the arrangement of desks in lines and the positioning of the teacher and the blackboard. This arrangement reflected the prevalent teaching methods (dialogic and didactic), the available teaching resources (blackboard and books) and the learning tools (desks, pens, exercise books and textbooks) that were used. The classroom was the place, the space and the container of the teaching and learning processes, and its layout was fixed. However, walk into any modern university and the preference for flexible and re-configurable spaces is much more in evidence.

Today's learning and teaching methods place a greater emphasis upon activity learning, problem-based learning and exploratory learning (Boud & Feletti, 1991; de Freitas & Neumann, 2009; Vygotsky, 1962). Often the learning resources are web-based and are accessed on mobile devices or laptops so that the functionality of these spaces is enhanced. Although they are still *containers* for learning processes, online and virtual learning spaces are not regarded as physically located places.

In this new consideration of the teaching and learning space, the unit of the classroom as a bounded space with a fixed physical layout for the placing of teacher and student is being challenged by the idea of flexible learning spaces that can be re-configured and adapted for group work and activities. At the same time, the basic spatial relationships of the pupil and teacher are less hierarchically determined. As an example of a new *physical* learning space, the Creativity Lab at Sussex University illustrates how open spaces, collapsing desks, user controlled lighting and moving walls allow for open and flexible learning spaces where students can sit with laptops and tablets and be arranged in casual seating groups for group work and social interactive learning. Figures 1.1 and 1.2 show a very flexible learning space, all in

Figure 1.1   The University of Sussex's Creativity Zone. Reproduced with the kind permission of the University of Sussex.

Figure 1.2   A teaching session at the University of Sussex's Creativity Zone. Reproduced with the kind permission of the University of Sussex.

white, with walls that can be written upon, touch control coloured lighting, movable walls, the use of projectors for front and back projection, re-configurable seating, wireless connectivity and under-floor wiring. The space has been used with both undergraduates and children and offers a new approach to design that is geared towards multiple uses and purposes.

Today, learners expect more flexibility in their interactions and learning transactions, and with the advances in Internet and mobile connectivity we are now able to access learning content and materials from locations other than our formal education institutions. The place of learning is changing: as well as providing more freedom to use different spaces—be they physical or virtual—the locations where learning takes place today are not all still organized according to the roles and rules of the 19th century lecture theatre or school classroom.

The context of learning includes institutions, policies and learning processes but the *context* is also, as it were, the container of these relationships and interactions. The teaching or learning space and how it is organized and designed, as we have discussed above, has an impact upon these relationships. With more flexibly designed university and school spaces emerging, the opportunity for more flexible learning approaches is enhanced (Collis & Moonen, 2001)—for example, allowing and promoting problem-based learning online (Barrett & Moore, 2011; Savin-Baden & Wilkie, 2006) through the use of handheld and laptop computers or group work activities and social interactive learning.

There are examples in the wider world which blur the divisions between physical and virtual boundaries, and these can be found in what is called the 'mixed reality' approach. The relatively recent emergence of 'street gaming' or 'social gaming' involves individuals playing games in urban spaces. Mixed reality or alternate reality games, as they are known, are games that cross various media and blur the line between the game space (*diegesis*) and the real world experience (examples are provided in McGonigal, 2011 and Petridis et al., 2011). These forms of social gaming often make use of mobile devices and utilize location-based geo-positioning of players to prompt game play and missions, and this type of functionality may have potential uses for education.

An acknowledgement of this trend was highlighted by a cooperative game play experiment undertaken at the University of Southern California, which included a three-day workshop and play day led by Bernie DeKoven (DeKoven, 2002; Fullerton, 2005). Another form of street or social gaming is *Big Game*, which crosses over into alternate reality games; these are usually large-scale multiplayer games that blend electronic and virtual elements with real-world presence (Ruberg, 2006). An early example of this is the game *Majestic*, which used telephone calls to the player to blur the game space with the real-world experience, in echoes of the David Fincher film *The Game* (Szulborski, 2005). This play between real and virtual spaces reinforces the notion of traversal between different states and different identities, helping us to suspend our disbelief. The sense of 'flow' between different states or identities reinforces that disbelief and the pervasiveness of the game in this way supports a more immersive experience.

The emergence of social online communities, mobile applications and alternate reality games, indicates a general crossover trend—from niche to mainstream–for social interactive applications, which utilize *different* media forms. These mixed forms may have deeper uses for formal learning, though they require significant knowledge on the part of the tutor as well as new creative approaches to lesson planning and assessment; crucially, however, these are beginning to emerge. The convergent forms of gaming rely upon multiple media channels and sources and thus parallel developments in social software (e.g. blogging, wikis and social shared spaces) and do support wider opportunities for collaborative activities. Yet another related approach involves blending augmented reality interfaces with games, providing overlays of information onto the real world (e.g., *ARQuake*, *EyeToy*; Liarokapis et al., 2009). Mobile devices and applications, therefore, open up new potential for learning in different places but also allow us to adapt *new learning techniques and approaches to our learner groups.*

The places and spaces for learning are as much part of the overall context of learning today as they ever were, though now we have 'discovered' new spaces where learning can take place. However, while CGEs offer a new *potential* for more creative teaching and learning, they also set significant challenges for teachers and tutors that may require the development of new skills and wider insights. All the same, they are teaching tools just as the blackboard and smart board are tools. The key difference is that they allow us more of an ability to engage with students and inspire them to become excited about learning.

Additionally, the emergence of CGEs provides an opportunity for more *exploratory learning* through which learners can roam new environments and tutors can actively choreograph and participate in those experiences. An interesting example of this is found on a programme of learning in *Teen Second Life* in an area called Schome Park, where 149 students from the National Association of Gifted and Talented Youth participated in an Open University study to evaluate the value of learning in *Second Life*. (See Call-Out Box 3: Second Life and OpenSim.) As one teenage student participating so eloquently expressed it,

> I think that what Schome is doing through breaking down the barriers between teachers and students, making it hard to see where one stops and the other begins, is fantastic because, when everyone is on the learning curve together, it brings about less of a feeling of segregation and a greater feeling of equality, and this leads to trusting people more (Twining, 2007: p15).

Whether this vision of learning can be accommodated in the wider apparatus of current systems anytime soon is a moot point. Clearly, any new vision for learning must first be able to demonstrate that it can meet our societal expectations for education before it is officially incorporated into the assessment and accreditation system. But this can be challenging, particularly where the opportunities to trial and test new approaches have been limited. Increasingly however, we are testing new approaches, and in many areas new forms are not only offering new levels of qualitative effectiveness and economic efficiency but also more preferable and engaging experiences for some learners.

The *vision* for the future of learning is thus not so far from where we are today, but while learning practices currently tend to centre upon single disciplinary perspectives, working within silos in educational institutions, I believe greater opportunities for cross-disciplinary (and cross-sector) learning will emerge over the next decade, which will increasingly utilize team-teaching, collegial collaborations, group learning in CGEs, participatory and flexible approaches to curriculum assessment and accreditation, greater participation of the learner through personalized approaches, greater use of commercial and learner-generated content and shared collaborative tools and applications.

Box 1.3   *Second Life* and *OpenSim*

Just as Facebook is gaining market share in social networking, the statistics for usage of *Second Life* have been in negative growth for several years. The fortunes of *Second Life*'s decline match the uptake of *OpenSim*, a similar venture but with much lower set up costs ($10 as opposed to $300). But *Second Life* is a venture worth noting here because it provides an early model for virtual worlds. Cory Ondrejka and colleagues at the Linden Lab in the United States developed this multiuser community in 2003. Since then it became popular in the online world, with over one million residents and a GDP (gross domestic product) value of $64 million at its peak.

The 'metaverse' was inspired by Neil Stephenson's cyberfiction novel *Snowcrash* (1994). Stephenson was the first to describe an online environment, a 'metaverse', that was a real place to its users—a place where they interacted using the real world as a metaphor and were entertained and socialized and conducted business (Ondrejka, 2004: 2). The environment supports the building and development of an online world, and its virtual real estate can be developed by users and bought and sold online (Ondrejka, 2004, 2007).

The main difference between *Second Life* and *OpenSim* is that *Second Life* is a single world with a large community, while *OpenSim* is software used to run hundreds and thousands of public and private worlds. In both, users can populate their real estate with objects, clothes and artefacts that they create and own but can also share and sell. Interestingly, the demographics of users of *Second Life* show an equal gender

Continued

Box 1.3   *continued*

split, and when regularly polled the users are also equally split when asked if *Second Life* is a game. One notable aspect of the online world is that creation takes place in real time and in the real world, not using separate programmes; this 'encourages teams to work together on larger scale projects and creates the strong interpersonal bonds that are critical to online world success' (Ondrejka, 2004: 10). Notably, over 95% of the objects in *Second Life* are user created. The commitment of users is evidenced by the amount of time they spend in the online world: 25% of users spent more than 30 hours per week at the peak of *Second Life*'s popularity (Ondrejka, 2004).

Perhaps most intriguingly, *Second Life* is a direct product of academic collaboration—notably, the decision to allow residents to create their own objects was a result of an academic roundtable. Linden Lab's development of *Second Life* provides an inside look at academic collaboration because academic feedback has been critical to several important decisions during its development cycle (Ondrejka, 2006: 113). *Second Life* provides an immersive space for supporting user communities and their varied activities, including events and seminars. Whilst the vast majority of activity there is commercial and entertainment orientated, a range of communities have developed in *Second Life* to meet a wide range of educational and therapeutic challenges.

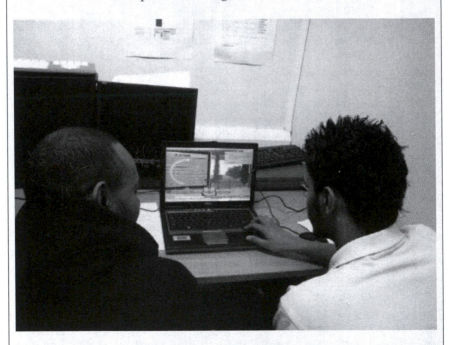

Figure 1.3   Students using *Second Life* for learning purposes. Image courtesy of the author.

Figure 1.4   Second Life being used for a study session. Reproduced with the kind permission of David Burden.

In a study undertaken by this author and colleagues, we analyzed learning activities around educational and career choices in *Second Life* (De Freitas et al., 2010). The study found that there was negative transfer for using a virtual world with the more experienced gamers, but that 81% of those using *Second Life* could see its use for supporting international collaboration (see Figures 1.3 and 1.4).

The educational uses of Second Life are notable. Campus: Second Life was an initiative to support schools, colleges and universities to utilize the game-environment to teach different subjects. Early projects have included areas of study such as the Media Studies Department at Vassar College, Trinity University, the University of Buffalo, the Department of Design and Industry at San Francisco State University and the School of Architecture at the University of Texas–Austin.

As Anne Beamish, an assistant professor in the School of Architecture at the University of Texas–Austin has commented,

My students set out to investigate the early development of the resident community within *Second Life*. . . . They became residents of the *Second Life* world, contributing their different skills and testing the limits of the system. They worked together in real time and addressed a variety of issues, including economic structure, social architecture, building density, and traffic patterns. *Second Life* gave my students a laboratory for testing their ideas that just isn't readily available anywhere else (Linden Lab, 2004).

Continued

Box 1.3 *continued*

These communities are operating in new and often creative ways to support a range of learning processes that are usually not curriculum-based, and are developing interesting experiences that broadly inform development and communications that extend their current competencies and skills.

Further research into *Second Life* and *OpenSim* is being undertaken to assess educational potential for learning in virtual worlds and how they might open up new opportunities for underserved learners as well as informing the development of formal immersive learning experiences (Allison et al., 2012; Warburton, 2009).

Learning in the context of immersive worlds is beginning to have wide ranging uses and applications beyond learning basic skills, and as *Second Life* and *OpenSim* communities demonstrate, interactions within and between groups are opening up new opportunities for learning beyond the confines of the classroom.

2 Social Play and the Virtual World

Learning is an integral aspect of all our lives; it enables us to adapt to our environment, benefit from social interactions and enrich our understanding of our lives and our experiences. The science of learning (mathetics) aims to explore *what learning is, how we learn* and the *best methods for learning*. However, it is fair to say that more research in this field goes into exploring the best methods for learning than goes into defining what learning is or how it takes place. Fortunately, this is changing with the emergence of neuroscience and learning studies. This, in my opinion, is vitally important because *learning theory* is our best tool for the development of the most effective learning methods *and* for linking and applying effective new theories to everyday practices.

Historically, most learning theories consider learning in its application (for an overview of learning theories, see de Freitas & Jameson, 2012). When we group these theories and trace their historical trajectories, most fall into a few category areas. In work around the grouping of learning theories, for example, most have fit into one of three categories: associative theories, cognitive theories and situative theories (Greeno, Collins & Resnick, 1996). *Associative* theory reflects task-based approaches where learning is broken down into component parts. *Cognitive* theory focuses upon higher-level cognition, such as constructivist learning, where learners build up a picture or 'map' of understanding based upon their pre-understanding and conceptions. *Situative* theory has its focus upon social learning—learning in groups (Greeno et al., 1996).

What I and my colleague found in our study of theory as it relates to e-learning was that situative learning theories were the least in evidence (Mayes & de Freitas, 2004; 2007). However, since that study was undertaken, a revolution in social software has altered our expectations and the understanding of *how we learn*. Social interactive learning has become much more common, and new learning theories in this area are now expected and needed. However, it is notable that while social software tools have become pervasive in our everyday lives, in terms of their capability to support *learning*, more conclusive research findings need to be derived. While studies exist that show the efficacy of game-based approaches over traditional learning, the same cannot be said yet for social software tools. This could be because these tools have not yet evolved enough to support learning. Yet, when blended within a computer generated environment (CGE), social software does appear to be an invaluable tool for supporting open discussion or debate and it does seem to have a potential for promoting reflection and adding a blend of human interaction into pure online or in-world learning.

Social learning clearly has some potential for supporting learning communities, and it is a good match for the use of CGEs for mediating social interactions and learning through social groups (de Freitas et al., 2010). Why, then, has social software not as yet been proven to be effective at supporting learning in terms of *measurable learning objectives*? Conversely, we can also ask, why are CGEs—in particular, game-based environments—proving to be better (more effective) than traditional learning in the scientific studies undertaken (Brown, Bayley & Newby, 2012; Kato et al., 2008; Knight et al., 2010)?

To answer these questions we need to step back and consider what learning in CGEs is—that is, what it consists of—and how it differs from traditional learning; this involves considering how we learn through *play*. Thereafter, we need to consider how *the roles of learning* have changed in CGEs, and lastly, we need to consider how social interactive learning is being used and how it may change some aspects of how we learn in the future.

PLAYFUL LEARNING

Learning can take place in many ways, contexts and sequences, involving task-centred approaches, cognitive learning and social interactive learning. But one of the earliest ways in which we learn, is through play. That predisposition for *playful learning* provides at least one clue for *why* game-based learning is so effective.

Computer generated games offer structured rule systems within which individuals can discover and accumulate information about the game world around them, using that information to explore the in-game environment. As in real life, game players can use that information to inform decisions and to support subsequent steps and actions. This type of play relies upon the development and testing of skills and the navigation of the environment to create a plotted narrative or journey for the player. What links computer generated games and playful learning in general is the fact that in both, all the actions and interactions of play are undertaken in a kind of safe 'rehearsal mode' where there are no real-life implications from any actions taken. In computer games this characteristic of playing is taken to new heights where any real-life physical harm is ruled out and where the player has a rewind button (multiple lives) with which mistakes can simply be undone and tasks can be attempted or re-attempted, in quick succession.

This is a powerful component of game play and why it has such a good synergy with learning. By learning in non-threatening environments, we have time to rewind and re-consider our actions and interactions, time to reflect upon what we did and how we did it and to examine valuable lessons as a result.

But while games and play are linked, of course, they are in fact different concepts. Generally speaking, games are rule-based and structured competitive *systems* that reward players for the application of the game skills and for achieving the game's objectives; at the same time games systematically penalize players for failing to apply the game skills or for failing to adhere to its rules. Games, then, in learning terms, are structured systems that organize the practice and testing of skills or knowledge. Play, on the other hand, is a *method* or type of learning and practicing and is curiously unstructured. Play in many ways is the cornerstone of learning. It is our first experience of learning, and at the heart of childhood play there is often an interplay between an imaginary space (*diegesis*) and the real world. This type of play can also involve the imagining of a *notional* space (*mimesis*) or objects (*sacra*). For example, a girl playing with a doll imagines the doll to be alive and sentient and imagines the doll's interaction with objects and others. The doll, of course, is a real object but her animation and social interactions in an imagined world are inventions of the child's mind. This interplay between real and imaginary spaces and scenarios thus allows the child to practice social interactions and experiment in a range of purely imaginary scenarios, just as in game play. In effect, the child is learning and practicing social skills through rehearsal in a non-threatening and safe environment (Chudacoff, 2007; de Freitas, 2006). This unmediated form of play is described by Peter Gray as 'free play'; he argues that it is vital for children's psychological development and emphasizes its 'self-directed and intrinsically rewarding nature' (Gray, 2011: 444).

Play, like learning, has historically been a notoriously difficult concept to define and analyze but it has undeniably been an important component of human culture. Many notable ethnologists, philosophers and educational psychologists have considered play as at the heart of the development of learning and cognitive processes (Bekoff & Byers 1998; Caillois, 1962; Huizinga, 1980; Piaget, 1999; Plato, 1992; Wittgenstein, 1972).

The introduction and widespread popularity of computer games and simulations has, if anything, increased the interest in play (Copier & Raessens, 2003). Therefore, through a better understanding of play as a 'culturally defined concept', it is hoped that a more rigorous comprehension of how the elements of play relate to learning might be established (Baron-Cohen, 1987). That comprehension needs to integrate a range of disciplinary perspectives on the way that we define and classify games (Aarseth, Smedstad & Sunnana, 2003; Aldrich, 2009; Amory et al., 1999; Garris, Ahlers & Driskell, 2002; Juul, 2003; Salen & Zimmerman, 2004).

The preoccupation with the element of play in our cultures began in the classical era, most notably perhaps, with Plato. Arthur Krenz notes, for example, that 'play is central to the interaction of the characters, the setting of the dialogue and at all levels of learning in the Republic' (1998). He also highlights the etymological connection between the Greek terms for education (*paideia*), play, games and sport (*paidia*) and children (*paides*). This connection goes beyond the use of play in children's education. Crucially, some of the notions or elements of play are hard wired into the constituent notions of pedagogy.

To understand the philosophical message of the *Republic* requires a close attention to the connection between education/culture (*paideia*), and the pedagogical approaches (*paidagogia*) to teaching and learning that are to be carried out in the community (Plato, 1992). As a kind of antidote to disciplinarianism, the central aim of pedagogy is to *encourage* learning as a form of play, which is the most persuasive and effective approach to learning for the free citizens in a society which honours philosophers (Krentz, 1998). As Plato suggests, "[D]on't use force (*bia*) in training children (*paidas*) in the subjects, but rather play (*paidzontas*). In that way you can better discern what each is naturally directed toward (*Republic*, 7.536e–f, quoted in Krentz, 1998).

Play in this sense is used both as a method for instruction as well as a source for activities used in an educational context. Notably, Plato separates the notion of play into play for amusement and play which is serious in a way that is similar to our current definition between games for entertainment and serious games for non-entertainment purposes. This distinction between 'frivolous' play and 'serious' play continues to intrigue many theorists working in this field (for references, see de Freitas, 2006).

Opposing the Platonic perspective, and possibly reflecting a general societal perception, Johan Huizinga's work (1980) considered play in culture purely in terms of 'non-seriousness'. Certainly this early work and the general association of frivolity, amusement or diversion with play has led to a legacy whereby play has been the subject of very little sustained scientific analysis in any of the disciplines (Brown, 1998). That however, has recently started to change with the publication of sociological and psychological studies of play in children (Gray, 2011; Twenge, 2006) and an excellent history of play by Howard Chudacoff (2007). The historical dearth of studies is, I think, explainable because of a perceived association of non-seriousness with unimportance (Burghardt, 1998). However, while an acknowledgement of the importance of *children's* play is now noted in the literature, it is still for the most part the case that game play by older students or adults is still associated with the notion of frivolous or non-serious diversion; in other words, games are for amusement, not learning.

Jean Piaget was an educationalist who considered in depth the link between learning and play in children:

We do in fact know that the young mammal plays, and that this play is not . . . simply an instinctive exercise but a general one of all kinds of behaviour possible at any given level, within any utilitarian purpose or consummation at the time. Now play is only one pole of the functional exercises which take place during an individual's development, and the other pole is non-playful exercises in which the young subject 'learns how to learn', not only in the context of play but in that of cognitive adaptation (Piaget, 1999: 844).

Piaget equates play with learning for development and while he does not explore this in the context of adult learning, other recent work *has* indicated the importance of play for development, to the extent that an absence of play can lead to social dysfunction, violent behaviour and even psychosis; as Stuart Brown notes, 'I now perceive healthy varied play in childhood as necessary for the development of empathy, social altruism and the possession of a repertoire of social behaviors enabling the player to handle stress, particularly humiliation and powerlessness' (1998: 250). Brown's clinical study of violent males led to his finding that 'normal play behavior was virtually absent throughout the lives of highly violent, antisocial men regardless of demography' (Brown, 1998: 249).

The position of play as fulfilling a social function is now gaining ground in a range of disciplines, but the field is still hugely under-researched, a factor that became apparent when John Byers conducted his research into animal play: 'I was astounded to find that there appears to be no comprehensive data on rates of human locomotor play from birth to sexual maturity' (Byers, 1998: 216).

Byers's research into the age distribution of play focused upon consideration of an ungulate, a rodent, a primate and a carnivore:

> There are three points to notice. First, play does not occur immediately after birth; it appears sometime later. Second, after play appears, its rate of expression rises quickly to a peak. Third, the peak of expression of play is brief, compared to the life span of the species. Play may appear sporadically later in life, but usually unpredictably and at a low rate, compared to peak rates in juvenile life. (Byers, 1998, p. 207)

For Byers, the finding of such a tight age distribution demonstrates 'a sensitive period during which the performance of certain motor patterns can alter development' (Byers, 1998: 208). His work demonstrates a link between play and development, as Piaget had noted. For Byers, the 'sensitive period' in behavioural development 'refers to a window in development during which specific types of experience permanently alter the course of development of the brain or other systems that support behaviour' (Byers, 1998: 210–211).

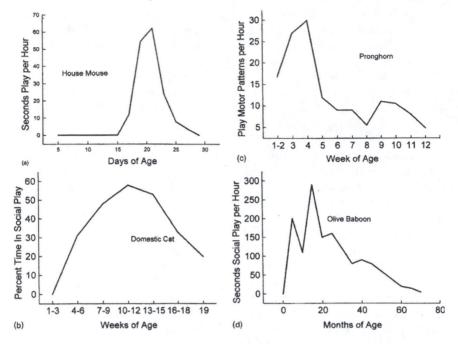

Figure 2.1   Age distribution in four species of mammal. Data re-drawn from the following sources: (a) house mouse: Byers and Walker, 1995; (b) domestic cat: West, 1974; (c) pronghorn: Byers, 1997; (d) olive baboon: Owens, 1975. Reproduced with the kind permission of Cambridge University Press, from Bekoff & Byers, 1998: 208–209).

Figure 2.1 shows how four species of mammals have a short early phase in which learning is particularly active. Byers regards this period—denoted by the sharp peak—as the 'sensitive period'. This important finding ostensibly supports Piaget's earlier assertion about the purpose of play for increasing development and indicates the importance of play in this development. But while the use of play does correlate with a period of increased mental functioning and development, can the increased use of play in other age ranges create accelerated development or sensitive periods? In other words, how crucial to development is play in humans at later ages?

Lev Vygotsky, in the constructivist tradition, also supported this link between play and development:

> The relationship of play to development is that of learning for development. Behind play are changes in needs and changes in consciousness of a more general nature. Play is a source of development and it creates areas of immediate development. (Vygotsky, 1933, quoted in Ortega, 2003: 108)

Vygotsky also noted that 'play contains all developmental tendencies in a condensed form and is itself a major source of development' (1978: 102).

It is an interesting observation that the role of play in modern culture is in fact increasing beyond childhood and increasingly into adulthood. This may be a significant factor for society and may have educational advantages for increasing and widening participation within learning, particularly if the motivation and engagement of play could be effectively integrated as part of 'blended learning' (blending face-to-face and technology-enhanced learning). Furthermore, if play was absent during the 'sensitive period' can it be replicated at a later age? If playing is encouraged in older learners, would that help some individuals with disrupted educations to learn more effectively?

Intriguingly, the newer studies on play—in particular, the work of Jean Twenge—have indicated a link between the reduction in free play time for children, at schools and in general, with the rise in narcissism, psychopathology and depression (Gray 2011; Twenge, 2006). Reduction in playtime is attested to in studies undertaken by sociologists in the University of Michigan: they compared playtime in 1981 and again in 1997 and found that for six- to eight-year-olds, there was a reduction of 25% over time (Hofferth & Sandberg, 2001). In Twenge's study (2006), 85% of young people sampled had anxiety and depression scores *higher* than the average scores for young people in the 1950s.

Twenge's studies also indicate a reduced sense of control in young people; here 'the shift was so great that the average young person in 2002 was more . . . prone to claim lack of personal control . . . than were 80 per cent of young people in the 1960s' (Twenge, quoted in Gray, 2011: 450). Increased narcissism and 'shifts towards greater materialism' (Gray, 2011: 451) were also noted in the studies. Twenge herself suggests that a move from *intrinsic* to *extrinsic* goals provides an explanation for the rise in psychopathology (Twenge & Foster, 2010). Gray defines the difference between intrinsic and extrinsic goals in this way:

> Developing competence in an activity that one enjoys, making friends, finding meaning in life, and pursuing a heartfelt path are examples of intrinsic goals. Getting high grades in school, making lots of money, achieving high status, and looking good to others are examples of extrinsic goals . . . the pursuit of extrinsic goals at the expense of intrinsic goals correlates with anxiety and depression. (2011: 452)

Gray argues that play enforces the development of intrinsic goals and competences, and that it allows children to make decisions and solve problems, 'exert self-control, and follow rules', support regulated emotions, make friends and value equality as well as experiencing joy (2011: 454). These aspects collectively ensure good mental health for our children. The notion of play as frivolous seems much less appropriate in light of these considerations—both in terms of a child's development and in terms of the health and welfare of the adult that the child will one day become. The obvious suggestion here, then, is that parents and schools should be very wary of obstructing or preventing opportunities for free play. One recent study of sixteen nations showed that 51% of children still rated outdoors play as their preferred activity, scoring higher than watching television, films or videos (41%) or playing computer games (19%; Singer et al., 2009). Similarly, Mihaly Csikszentmihalyi and Jeremy Hunter undertook a recent study with public school students to detect happiness and unhappiness; they used self-reported surveys with 800 students in 33 schools to measure levels of happiness over the period of one week. They found that the lowest levels of happiness occurred when the children were doing homework or attending school and the highest levels occurred when they were playing and socializing with friends and out of school (Csikszentmihalyi & Hunter, 2003). If that seems like a statement of the obvious—that we accept that this would likely be the case—it really does force us to ask *why* we take such a thing for granted.

Ironically, the more control adults have exerted over children, the less children have had opportunities for free play, and this can be damaging. Gray suggests that children need a little more control of their own development and much more time for free play. This, he suggests, would make them happier, would allow them to learn more, to be more intrinsically motivated and less narcissistic, and would ultimately help them to feel empowered instead of controlled.

To many this argument may seem counterintuitive. However, if we are to raise the next generation to solve social problems and to take care of each other—which rests on the development of altruistic rather than narcissistic qualities—we need to urgently consider how we can build the benefits of free play into our educational systems. According to educational theorists from Piaget to Vygotsky, play is a valuable tool and social play is a powerful mechanism for social change. Games provide one sensible method for structuring this natural human method of learning that is increasingly becoming accepted and validated.

It is perhaps most shocking to learn of how school in its present form is making some children unhappy. Of course, there are other factors involved here, but an environment which is prohibitive, restrictive or lacking in opportunities for play will not help. The growth of home schooling and the emergence of online learning offer alternatives, but these may also take control away from children and remove natural opportunities for free play on their own and with other children. A balance between study and play is necessary in our schools and ways that promote this balance urgently need to be explored and supported in our societies. As Gray notes that social play seems to offer the best available means to combat the feelings of superiority associated with narcissism. Parents may put their children on pedestals and tell them how special they are, and teachers may offer excessive praise and high grades for mediocre accomplishments, but children themselves do not overestimate one another in their play. (2011: 457)

THE LEARNER, THE TEACHER AND SOCIAL PLAY

The previous section demonstrates another aspect of the social context of learning—that is, the importance of childhood play and play-based learning to the development of altruistic behaviours that are key to the health and maintenance of the society. This section builds upon this notion of social learning, in particular, in respect to the roles of the learner and the teacher.

At the heart of social learning is the designated relationship between tutors and learners. The work of Etienne Wenger follows the social learning theory of Vygotsky, with the same emphasis upon social interactions, and highlights the role of these social interactions as an integral part of the individual's development process. In Wenger's study on workplace learning (1998), he argues that learning was taking place in the workplace according to 'communities of practice'. This allowed the learner to advance from novice to expert status through 'legitimate peripheral participation', predicated upon interactions and proximity with experts. This echoes some of the observations that can be made in the changing relationship between tutor and learner about the potential for learning from each other. This kind of interaction is sometimes referred to as 'horizontal learning' between peers and mentors. The context of professional working and learning practices is a good one for highlighting the way learning takes place, as professional or commercial training necessitates forms of learning that routinely result in the demonstrable acquisition of new skills, knowledge and behaviours.

One of the reasons why social interactive learning has taken a back seat, I believe, may be because of the reticence to consider alternatives to the traditional dyad between tutor and pupil. A search for literature that compares tutor-based learning with peer learning, for example, reveals comparatively few studies, and these are relatively under-cited in the rest of the educational literature (Schmidt et al., 1994; Woltering et al., 2009). Work on peer learning is also relatively under-represented in the literature, although interestingly one early study found that syndicate work had 'striking results in the development of higher order cognitive skills' (Collier, 1980: 55). Peer *teaching* articles are also hard to find. One systematic review has suggested that many studies of peer learning do not make it into scientific publications. Interestingly, that review suggested that one of the strengths of peer learning was to enhance intrinsic motivation (Ten Cate & Durning, 2007). Anders Fransson found that strong interest and low anxiety provided the best environment for good factual recall (1977) while Erika Patall and colleagues (2008) found that *choice* enhanced intrinsic motivation.

Despite the central role of the teacher in education, 'we know relatively little about them', Philip Gardner argues, and this, he says, is paradoxical because the 'entire understanding of formal education was constituted through the agency of teachers' (2005: 214). Furthermore, as Gardner outlines in his study of school teachers from 1876 to 1996, their role was often a peripheral one where they were unable to effect change in policy. Where teachers had received less intervention from local government and government inspections in the pre- and inter-war years in the United Kingdom, after that time, with greater governmental intervention, many of them 'felt a sense of impotence and resignation' (Gardner, 2005: 224). He adds, 'Politicians and public were increasingly unwilling to be excluded from what went on in the classroom' (Gardner, 2005: 225). Even the 'secret garden of the curriculum' was under scrutiny (Simon, 1991: 312). Gardner notes,

> The claims of parents and children impinged upon teachers' historic class-room autonomy from the late 1940s onwards. From the 1970s on the principal impact of policy on teacher autonomy culminated in the removal of collective bargaining rights, the imposition of new conditions of service, the introduction of the national curriculum and new regimes of testing and inspections (2005: 223).

The changes in the wider society were impinging upon the central power relationships in the classroom, and the autonomy of teachers was replaced by a culture of inspections and monitoring, more consistent with 19th-century Victorian models than post-war egalitarianism. But now it was the teacher under the gaze of society, not the student under the gaze of the teacher. Gardner comments on the impact upon discipline in the classroom in his study, and suggests that there was far less discipline after the war. Larger class sizes impacted upon this worsening situation, and the favoured 'chalk and talk' model for learning was increasingly becoming less effective and engaging. At that same time, the teacher's role started to become more peripheral.

The closeness of the relationship between the teacher and student, which has become quite normal in modern classrooms, was in fact eschewed by teachers in the pre-1960s era in favour of a more distant and formal relationship (Selleck, 1972). In the modern era of teaching the old asymmetrical relationship, based upon an organization of the tutor's power with disciplined classrooms and 'chalk and talk' pedagogy, was breaking down. Over time, a more symmetrical relationship between tutor and learner, with less discipline and more flexible learning strategies, developed. Learning in the new era is less concerned with a power structure than it is with a power balance—a *horizontal relationship,* to use Wenger's term (1998). It is natural, then, that the tutor-student dyad has given way to other socially mediated relationships, such as peer learning and team teaching, designed both to re-engage the learner and to enrich the roles of learning by making them more equal, diverse and plural.

Dialogue and social interactions were always at the heart of the formal learning relationship of tutor and student, but those social interactions were underwritten by power structures—albeit ones that made sense in a Victorian context of learning. Our understanding about the role of social interactions has developed in parallel with a wider shift away from a *didactique* teaching model that merely entails the dissemination of knowledge. And the fact that we *can* and *do* learn collaboratively through dialogue and interaction underlines the importance of the role of peers in the learning process (Laurillard, 2002). The flatter hierarchies of social learning and the more horizontal learning opportunities (Wenger, 1998), mean that learning can be expressed as *shared activities* or *constructive process* rather than as 'a state of knowing' versus 'a state of not knowing', as had previously been posited.

The shift away from the authoritarian approach and an idea of the teacher as 'all knowing' was already occurring by the end of 1960s. In our own time the idea of the tutor as the producer and deliverer of the learning content is also in decline, and the disaggregation of the development of learning content from the role of teaching is increasingly evident. At the same time, the relationship between the teacher and student has undergone a significant transformation and further changes appear to be well underway.

To an extent, we can also look at the relationship between the theories of learning and practices of teaching. Many practitioners are unaware of the pedagogic strategies they are employing when teaching, and often do not have much time structured into their day to reflect upon their practices. They have built up their approaches through their experience of real-life interchanges with students, and that has allowed them to develop strategies that work for them, their learners and their discipline. Much of this experience-based approach will come from their own experience of teaching, but some strategies may reflect their own personal experiences of learning. Equally others may derive their strategies from the tutors who taught them when they were training. Ultimately, many teachers will employ a mixture of these influences along with any professional guidance that can be gleaned from books and articles.

As was stated at the outset of this chapter, the science of learning explores *what learning is, how we learn* and the *best methods for support learning*. But with more research undertaken that explores the best methods for learning rather than what learning is or how we learn, there is a perceptible gap between the theory and practice of learning. While learning theory is our best tool for supporting effective learning practices through applying and linking theories to everyday learning practices, it can be a blunt tool if teachers and tutors find it hard to understand that link. In fact, our understanding about how we link between theory and practice in learning is a relatively under-researched area (de Freitas et al., 2008).

While schematic models can help us to understand the relationship, these are not always helpful. Traditionally, we linked theory and practice in learning and education via pedagogy and learning frameworks, and our working definition of learning was the accumulation of knowledge or skills. Following on from the logic of this definition, the traditional role of teacher was as the 'possessor and voice of knowledge' and the students could be considered as 'receptacles' for that knowledge. But that assumption fails with the modern conception of what learning is—that is, as a construction of individual understanding rather than just as the acquisition of notional knowledge (de Freitas & Jameson, 2012). Here, then, the traditional dyad between teacher and student breaks down in favour of more equal 'horizontal' relationships.

Modelling is all about creating maps or 'referents' (likenesses) of practices and conceptual descriptions, and this is why the value of modelling—whether in 2D or 3D—is so important not just for communicating ideas and practices but also for rehearsing (and therefore learning) ideas and practices. Whether modelling takes place in real situations, collaboratively or in isolation, creatively or scientifically, the value of modelling experiences, ideas, abstract concepts and particular problems or challenges, conflicts or scenarios can aid with supporting the learning processes (Hays, 2005). This gains credence with the modern idea of learning as *a process of individual construction of understanding*, as each person constructs different maps of the world according to his or her own experiences, social interactions and level of engagement in social play (Edelman, 1992; Piaget, 1999; Vygotsky, 1962). Learning facilitates that construction, scaffolding development through social play and experimentation. At the heart of learning, therefore, the crucial social interactions—between tutor and learner, learner and learner, parent and child or novice and expert—are key considerations for the development of learning theories and practice and for the development of effective teaching practices.

It is easy to see how the role of the 'master' presented an effective method for supporting learning, particularly when the notion of knowledge as *connaissance* (a body of knowledge) was foremost. Now however, information rather than knowledge lies at the heart of our understanding of what learning is, and our needs to marshal and process information take into account our social interactions and wider life experiences. Consequently, social interactive learning and learning through experiences now seem more obvious and logical methods of delivery for certain aspects of learning.

Bridging the gap between the practices of learners and the practices of tutors is today probably one of the greatest challenges for educational providers, and it is important to note that practices are still very much in flux. At the heart of these debates, particularly in the field of e-learning, has been the debate about the changing role of the tutor and the drive towards more 'learner-centred' processes. However, as with the debates about 'inter-disciplinarity', the debate here has often paid lip service to a learner-centred approach whilst practices on the ground often remain unchanged. Nonetheless, in the current environment there are real opportunities for shifting the balance of the relationship between pupil and master to one of learner and mentor, or learner and tutor-practitioner, or even learner and learner in parallel. There is a chance to experiment with cross-disciplinary interchanges, team teaching and a range of other approaches to learning, which may innovate current practices, helping to engage a wider range of learners into tertiary education, vocational training and workplace learning as well as facilitating new approaches for personal lifelong learning.

Online social interactions often centre upon sharing content, playing games, joining quests in online games, exchanging text and audio messages and producing multimedia content. These interactions, then, *can* be co-opted to support forms of learning that deliver significant societal benefits along with the acquisition by the individual of personal social skills. If learning can be expressed as part of development and as the preparation of the individual to take on an active role in society, then surely situative learning approaches based upon social interactions and focused upon vocational learning practices *are* desirable. Social software is being taken up widely by tutors, but this surely can only be a part of our learning and training needs (Conole et al., 2008). While the power of social software and simulation-based tools is clear, in pre-work situations we must also fully appreciate the link between theories of teaching and theories of learning, the relationships between the tutors and learners and the importance of the social context in the objectives of education.

CHOREOGRAPHING SOCIAL LEARNING PLAY

Building upon this wider contextual consideration of play, work in social psychology, computer science and education science is emerging that deals with *immersion, flow* and *spatial presence*. In particular, work undertaken by Mihaly Csikszentmihalyi on *flow* (1992), Mel Slater and Sylvia Wilbur on *immersion* (1992), and Steve Benford and colleagues on *presence* (1998) is illustrative. Although many studies have focused upon *immersion* as a critical category for effective learning in computer generated learning environments, understanding exactly how immersion enhances *learning* that takes place in them—for example, where the learner can control an avatar and move it around a virtual space—is the subject of ongoing study and debate. Initial indicators are that the sense of presence or spatial presence in CDEs *does* have a significant impact upon the overall efficacy of these environments (Willans, 2012) and may, at least in part, explain the greater efficacy of these over *traditional* learning approaches. However, their efficacy could also be attributed to their playful and social appeal (Kato et al., 2008; Knight et al. 2010).

Social learning play can also be supported or enhanced by the identification of learners with their avatars. As in a film or book, the avatar represents the learner in the virtual world. This is another interesting indication of the differences between virtual and physical learning environments (Van Looy et al., 2012). Two studies have demonstrated that younger people find it easier than do older players to identify their avatars as themselves (Allison et al., 2006; Blinka, 2008). It is curious that adults see their avatars as a detached 'other' whilst children see the avatar as themselves, but it does give us an indication of why children like games, such as *Habbo Hotel*, in which they can easily identify with the cartoon-style characters that represent them in the game.

The role of avatars for supporting social learning play has powerful applications. One study involving children with autism found improvements in facial and emotional recognition *and* in social interactions when using an avatar assistant (Hopkins et al., 2011). Hypothetically, control could be a factor here; it is an important component in learning, and particularly for gaining confidence. Thus, theoretically speaking, the more control exerted by the learner, the more effective learning in CGEs should be (Kiili et al., 2012). While focus in the literature has centred upon notions around *identification formation* (Bessiere, Seay & Kiesler, 2007), there has been less study into the role that control plays both in identification and play behaviour. It does appear that it helps children to learn, if they have a perception of control over their avatar, whether that representation of themselves in the CGE is a cartoon animation or a lifelike character. We should therefore acknowledge the potential influence of the learner's general sense of control over and within the environment.

Interestingly, one recent study found that virtual environments also allowed young children a good many opportunities for free play or offline play (Marsh, 2010). Building on the findings of the literature, the growing popularity of both online and offline virtual environments and free play may be due to a combination of several contributing factors, for instance: flow and immersion, a sense of control (e.g., over the avatar), playful and competitive elements (e.g., narrative, leader boards), the facilitation of social interactions (e.g., in-game chat and multiplayer missions and tasks) and immediate feedback in the system to the user (e.g., levelling up, points gained).

In his other work, Van Gennep has noted how narrative can support transitions between developmental stages, or 'liminal states', as in rites of passage when individuals move from child to adult (Van Gennep, 1960). Narrative can help us make the transitions more easily, because we can benefit from others' experiences by taking on their role or position in a book or film, for example, without any negative consequences in our own lives. This resonates well with the Piagetian notion of learning as 'phasal' development, and Lave and Wenger's notion of 'legitimate peripheral participation' with learning in groups (Lave & Wenger, 1991; Piaget, 2007a). Whether within a narrative structure or a community of practice, these are 'scaffolds', or forms of rehearsal, for individuals as they progress through their maturation. Narrative frames the previous cultural and social experiences of others, which provide useful information on how to move through different life phases. Interactions within social groups allow for sharing of common human experiences, providing necessary scaffolds for development. Social play in this sense can thus combine immersive experiences that promote a sense of spatial presence, together with narrative structures and mediated social interactions, for 'sense-making' and overcoming pitfalls in human development (Dervin, 1983).

The power of CGEs is that they lend so well to incorporating these elements of immersion, interactivity, sense of control and feedback in one environment. Social play and social interactions can be easily framed in game environments, and structure, control and identification all contribute to producing a scaffolded learning system that can map against many different learning scenarios and learning activities. In the face of quite radical changes to learning practice, learning conceptualized as *exploration* and *play* is becoming more prominent. In parallel, how tutors and trainers approach learning is altering as well. In new simulation-based approaches, rather than simply producing learning content and mediating dialogue about key concepts and issues, tutors are increasingly creating or choreographing social, playful learning interactions, as evidenced by the *Ardcalloch* exemplar, in which legal trainees are taught key methods through a simulation of an imaginary town. (See Case Study 1: The *Ardcalloch* Simulation Game.)

Box 2.1   The *Ardcalloch* Simulation Game

While simulations have a long history of use with certain professions, such as legal, medical, military and business training, uptake in other educational areas has been slower. While it is not definite that this is because of the vocational dimension and effectiveness of simulations in those particular contexts, there is a clear link between effective use of simulations and vocational practices. However, in a climate where greater relevance of work-based learning is being heralded as important both for learners (and their orientation into work) and industry (and its requirements for specific skill-sets), this area of educational practice may well become more widespread, particularly as the use and application of virtual-world applications and software development tool kits becomes cheaper to deploy and the skills of tutors (through continuing professional development) increase to match these innovative uses.

The main challenge for colleagues at the Glasgow Graduate School of Law (GGSL) at the University of Strathclyde was how to best utilize information and communications technologies to aid law students to make a smoother transition from their academic study of law into vocational legal practice. The diploma in legal practice offered at the CGSL

Continued

Box 2.1 *continued*

is a vocationally orientated postgraduate course. The course aims to introduce learners who have completed their undergraduate studies in law to the knowledge, skills, attitudes and values required to become advocates and solicitors in Scotland. The course is mandated by the Law Society of Scotland, and involves eight compulsory subject areas and one optional subject choice. Following the course, students then enter a two-year traineeship, on successful completion of which they are deemed 'fit and proper' to enter the legal profession.

To support their students, Karen Barton, Paul Maharg, and colleagues at the GGSL developed a blended learning solution evolving a traditional lecture- and tutorial- based course with academic examinations into a highly interactive and practice-based set of activities supported by online collaborative assessments. The main focus of the diploma is the fictional west coast Scottish provincial town of Ardcalloch. The virtual town includes businesses (among them virtual law firms), institutions and citizens—in short, the 'realia' of local urban life. The town—accessed via the university's intranet system—allows learners to take up the role of legal practitioners operating in Ardcalloch, supported by databases of legal documents and templates, forums for discussion with tutors (who, being practitioners, double in their roles within a transaction), e-mail communications with other firms and supervisors, and activity and personal logs. In addition to these resources, learners can also access course lecture videos, multimedia presentations, online drafting tools, notes, documents and assignments through this means. Tutor-practitioners, in seminars as well as through online support and communications, support the learners throughout the simulated transactions.

According to the designers of the course (Barton & Maharg, 2006), the simulation depends upon three main factors:

- Design of learning outcomes and activities.
- Type of simulation field (e.g. bounded or open).
- Organization of communities of practice supporting the simulated activities.

The type of simulation used depends upon the learning outcomes desired and the type of transaction that is the focus of the simulation. Thus, certain transactions are fairly linear—winding up the estate of a deceased client, for instance—and produce a 'bounded field' of simulation that relies upon more 'specific and precise' outcomes. Other transactions are more flexible and less well structured.

This open field of practice does not require specified learning outcomes but instead specifically wide-ranging activities and bodies of evidence in the form of a transaction file. It is noteworthy that both types of simulated activities warrant assessment, the type of assessment being real-world based and consistent with legal practice outcomes, such as winning an adversarial case, following correct procedures, managing risk and being aware of ethical and client-centred practice. In this way, Barton and Maharg argue that it is the 'realia'—that is, the choice of which items learners will want to use, the 'virtual objects'—that lends authenticity to the activities, allowing the learners to have a more realistic set of experiences.

Barton and Maharg suggest a notion of the 'depth of field' as a way of assisting designers of complex simulations. This depth of field—similar to that of the photographer or cinematographer, and to the notion of *diegesis* (in this case, the internal space within the game; see De Freitas and Oliver, 2006)—allows designers to place 'realia' and objects within the simulation to allow learners to have a freer opportunity to explore the simulation. This includes intended objects as well as incidental ones. As in diegesis, the realism of this allows the learner to become more immersed within the space, a factor that is non-dependent upon the fidelity or verisimilitude of the simulation—that is, the realism of the look of the space, but more dependent upon the realism of the experiences within the space.

The organization of the user communities in the *Ardcalloch* game is supported by the realism and immersive nature of the activities per se. This allows and facilitates an identity change through role play from the undergraduate student to the legal practitioner—as in the historical game modification of *Neverwinter Nights*, *Revolution* in which the student plays the role of a slave in the 18th century. This process of change is critical in this course, which is organized to provide a bridge between academic study and vocational practice (Barton & McKellar, 2011). The simulation allows the learner to make these changes in a safe and controllable environment without adversely affecting any claims of real clients. The identity formation that takes place in the learner allows for a scaffold on the part of the tutors and designers who 'enable learners to work within the problems and issues that arise when professional identity is first formed' (Barton & Maharg, 2006); that is, scaffolding for learning assists learners in constructing more complex thinking tools for learning.

Vocational practices, as noted in *Ardcalloch*, indicate that the use of simulations not only inform the process of learning but can also provide a clear structure for how simulations can be used effectively to support identity change and professional development within a formal educational setting. The link from academic endeavour to vocational practice has been well conceived in this exemplar, which also demonstrates that effective use of immersive worlds needs to be carefully planned into group activities and social interactions, through scaffolded learning, discussion and post-exercise reflection.

Box 2.2   The Quest to Learn School

The Quest to Learn (Q2L) School opened in New York City in September 2009 for grades 6–12. The school is the world's first of its kind, and came out of work between the MacArthur Foundation and Katie Salen (who is based at the Center for Transformative Media at Parsons the New School for Design as well as the Institute of Play in Brooklyn). The idea that emerged was to set up a school 'using "gamelike learning" to empower and engage students from all walks of life' (Salen et al., 2011: 1–2).

> Design and innovation are two big ideas for the school, as is a commitment to deep content learning with a strong focus on learning in engaging, relevant ways. The school is a place where digital media meets books and where students learn to think like designers, inventors, mathematicians and more. (Salen et al., 2011: 2)

In the United States, as in other countries, a trend towards dropping out of high school, not taking science and engineering classes at university and a general disengagement within the classroom are leading to severe social issues that need to be addressed. But as in the United Kingdom and internationally, the United States has found it difficult to rethink its education system, and the comprehensive system as a whole seems to let down a large proportion of students. Q2L is an experiment to see how standards could be driven up, interest in science, technology, engineering and mathematics increased and drop-out rates reduced by re-engaging students through games, 'gamification' and digital media. While engagement in school has reduced, the use of digital media has conversely increased significantly. Q2L sets out its rationale to engage its students through immersive dynamic games by providing constant feedback and supporting new ways to think about and see the world.

Interestingly, perhaps, the school addresses 'learning spaces' in an unbounded and original way: 'several kinds of learning spaces are identified: home, lab [before- and after-school spaces located in proximity to the school building], School Day [the "formal" space of the school], global communities [social networks, virtual worlds, etc.], and local communities [the soccer team, the neighborhood library, the youth club, etc.]' (Salen et al., 2011: 13). This arrangement allows the school to understand and actively design for learning that crosses the boundaries between school and outside school activities. They see 'learning as *practice* and Q2L as a *practice space*' (Salen et al., 2011: 13).

The curriculum used follows one adopted by a New York State maths and science foundation, but its innovation comes into play with 'Discovery Missions', which are 'questlike challenges that require students to plan, collect data, create theories, test their results, and document outcomes' (Salen et al., 2011: 14). Each Discovery Mission comprises mini-quests, designed as 'data expeditions' involving collecting data and analyzing it. For example, a student might be required to find key terms online and would be expected to 'learn the basic syntax of HTML, become fluent in the use of search engines, and learn how to assess the credibility of sources' (Salen et al., 2011: 75). Each Discovery Mission involves between four and ten quests, and each quest can be completed by individual students or in groups. The mission goal is known at the outset, and developing and designing quests for the younger students is also part of the curriculum. Some quests may be more informational whilst others more problem-based, such as researching questions or experimentation.

At 75 to 90 minutes in duration the daily sessions are longer than those of most schools, thus allowing for longer project work and learning experiences. The school also has small class sizes (on average 25 students per class). Games are used in different ways to frame the school activities, and Q2L utilizes a range of different games, tools and languages such as *Alice, Scratch, Quest Altlantis, SimCity, Civilization,* and *Animal Crossing.* Ongoing evaluation work has shown marked improvement in student performance and drop-out rates and aims to validate the game model approach (Shute & Torres, 2012).

The school provides an excellent model for what schools of the future may look like and provides an innovation that is being tracked by many ministries of education with respect to grades and performance improvements.

Box 2.3   The Grange Primary School

Another instance in which innovation is being used in the school system is provided by the Grange Primary School in Nottingham, England. School head Richard Gerver arrived at an under-performing school (with only 50% achieving the benchmark grades at the end of Key Stage 2). The teachers in the school 'knew they were not providing a vibrant experience for the children and the children could see no purpose in their learning' (Gerver, 2010: 96). In order to get the school back on track he conducted a review to establish what the world was like for today's children and to explore visions of what the future might be like for them. This inquiry involved talking to both the children and local businesses as well as reviewing relevant papers and reports (e.g., National Advisory Committee on Creative and Cultural Education, 1999; Robinson, 2001; Royal Society of Arts, 1999). Gerver was trying to establish what skills were needed for the 21st century and looking at innovative ways of engaging his students, who were consistently under-performing.

The challenge for the school was how to motivate children and how to raise standards to higher levels to support greater opportunities to

Continued

Box 2.3   *Continued*

better reflect the more dynamic global economy that the children would grow up and work in over the coming years. The result of the synthesis of the review and consultation undertaken was an innovation not only with how the school was organized but also with what the children were taught. Based upon the review, clear messages were found: 80% of future jobs do not exist yet, costs of computing will reduce considerably and employability patterns are changing.

To facilitate this need for different kinds of skills, and in order to motivate his students, Gerver decided to employ the use of computer games. This approach would engage the students and provide opportunities for developing greater creativity, problem-solving ability and leadership potential.

Building upon notions of children as at the centre of a design process, as noted in the work of Druin and participatory design strategies (Druin, 2002; Guha et al., 2004), the wider notion of the efficacy of games to motivate learners, and the notion of multiliteracies (Kalantzis & Cope, 2000; Pelletier, 2005), Gerver identified a range of games that could be used to support learning, including *Theme Hospital, Sim City, The Sims* and *Roller Coaster Tycoon. The Sims* was chosen as the best metaphor for the school due in part to its widespread appeal. Gerver set about transferring *The Sims* onto his school, setting up the virtual town Grangeton, and today students have control regular broadcasts over their own TV and radio stations and run their own shop. *The Sims* school even includes a Parisian café where pupils have to converse in French, and there is also a school museum. The enterprises at Grangeton run all the time, and there are radio broadcasts five days a week run by six- and seven-year-olds.

Gerver argues that games provide a rich educational tool that offer scope for wide opportunities to consider real-life scenarios in a safe and immersive world. Hence, Grangeton has its own council, with local mayoral elections, thus supporting an emerging understanding of citizenship. Understandably, Grangeton has been extremely popular with the students and has significantly changed the roles that teachers employ to support learning. The models adopted permit tutors to guide learners, allowing them to develop independence and take on responsibility, taking risks in a safe and secure environment. While seven-year-olds can apply to work in the enterprises, even children in the nursery are engaged in media-based activities, producing their own DVDs.

Future plans for the school include as its main goal to move away from a curriculum-based approach with defined age groups towards a system based upon four themes: communication, culture, enterprise and well-being. All learning will fall into these themes, with additional literacy and numeracy classes. There will be 30 simultaneous workshops (six-week courses; e.g., in filmmaking) and the groups will include students of mixed ages and abilities. Career entry profiles will be produced, with certificates and accreditation points built up throughout their time at school.

The approach of using sessions of longer duration, and the move away from 'age and stage' structures, is reflected in other innovative approaches for school education—for example, the work of Wim Veen, who argues along the lines of Diana and James Oblinger (2005) that young children are becoming more conversant with the new technologies, transforming the learning paradigm (Veen, 2006; Veen & Vrakking, 2006). The new paradigm is leading to a need for changes to how formal learning takes place, as outlined in Table 2.1, in which Veen compares traditional and future schools.

Table 2.1   Comparison of Current and Future Schools

Traditional schools	Future schools
•50-minute classes	•Four-hour periods
•Subject specific content	•Interdisciplinary themes
•Classrooms for 30 students	•Areas for 90 to 120 students
•Age-based groups derived from yearly cohorts	•Continuing individual learning paths

Source: Veen 2006.

The Grangeton model shows how motivating games can be as metaphors for learning, allowing children to learn in less structured and more practically applied ways supporting creativity and problem-based learning and allowing them to acquire higher-level cognition through role play and experiential and contextualized approaches to learning. The virtual town within a school not only offers children an overarching narrative but allows the children time to problematize activities and work within that context as well as supporting opportunities for meta-reflection within a virtual environment. The innovations have had a positive impact upon grades, and the Grange Primary School has gone from the bottom quartile nationally to the top 10% of primary schools (Gerver, 2010).

Education is moving towards these more immersive, experience-centred and media-enriched approaches in which social interactions and play become critical components of a *new learning* (Simons, Van der Linden & Duffy, 2000).

So far we have considered immersive learning as sets of experiences and activities that guide individual development through social play; this has been supported through new methods of learning that include play as an organizing principle. This, however, certainly does not mean the end of face-to-face learning, and in some senses the changes imply greater emphasis upon one-to-one interaction, greater opportunities for e-mentoring with experts and more scope for team teaching and collaborative learning.

However, CGEs and their use in formal education do imply a need to re-consider many of the basics about learning. This need centres more on learning processes and changing epistemological influences than on any technologies or forms of CGE *per se*. Knowledge as a corpus (*connaissance*) is no longer the only discourse, and the questioning of traditional curricula indicates a shift towards more dynamic orderings and a deeper understanding of the *processes of information* (de Freitas, forthcoming). *Memorized information is not the only unit of learning today; social interactions and transactions are now also central to learning.* Information processing is still an integral part of learning, but increasingly 'social interaction' is becoming a unit of learning in its own right. The future of this trend will ultimately rest, however, on our ambition and imagination in developing more models of communities of learning and on our will to work on the pedagogic and didactic approaches that best exploit and combine the powers of new developments.

In this transition to *new learning*, the learning relationships that lie at the centre of learning are not wiped away; in practice, in immersive worlds they become even more central to the processes of learning. Tutor-learner relationships, and those between learners themselves, are amplified by other sets of relations including the roles played in learning by friends, family, other practitioners and the wider society of learners. As the author is the first reader of his or her own book, so too is the teacher the first learner of his or her own lessons; the importance of the teacher's role is not diminished in the re-ordering of the educational landscape—it is heightened by the plurality of that role. The 21st century teacher increasingly has many skills, some of which are not fully acknowledged by the wider public and some of which are not fully exploited by the traditional system. The modern tutor acts as *choreographer* of learning experiences, as guide, mentor, learner, expert, facilitator, mediator, consultant and researcher. And these skills are not just delivered to inculcate disciplinary knowledge; they are key to mediating the practicing of social interactions and the development of social skills.

I began this chapter considering the learner at the centre of the learning process, through a consideration of learning in CGEs and through social play. I end the chapter with a consideration of the tutor. As we have seen with the *Ardcalloch* study the complexity of learning in different worlds is prompting the development of new teaching skills and more complex *learning patterns*. The tutor, as an active participant in the learning scenario, requires the skills to guide activities and learning experiences that allow the learner to feel control but which also drive the learning process. Approaches like those adopted in the Quest to Learn and Grange Primary schools illustrate how media and games can be used to engage and immerse learners, making learning more fun and relevant for the 21st century. Crucially, though, debriefing, discourse and reflection upon these activities are still central components of learning in virtual spaces and in CGEs and require careful *tutorial* mediation and feedback.

3   Designing Learning

One of the challenges that teachers and tutors face when using computer generated environments (CGEs) in their classrooms and seminar rooms is how to effectively deploy them with students. But when we consider the best ways for designing learning experiences inside the game, simulation or learning environment, we need to consider all the same elements we did for designing face-to-face learning, including understanding the *roles* of learning (e.g., teacher and learner, teaching assistants, other learners), the *theories and methods* used to underpin learning (e.g., experiential learning, inquiry based learning, exploratory learning) and the *models for deploying the results* of learning (e.g., classroom exercises, homework assignments). But in addition to these considerations, within CGEs there are added design principles to consider, such as the design of the look and the layout of the virtual space and, importantly, the interactive design elements such as challenge or mission design, narrative, the competitive element and the staging of different levels (Dickey, 2011; Harteveld, 2011, 2012; Salen & Zimmerman, 2004).

When we design learning activities for the classroom, we are limited by the extent of the space there, the immutability of its physical architecture and the time we have available to use any such physical space. In other words, we are limited by real world physics and economics. CGEs help us to overcome some of these limitations because we can simulate different spaces and environments without the costs involved in building or even visiting real world spaces. Crucially, this sense of economy is a vital factor in our considerations. For example, physically rebuilding the actual forum of ancient Rome (c. 200 CE) would be incredibly costly and even visiting such a renovation—say, for a class field trip—would still be prohibitively expensive, in an international sense. A simulation on the other hand can offer a virtual 3D rendering of the renovated ancient forum, to a global audience—and to a school or class—for the price of a standard game (around $40/€35/£30). This new economy means that we can provide students with a variety of immersive, interactive and high-fidelity learning environments and tools that can *all* be accessed from their classroom or their homes. This, in turn, means that we can use both formal and informal time frames to learn and to deploy the results of learning. This chapter focuses upon these elements of *immersion, interactivity* and *fidelity* as key design criteria of CGEs and explores the ways in which learning in CGEs can enhance classroom-based learning, support learning outcomes and reduce the effort—that is, the student's effort—needed for learning transfer.

While we need to be careful that learning with CGEs does still stretch our students and doesn't spoon-feed them too much, the opportunities for enhanced learning in CGEs are significant. These opportunities are now starting to be acknowledged in scientific research, and increasingly that research is gaining a far better understanding of how and why these new forms help to enhance learning. In particular, the research on e-learning, technology enhanced learning and game-based learning is allowing us to gain a better overview of what works and what doesn't work (de Freitas & Maharg, 2011; Sharpe, Beetham & de Freitas, 2010). Early examples of simulation-based learning (the *Ardcalloch* simulation game; see Chapter 2), game-based learning (New York City's Quest to Learn School; see Chapter 2) and successful e-learning approaches (online learning delivery of courses, massive online open courses and OpenCourseWare), are already providing a glimpse of what school, college and university education may look like in the future. What the current research is telling us is that new methods of learning, or *new learning*, can certainly deliver: greater opportunities for personalizing learning for students; more flexible learning opportunities; more informal opportunities for learning and testing learning; lifelong learning capabilities for professional training in the workplace; and the opening of new international markets for overseas students (Barton & Maharg, 2006; Collis & Moonen, 2001; de Freitas & Yapp, 2005; Salen et al., 2011; Walsh, 2011).

It is interesting to note that while there is a significant and growing body of research and literature that addresses *game design* (Rodgers, 2010; Salen & Zimmerman, 2004; Schell, 2008), there is a limited body of work that looks at *game design for learning*, and this has only really emerged more recently (Dickey, 2011; Harteveld, 2011). *Simulation design*—that is, the design of a simulated environment or object, as opposed to game design—also has a compact but well developed range of literature that has evolved over the last twenty or thirty years (Brannick, Salas & Prince, 2009; Jones, 1985). More recently, in light of the similarities of design principles and production of computer games and computer simulations, some authors have tried to bridge the conceptual gap to bring simulation design and game design together (Becker & Parker, 2012; Quinn, 2005), and this sort of approach reflects a wider attempt to consider design in CGEs more comprehensively. In other areas, the quantity and quality of the literature around *e-learning design* is growing, as more academics and instructional designers have become aware of the possibilities of using technology enhanced learning capabilities (Horton, 2012; Sharpe & Beetham, 2007) and *multimedia design* also has its well established specialist titles now (Druin &

Solomon, 1996; Moggridge, 2010). Lastly, a consideration of *interaction design* and *human computer interaction* has started to emerge, providing guidelines and best practices for usability and heuristics (Benyon, 2010; Nielsen, 2000).

When it comes to learning design using CGEs, we need to draw on an understanding of best practices in design from games, simulations, e-learning, interaction and, of course, learning design. These guides to practice can assist us with the process of design, but most teachers and tutors will be less interested in how to design the simulated environment or even the game and more interested in how to design a useful *learning experience*. The main focus for teachers, then, is that the experience (simulation and game) will be engaging for the learner while promoting learning outcomes that can be measured and assessed accurately. Learning in CGEs offers us a new set of challenges for designing *learning experiences* rather than lesson plans or learning outcome schedules. Those *learning experiences* can be freed from the constraints of time, space and location and can integrate different elements and levels of *fidelity*, *interactivity* and *immersion*. Crucially, CGEs can also build in the task of assessment (testing), taking laborious marking duties and responsibilities away from staff, and allowing them instead to focus upon higher cognition exercises and learning design.

Choreographing learning experiences in different kinds of CGEs, be they games or learning management environments, relies upon an understanding of the world 'inside' the game, simulation or interactive environment. Readers may be familiar with this idea from their experiences with viewing films, where the locations and events that are depicted constitute a kind of mini-world. In film studies this notional world is sometimes referred to as the *diegesis* of the film (Burch, 1982; Stam, Burgoyne & Flitterman-Lewis, 1992). This sense of a notional world, it should be added, is more the by-product of the description or depiction of the spaces and places of the narrative story than of the events and happenings or the dialogue of the characters. Etienne Souriau proposed the term *diegesis* in 1948, 'contrasting the diegetic . . . universe [the place of the signified] with the screen-universe [the place of the film-signifier]. Used in that sense *diegesis* is indeed a *universe* rather than a train of events [a story]' (Gennette & Lewin, 1990: 17).

It is similar, if not the same, in the world inside the game or simulation. *How* the notional world is represented is a significant aspect of why we feel so engaged when playing a game or undertaking a simulation. The fact that *we* are represented in a virtual environment is, however, a significant difference from the example of the narrative film. While in the film we identify with the main protagonist, in the game we *are* the protagonist, and we can be represented by an avatar that can be customized to look more or less just like us. The avatar, and the important fact that we can control it, allow us to identify even more easily with it than we can with the protagonist in a film. The fact that we can control our representation in the game environment to interact with that environment and with other characters, also helps us to perceive and believe in the notional space—the game world—as a real-world space.

In a recent study of *the flow of games*, when testing students, Kristian Kiili and colleagues found that 'sense of control', 'clear goals' and 'challenge-skill balance dimensions' scored the highest with players (Kiili et al., 2012). This idea of *flow* is used to describe a sense of the narrative progression through the notional game world and is linked, in design terms, to the interactions of the player's in-game character. The direct representation of one's self within the environment, coupled with the effective and engaging narrative flow that a well designed game can present, provides the combination of *incentive*, *control* and *interactivity* that makes CGEs such unique training tools and forms. If the balance between fun and learning is correct, then, all the positive aspects of watching a film or playing an entertainment game come into play but with the added advantage that active participation and interactivity produces an active involvement of *the player or learner* rather than the passive involvement of the viewer of a film. As is evidenced by entertainment games such as *Call of Duty*, if they are designed well, digital games can deliver the entertainment of top budget films, the same sense of immersion into the narrative as a good book and the interactive elements, including competition, that characterize all the most popular real-world or physical games and sports.

For those who have never played a computer game, it can be difficult to understand how there can be any symmetry between the experiences in a game—with what looks to the casual observer like a cartoon version of world—with experiences in the physical world. This is to miss the central design consideration of computer games, which is not to deliver a photo-realistic duplication of our physical world but instead to deliver, through the game, experiences that we could never otherwise have. At the same time, all the most popular games and game genres use narrative structures that progress through challenges or competitions, and this means that game players *are* learning and acquiring skills or knowledge in their game play. And crucially, in some players it is a rapid acquisition of skills. Of course, these game 'skills' are not usually transferable to everyday life, but then neither are the skills we learn in physical sports or board games. These games weren't designed to produce transferable skills. The point is, in any type of game—football or chess, *Halo* or *Far Cry*—learning it involves playing the game and playing the game involves learning it.

If we carry the logic of digital game design into educational games, we can see that the potential exists to identify and exploit the sweet spot between entertainment and learning by innovating games that *are* designed to produce transferable skills. The design of learning games or learning experiences in CGEs brings together the traditional blend of different media elements—such as visual and audio realism—with the new elements of greater identification (e.g., through control over one's avatar) and interactivity (e.g., through involvement in challenges and missions). This requirement for complex combinations sets the designer specific challenges that need to be considered and used to make the learning experiences realistic, fulfilling and effective in terms of what is learnt. When these design criteria are addressed successfully by the game or simulation, the player, learner or trainee is properly motivated *and* more able to extend a sense of identity into the world of the game—the simulation. This element—*immersion*—aids the intuitive performance of the activities and the acquisition of skills, but an understanding of the centrality of *incentive and motivation* to the structuring and design conventions of existing digital games and learning games is vital.

Ultimately, however, the requirements of educational games are more demanding than those of entertainment games in that learning games need to produce skills that transfer between the learning game or the learning environment and the real spaces and places where these skills need to be applied—for example, the workplace. This is a central challenge for learning game designers.

While simulations replicate realities, games place control systems—and sometimes game specific, unrealistic or arbitrary rules—inside 2D and 3D environments. While we may seem to be in control, the designer has carefully structured our interactions to ensure that we experience a certain thing, see a particular problem or undertake a specific mission with proscribed learning outcomes and experiences. Moreover, these rules and structures are, arguably, one of the reasons why games work so well.

Unsurprisingly, perhaps, early attempts to explore the idea of learning in virtual spaces have often lacked structure, and this contravention of the key design principles for both games and learning experiences was critical. For example, in a study undertaken by this author and colleagues, very little structure was provided in one *virtual world* learning scenario; as a result, learning outcomes were often difficult to measure or were not satisfactory in terms of learning transfer (de Freitas et al., 2010). One conclusion here might have been that open-ended unstructured learning in a virtual world does *not* promote learning transfer. However, it is important to remember how recently these learning tools have been developed and that we are still learning how to deploy and use them effectively in learning contexts. I believe that the key here is attention to design and structure. Studies on game environments have demonstrated consistently positive learning outcomes and this, in my opinion, is attributable to the rules and structures implicit in game environments that have not as yet been incorporated into the use of open-ended virtual world environments.

There appears to be a clear lesson here for good learning design; in general, structured learning *is* more effective than unstructured learning, but crucially there must be a balance. A sense of control over the environment and our avatars, as I have noted earlier in the chapter, enhances the individual's sense of immersion into the environment and their engagement with the learning or gaming experience.

To enhance the learning design experience, the learning designer in this context becomes a game designer or learning *choreographer*, designing learning experiences that have a distinctive look and feel that at once supports engagement, flow, narrative structure and learner control. This is where the area of 'experience design' overlaps with learning design. Experience design incorporates all the conventions of game design but also integrates an understanding of the principles of learning design—for example, building in learning assessment according to learning outcomes (Shedroff, 2001). At the same time, designers need to craft activities that map against validated curriculum objectives, utilizing the value of engagement and immediate feedback for scaffolding learning in the CGE; the lessons from game design suggest that can easily be achieved through the conventions of challenges, missions, points, multiple lives and level-by-level progress.

By bringing together learning design, game design and experience design, the teacher can gain the notable benefit of integrating feedback and assessment into game missions, thereby lessening their workload with respect to assessing learning, marking and testing.

This chapter focuses upon the creation of the *world inside* the CGE and looks to the overlaps in game design, learning design, experience design and learning game design for the tools to make learning as effective as possible in terms of what is experienced, learned and assessed. In the first section we have looked at immersion, control, interactivity and incentive/motivation as key elements that create the *world inside* the CGE. In the next section, I want to explore the notion of traversing through 'liminal stages' as a method for human development and why narrative and imagination are such important social constructivist tools, for creating these worlds and universes and for scaffolding social learning environments in new learning.

LEVELING UP: CROSSING BOUNDARIES

The term *liminal stage* is an ethnographic one and is used to describe the transitional phases—in particular, those between maturity stages—of human development. The term is an apt one with respect to learning, particularly when we take learning to mean development, as in the constructivist expression (Piaget, 2007a; see also the section on *developmental learning* in de Freitas & Jameson, 2012). Arnold Van Gennep, in *The Rites of Passage* (1960), expressed this transition in terms of human development, such as the transitions from girl to woman and from boy to man. In ancient cultures, passing through these key phases in the individual's life was ritualized and became part of a group expression, echoing the deeply social ties of the community and aiding in the actual transitions (Frazer, 1991; Turner, 1987). In modern societies, these transitional phases can be problematic to individuals even today, such as the transitions taking place during the teenage years or during a mid-life crisis, and they can be long in duration. In the learning and training contexts, the phases between novice and expert include initiation into an expert group and involve a lengthy process of 'scaffolding' to attain expert status (Vygotsky, 1978; Wood, Bruner & Ross, 1976).

Learner-practitioners set a range of different parameters for the individual to traverse. Often this transition takes place in the workplace, but it is no less challenging as a result. The central transition in the learning context, then, is the transition from pre-school to school to university and then into the workplace, and the role of education is, arguably, to provide students with the skills and knowledge that they need to fit into and succeed in the workplace. An understandable problem in the modern 'information society', however, has been that schools didn't know exactly what skills their students would require in the fast changing, high-tech, knowledge society—but then, neither did anyone else.

The recent response to this has been a new global movement which attempts to define the new learning. The definition and adoption of new skills, as defined under the Partnership for 21st Century Skills, attempts to re-engage learners and better reflect the constructivist tradition in learning: 'By posing open-ended questions and posing intriguing problems engage children's imaginations and help motivate them to explore, discover, create, and learn' (Trilling & Fadel, 2009: 94).

But these skills often seem quite broad and hard to integrate into modern learning, even with the use of activity learning and a greater emphasis upon constructivism, a solid understanding of what the curriculum was and what the required skills were for any given generation were critical (see Table 3.1).

Table 3.1   21st Century Skills

Learning and Innovation "The 4 C's"	Digital Literacy	Career and Life
Critical thinking & problem solving	Information literacy	Flexibility & adaptability
Creativity and innovation	Media Literacy	Initiative & seld-direction
Communication	ICT Literacy	Social & cross-cultural interaction
Collaboration		Productivity & Accountability
		Leadership & responsibility

Source: Reproduced work of Charles Fadel, under Creative Commons licensing

As an example of the perceived problems facing education in the United Kingdom, Michael Gove, the minister for Education, has recently announced the move towards the more generalized English baccalaureate with a return of the 'O' Level–style, end of two years, summative examination (UK Department for Education, 2012). This move rings in the changes of a more generalized curriculum and away from the more specialized general certificate of secondary education (GCSE), and is a response to the perception of the 'dumbing down' the educational qualifications, particularly in the science subjects (Kitchen, 1999). Arguably, this perception of the problem of 'dumbing down' began in 1988 in England, Wales and Northern Ireland with the move over from the two-level qualifications framework of the general certificate of education (GCE) and the certificate of secondary education (CSE) to the single-level GCSE for students between 14 and 16 years of age.

Here the twin tracks of qualification separated the more academic children (those with the GCE) from those who were assessed to be better suited for vocational training (those with the CSE). The reason for bringing these tracks together into one system was the barriers experienced by CSE students when it came to getting into university. Ironically, perhaps, the same reason is provided on the Department for Education's webpage explaining the government plans to scrap the GCSE:

> The number of non-academic qualifications taken up to age 16 had risen from about 15,000 in 2004 to about 575,000 in 2010, with a higher take-up of vocational qualifications by young people from deprived backgrounds. Many of these qualifications do not carry real weight for entry to higher education or for getting a job (UK Department for Education's, 2012).

The initial use of the English baccalaureate was to be as a performance measure, but the announcement by Gove in September 2012 has indicated that the English baccalaureate certificate will be adopted in 2017 (Coughlan, 2012). The move is being dubbed as a return to the 'O' GCE level however, it recognizes the failure of GCSEs to drive up academic standards and their failure to address the issues with the old two-tier system.

The knowledge economy requires higher skilled students coming into the workplace, and the recent need for more *adaptable* skills reflects changes in career patterns. Defining 21st century skills is one part of the problem, but the move towards a skills-based education system rather than a knowledge-based one creates additional problems for how to define and teach these skills. There are dangers if we get the balance wrong between producing rounded and socially responsible individuals and producing workers, but that can't mean that we shouldn't aim to do both things effectively. Where schools can't deliver training for every sector of employment, it seems clear that there is a need for additional lifelong learning for 'upskilling' young people coming out of education and going into the workplace *and* for the training needs of adults in their career development.

The scale of the challenge is not just seen in terms of the *levels* of unemployment amongst young people coming out of school. In the United Kingdom, we have just under one million unemployed, but this is set to reduce; the problem in the Eurozone is far greater, with unemployment amongst 18–25 year olds in Spain at 46.4% (European Commission Eurostat, 2012). This situation has, of course, been exacerbated by the global economic downturn. However, it is curious that in an age dominated by the emergence of entirely new sectors, technologies and skills—for example, the video game sector and social media sector–young people who have grown up with these things and who are much more familiar with them should end up so under-employed. Our society's focus on *extrinsic motivations* in the education system—employment and career prospects—does not appear to have delivered the one thing that was meant to be the societal priority: the knowledge and skills that provide the platform for employment and good career prospects.

To correct this problem, we need to look at how children can deal with the transitions in their lives more effectively and gain the knowledge and confidence they will need to navigate their more complicated careers and life paths. One of the tools we can use for this purpose is the computer generated learning environment because of the way in which effective and engaging learning experiences like games rely on transitions in their design and narrative structure. For example, in games, the process of passing through different levels which require increasingly more conversancy and understanding of the game played is well understood by players—and is a familiar part of game play. Like the play levels in a game, learning in general may also be considered as the passing of different 'liminal stages', through sets of structured, semi-structured or unstructured experiences—utilizing challenges, social interactions and play within the learner's environment. Crossing between our 'liminal stages' is a process of transition, and in learning it is characterized by periods of greater discourse, interaction and reflection. The concept is a key one to understanding the complex processes of initiation, participation and active involvement displayed by learners and learner groups as they develop and progress.

The use of CGEs relies upon scenario production and sometimes role play to allow learners to engage with the different set of practices represented in the learning environment. In the *Ardcalloch* case study discussed in Chapter 2, the students played the role of legal practitioners and undertook different tasks and activities to develop their skills and to succeed in becoming lawyers (Barton & Maharg, 2006). In Richard Gerver's Grange Primary School, also discussed in Chapter 2, the students play the roles of radio producers to develop their media production skills and to gain confidence acting as leaders (Gerver, 2010).

Both examples show how, by creating a notional learning space skills, roles and situations can be rehearsed and reflected upon to support learning lessons and to use imagination as a tool for smoothing the transitions of the child to the adult, the student to the worker and the novice to the expert. In *Ardcalloch* this takes the form of a fictional town in Scotland, and in Grangeton it takes the form of a created world within the Grange Primary School that the children have some control over. In both cases the emphasis is upon roles, from the role of the student to the more empowered guidance role of the *legal practitioner* or *media producer*. Once the students have successfully negotiated each set of challenges provided, they evolve their roles to become increasingly more empowered, learning new skills and maturing to meet the new and missions associated with each new role. Students can, in this way, use these learning environments and learning experiences to rehearse interactions and develop appropriate skills and responses. Crucially, these experiences provide an intuitive and natural pathway through the transition points of learning, that—with all the interpersonal interactions that mark and underpin development—feels far more akin to the real-life processes of human development than a regular and abstract exam paper does.

How the stages and roles are used in a CGE, then, is a prime design component not just for engaging learners and users of CGEs but as an organizing concept that may be used for *understanding* the processes of transition. Van Gennep's (1960) work breaks down the concept into 'preliminal', 'liminal' and 'post-liminal' phases to assist with understanding the processes of transition more analytically. These descriptors may be helpful for future studies of virtual worlds and may also inform the design of learning experiences and activities (Bardzell & Odom, 2008).

Aligning learning more closely with changing and evolving behaviours and activities makes sense not just because we now have tools that enable to us do this, but also because the resulting transitions through the stages of learning feel more intuitive. To put it another way, the gap between testing or examination in school and the application of skills and understanding in practice will be closed. However, if activities and social interactions are used to develop and test knowledge or skills, the quality—or constructive use—of the social interactions is pivotal.

The quality of social interactions the individual has within an environment can often depend upon the quality of the *orientation* of the individual in the environment. An assessment of orientation stations in, for example, *Second Life*, a pervasive virtual world, revealed particular common qualities, such as the use of four stages, guided trails, video and occasionally narrative to enhance engagement. The successful completion of the US TV show: *CSI's* virtual orientation area involved solving a mystery, and that resulted in gaining a badge to show that the participant had completed the orientation training (Wetsch, 2008). To become immersed in the activity the learner needs to feel engaged, and this can be achieved through designing engaging processes and activities, or through narrative flow, such as through quests for objects and information and through engaging interchanges or 'transactions' with other individuals (Barton & Maharg, 2006; Barton & McKellar, 2011).

In addition to creating directed activities for supporting the ease of engagement and induction into the virtual or online world, the way that the virtual world is represented in terms of its 'look and feel' supports the act of *crossing over* into the virtual world or space. This act of crossing—or entering the virtual world—requires a level of verisimilitude to facilitate the process. Moving into immersive worlds can become a process of initiation: entering the community, learning how individuals participate within the environment, the quality of social interactions and transactions taking place there and the duration of 'newbie' status. These are all aspects of the transition from 'newbie' to active member, not unlike Etienne Wenger's (1998) 'legitimate peripheral participation' in which the newcomer would take time to observe behaviour in advance of graduating to expert status. Virtual worlds, games and interactive environments have their own rules, regulations, etiquette and formalities. However, the anonymity of some of these environments means that the rules and regulations have to be enforced or mediated in some way—just as blog posts invariably need to be moderated. Just as in other learning environments, it is important that the tutor or guide has the ability to communicate freely with the learners to ensure that they understand the rules and regulations and that they are safe from invasive or disruptive outside interferences such as non-initiated learners. The extension of identity and the orientation of learners in these non-standard teaching spaces needs to be considered carefully.

While the research in the area of extended identities in computer generated environments is still in its infancy, preliminary research findings indicate that individuals *do* identify with their avatars closely, and that this identification can support better engagement and involvement in activities in the virtual world (Bessiere, Seay & Kiesler, 2007; Zagalo, Morgado & Boa-Ventura, 2012).

Referring back to Jean Piaget (2007) briefly, this may be explained in terms of developmental phases when identification may be used as part of the process of 'assimilation' and 'accommodation' with the external environment. When we are playing and learning, perhaps it is easier to distance ourselves from the environment; the distance allows for deeper reflection or meta-reflection upon the activities taking place. For example, in the case of citizenship education, Yam San Chee and colleagues argue,

> Effective education for becoming citizens does not consist merely of being told what one ought to do and to be. Neither does it primarily revolve around learning about the birth of a nation and its consequent development. Rather, effective citizenship education needs to focus on students' being and becoming: on how they understand themselves as persons—their identity and being—and on their developmental trajectories of becoming, projected into the future. (2011: 129)

The capability to imagine one's identity and sense of self in a different space or place supports more engagement and motivation, which in turn supports the learning process in terms of remembering what is learnt and being able to imagine how learning could be applied into real-life settings (Chee et al., 2011). Interestingly, one study found that *how gamers relate to their identity with their avatar affects how they self-report what learning gains they receive from the game* (Iacovides et al., 2012). In this way, the traversal from one space or stage to another, and how we identify with our avatar in the virtual world, affects how we perceive the learning experience. The traversal between real and virtual spaces, and between identities, seems to re-affirm a process of human development by reflecting it.

Another traversal relates closely to context—in particular, the context in which learning is taking place. Whether it is in a formal place such as a school, college, university or workplace, or whether it is in an informal place—for example, at home or in transit between work and home—learning may be occurring via portable devices such as laptops, tablets or portable game machines. With the advent of wireless mobile devices and the greater pervasiveness of higher-bandwidth wireless available for working via the Internet, the opportunities for learning in formal and informal contexts have opened up.

The formal setting and location of traditional institutional places of learning represents a Victorian and utilitarian set of architectural and epistemological considerations regarding where spaces organize functions—for example, at school for learning versus at home for recreation, sleeping and eating. However, the erosion of the logic of spatially determined activities in our own time has undercut the logic or necessity for designated functionally defined spaces. To illustrate, think online research in the home or in the park rather than in the library, or video conferencing from a desk at home rather than congregating in a meeting room. In these new designs, spaces are also freed from singular designated functions—to be more flexible, multipurpose and, in the case of computer generated spaces, to be interactive.

The other notable aspect of the blurring between formal and informal contexts for learning might be the use of boundary objects, or *sacra* in Van Gennep's terms. These are *objects* used to help us shift between different spaces and environments. In particular in the modern context, the use of mobile devices, sensor technologies in the environment and user tracking (e.g., global positioning system software) are opening up the possibility for connecting between our spaces of work, play and learning. In addition to providing bridges between virtual and real spaces (e.g., mixed reality) or real and online spaces, these objects can help learners to effectively traverse between different learning experiences and activities in the physical world and the virtual world. In the same way, they might also be used effectively to open up new possibilities that could be explored and exploited for educational and other purposes (Milolidakis, Kimble & Grenier, 2011).

Importantly, the concept of traversing between 'liminal stages' contextualizes an understanding of learning as part of a wider process of individual human development and in terms of the processes of transition that can be used to test the application of 21st century skills. The key design principles here thus relate to processes, not spaces—to the learning experience rather than its location.

The notion of correcting our education systems and adapting them to new learning is a daunting prospect, but we need to ensure that our children *are* able to adjust to the wider realities of more complex societies, new technologies and practices and new commercial and industrial sectors.

We need to reflect upon what children *really* need to support their effective development and how we can prepare them for the new global economy's competitiveness and cross-cultural meshing. If we really want to capitalize on a societal management of education, we need to deploy the tools we have much more effectively, and this requires an understanding of the developmental stages and phases of learning, the most effective methods of learning, new forms of learning and the wider socio-economic change in our societies.

There is plenty of scope for new scientific research to broaden our understanding of how CGEs and CGLEs may be best deployed. But if we consider the unit of learning as the experience and if we want to use learning to map *how we learn* to *how we behave*, then we need to understand how narrative, immersion and fidelity can help play a role in re-introducing 'play' into learning as a practice that facilities the rehearsal of skills, complex interactions and experiences that are unfamiliar or are outside of our own lived experiences.

THE LEARNING EXPERIENCE

To understand the quite abstract association between our own behaviour and wider social changes requires linking *how we learn* with *how we behave*. To achieve this we need to evolve new and existing tools for supporting advanced educational design. CGEs allow us to close that gap between learning and behaving or interacting, or learning and doing. Therefore, if we take new learning in the future to mean *designing learning methods and experiences*, then we find the single unit of learning is not necessarily at the level of the book or the piece of information. Rather, the central focus for design rests upon the roles played, the missions and the modes of social interaction created. To understand this approach to learning design, we need to give some consideration to *immersion, flow* and *narrative*.

Immersion is a difficult concept to define, but most closely relates to the idea of 'deep mental involvement' (*Oxford Dictionary of English*, s.v. "immersion"). Immersion can happen in CGEs taking the form of a preoccupation or absorption with an activity or set of activities. For example, games can be very immersive by their nature, holding a person's complete attention and engaging him or her to the point of exclusion of all else. Counter-intuitively, perhaps, this aspect of game play has been criticized widely in *entertainment* game play contexts, and the addictive nature of game play has been the subject of ongoing psychological and neuro-imaging studies and debate (Griffiths, 1999; Kuss & Griffiths, 2012; Van Rooij, Schoenmakers & van den Eijnden, 2012). This is, of course, less the case with educational games, where the design of activities is rarely as absorbing as in entertainment games, and obviously games for non-leisure purposes rarely if ever involve violent or aggressive behaviour.

Yet while 'serious' games can be less absorbing than leisure-based games, the potential for them to become compulsive or addictive is an area worthy of further investigation, as negative aspects such as 'withdrawal, conflict and relapse' have been noted in studies with entertainment videogames (Kuss & Griffiths, 2012: 366). Although getting the balance between involvement of the learner and not being too addictive may seem to be contradictory impulses from a games design perspective, in educational design it is the 'holy grail' to provide educational content and material that can be so absorbing that it is addictive to play. Yet it seems that with the current scale and budget available for designing widely used educational games this sort of achievement has still not been realized.

Designing for achieving greater absorption in learning experiences is thus complicated in practice, especially since immersion is such a difficult concept to frame. However, some early studies have suggested that *flow* is an important component of how individuals become engaged in games and other immersive formats (Csikszentmihalyi, 1992).

In his foundational work on the notion of *flow*, Mihaly Csikszentmihalyi has argued for the importance of creating 'a self-reinforcing loop' to maintain learner interest. He explores how the central components for producing pleasurable states often involve tasks that are pitched at *the correct level of difficulty and challenge for the learner*. These components also include design of tasks that the learner can complete and well-defined goals and immediate feedback in addition to a high level of learner control. Csikszentmihalyi has also argued for the importance of creating challenge, although this must be aligned with the skills of the learner and be pitched at the correct level of difficulty. If these elements are synonymous with absorption, they also perfectly mirror the design of games and simulations, explaining the engagement of games formats especially when compared with other media. However, the role of interactivity is also crucial. In games, for example, learners are placed in a position of autonomy, and although they may 'represent real-world systems . . . the *cost* of error for participants is low, protecting them from the more severe consequences of mistakes' (Garris, Ahlers & Driskell, 2002: 442; emphasis added).

Flows become seamless and continuous experiences, often with a basis in reality or lived experience. These experiences may be 'choreographed' or orchestrated by tutors, learning designers or others in different contexts (Barton & Maharg, 2006; Inal & Bagiltay, 2007).

Steve Benford and colleagues (1998) define play within the context of this relationship between physical and virtual space. They describe a spatial typology in terms of how physical and virtual spaces are mapped—or bounded—together according to transportation (immersion), spatiality (proximity) and artificiality (verisimilitude). They bring five categories of CGEs together: media spaces, spatial video-conferencing, collaborative virtual environments, telepresence systems and collaborative augmented environments. The emphasis upon spatiality and how physical and virtual spaces map together can be regarded as a substantial change in how play is categorized. This replicates the internal 'cartography of learning', in the sense that the child learns through active play within spaces (some bounded and others imaginary), but all are brought together to create a coherent mapping of space and the relationships that unfold within it. Immersion, proximity and verisimilitude are interesting subsets of the representational dimension of the 'four dimensional framework', and each merit some individual consideration. (See Box 3.1: The Four Dimensional Framework.)

Box 3.1   The Four Dimensional Framework

Alongside frameworks and approaches being developed to support the more effective design and study of games, several frameworks for selecting and using games are emerging from early research. These frameworks are often aimed at practitioners for supporting more effective use of games and to help them to avoid the pitfalls of game-based learning (Barab et al., 2005), although these often focus upon frameworks for game design. One recent example of a framework for practitioners is provided by this author and Martin Oliver (2006); we developed a four-dimensional framework (4DF) for selecting and using games in formal learning contexts. However, recent work indicates that the framework is also supporting the design and development process of games (de Freitas & Jarvis, 2007) and has been extended in other frameworks (Staaldruinen & de Freitas, 2011).

Building upon the centrality of learning as play and exploration, the 4DF sets out to inform the selection of games that may be used effectively by practitioners and picks out four generic principles—context, mode of representation, pedagogic approach used and the specifics about the learner—as in need of consideration in order to support effective learning outcomes. The 4DF builds upon earlier work (Mayes & de Freitas, 2004, 2007), advocating a pedagogic approach that utilizes associative, cognitive and situative approaches to learning through an alignment of learning outcomes with learning activities and modes of assessment (see Figure 3.1).

Continued

Box 3.1 *Continued*

Four Dimensional Framework

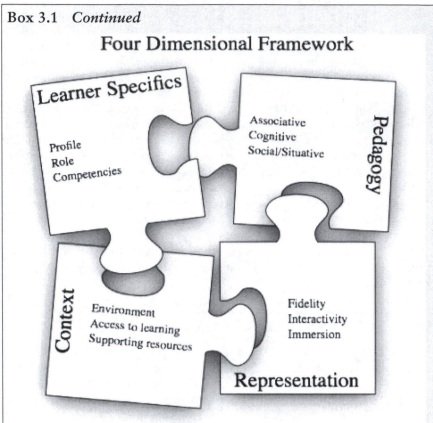

Figure 3.1   The four dimensional framework. Image courtesy of the author.

In the figure, four dimensions are represented: *context, learner, pedagogy* and *representation*. These are dimensions or factors that need to be taken into consideration when selecting and using games for learning.

The first dimension of the framework is the *context* dimension. As we know, the context of the game is central to the effectiveness of how the game is utilized. Contextual factors include where a game is used, what technical support is provided and what the general environment is for game play: is the environment conducive for play or not (e.g. classroom, home, outside)? The context will therefore have a direct bearing upon which game is selected. Socio-political contexts and institutional contexts may also play an informing role in selection and use of games, as does the context of discipline.

The second dimension of the framework relates to the *learner's* specification. The learner or learner group is also central to which game is selected and used. Aspects such as age, stage of study, demographics, conversancy with information and communications technologies (ICTs) and games technologies and past learning experiences will all have a bearing upon the selection of games used, indicating the efficacy of learning—for example, the level of engagement and motivation, learner control and impact upon the system as a whole. Also, groups familiar with using ICTs widely in their social lives may get more out of using integrated social software and communications to support game-based learning, providing greater opportunities for group interactions and meta-reflection in different contexts to support learning outcomes and activities.

The third dimension—*pedagogy*—aims to map the former two dimensions onto the fourth dimension, and provides the methods and theory for forming and shaping the learning experiences and bringing them into line with practical application. One of the main challenges of teaching in the context of virtual world applications is to ensure that learners and their specifics and the context of learning map correctly against the designed activities in the virtual world. If this is not the case, then there may be a mismatch that could lead to negative learning transfer that may impede further learning and may put learners off immersive worlds altogether. The main change in the role of pedagogy with virtual worlds, then, lies in the areas as highlighted—that is, the additional scope for learning as play, as exploration and as socially interactive interaction.

In earlier work (Mayes & de Freitas, 2004, 2007), it was found that that learning processes are supported by associative (instructivist and often task-centred), cognitive (constructivist) and situative (learning in communities of practice) modes; these three perspectives come into play rapidly at different points as learning progresses. Notably, learning with a game is rarely if ever a learning experience in itself; more often it is embedded into a set of activities and processes according to the pedagogic approach adopted—often experiential or problem-based (Boud & Feletti, 1991; Kolb, 1984;). Therefore, the role of debriefing is central to the use of simulations and it is also important for game-based learning; whether debriefing is through post-exercise discussion, reflection with peers or reflection with the tutor, this aspect of learning in immersive worlds is central (Crookall, 1995; Peters & Vissers, 2004).

The fourth dimension of the framework represents the interface between the learner and the game or virtual world; it is the *representational* dimension. The representation of the game—what I have described elsewhere as the *diegesis*—is the internal reality or world of the CGE. This dimension includes the fidelity of the environment, the level of immersion and the level of interactivity—in fact, everything to do with the creation of the world and how the learner interfaces within it.

The four dimensional framework offers a starting point for tutors considering using games in their practice, mapping well onto activity theory as well as other pedagogic theories (de Freitas & Oliver, 2006). The framework may be used to frame the selection and use of games in practice, as well as for supporting more critical approaches to considering game-based learning.

If immersion can be equated with Benford's idea of 'transportation', then flow is clearly a reinforcing aspect of this. The game acts as a method for transporting the user to another time, place or space, and this can reinforce learning, particularly when learning is considered as play, as social interactions and exploration in particular environments (e.g. physical, virtual or traversing between the two). Benford then considers spatiality as proximity or nearness. Games—and, in particular, virtual world applications—create quite artificial spaces through which users can navigate using keyboard keys or handheld console devices. The spaces can be realistic or, more usually, fantasy spaces which give an impression of the three-dimensional and which can be traversed as an avatar.

The avatar, as has been noted, is a kind of an extension of an individual identity within the virtual space and allows the user to experience the space vicariously but, importantly, with an element of user control. While many avatars are not realistic portrayals of ourselves, some can look quite similar to us—the choices of avatar are usually configured to generic human facial and body types. Crucially, the element of user control—of the avatar—has been found to be an essential aspect of learning, as when we are not in control over our learning we can feel helpless and disengaged (Francis, 2006a, 2006b; Greene, Bolick & Robertson, 2010; Kay, 2001). Having control over the avatar allows us to freely associate with the representation, and this engages us more fully in the space of the world. The element of freedom of movement and control over our avatar allows for a greater use of exploration and, particularly, *learning as exploration* (Choi & Baek, 2011).

Creating the visual expression of the virtual and immersive space for learning allows considerable scope for designing—or *choreographing* learning experiences. How realistic a scene or setting might be is clearly dependent upon the familiarity of that environment to its users, the level of fidelity or verisimilitude of the environment and the level of immersion within the construction of the learning activities presented. While learner control and the context of learning are central to the effectiveness of the setting for supporting learning, the design of the space, its familiarity and level of fidelity, will play a role in supporting the learning experience as a whole. Furthermore, the realism and accuracy of social interactions within the represented space are also critical for the flow of experience; anything that jars the experience may impede effective learning or, worse, create negative learning transfer.

Designing learning in virtual spaces therefore includes a need to consider three levels of 'artificiality':

- *Setting.* The spatial requirements that facilitate learning (e.g., fidelity, verisimilitude). In cinematic terms, this is the *mise-en-scène.* As in cinema, everything about this is artificial; it is a created environment. Whether it represents a real-life setting or not—*the virtual space is a created and artificial space.* The setting becomes an actor or component in the learning experience that is created.

- *Learning activities*. The learning activities that are developed may be supporting e-mentoring, reflection, learning through play, explorations or social interactions. Therefore, the activities need to be considered in relation to established learning and instructional design theories and practices, but may be less outcomes-based, more open-ended and collaborative. For example, undertaking challenges, missions or quests (e.g., the Quest to Learn school), involving changing roles (e.g., the Grangeton model or *Ardcalloch* game) or involving crossing boundaries between physical and virtual spaces (e.g., the use of *Second Life* for teaching).
- *Social interactions*. The social interactions that are facilitated within the virtual spaces need to be adequately structured and to conform to learning models and approaches, but these can be quite flexible, open-ended and creative, such as role playing characters from history (e.g., *Revolution*) or involving team activities or competitions in missions and quests (e.g., *OpenSim*).

Whether we define it in Benford's terms as part of the transportation, spatiality and artificiality, or as part of Csikszentmihalyi's *flow*, *immersion*—though hard to define—is clearly an important design component in learning. Just as in the qualities of a good book or an engrossing film, the trick of good learning design is to engage learners in an experience that allows them to become completely immersed.

While my clearest remembrances from school are certainly the field trips and hands on (experiential) science lessons that brought to life the subjects and concepts that we discussed and read about, regrettably, these were rarer experiences when I was a child. Today, CGEs open up numerous opportunities for young learners to mock up many different environments that can be realistic and engaging. Environments that previously we could not bring to life in any way other than through imagination are now enlivened by visualization and modelling in CGEs. The tool kits are available and usable for all of us, but we need imagination to design the learning experiences and make them lifelike.

At the moment we have new tools but we are still exploring how they can be used in a systematic way. What is critical here is to remember that new tools can add to our teaching and learning traditions, but we should not think that they must necessarily replace them. *New learning*, as I have labelled these new approaches, involves a *blend* of physical and virtual experiences—and of traditional and new approaches.

LEARNING THROUGH INTERACTIVITY

Additionally, interactivity and learner control are areas of design that can aid how embedded the learning experience is, how effective it is in conveying information and processes and how engaging the game or application may be in practice. Interactivity is, in many cases, about sense of control over the avatar and the learner's control over the environment. How much control the learner has in terms of exploring the environment, how much feedback from the system the learner is getting, and how much input the learner can make upon the environment are elements that require careful design and consideration. Interactivity often needs to go beyond a simple multiple-choice selection from limited choices to ensure that the learner will have an immersive and stimulating or *varied* experience.

For interactivity to be effective in a CGE, a close relationship between the learner and the simulated environment needs to be supported. But learning outcomes, if they are to be reinforced, need to be reflected upon outside the computer generated world as well, which is why blended learning solutions seem to be the most effective in practice. Constant and immediate feedback within the learning experience, needs to be incorporated either in the virtual world or in face-to-face sessions; ideally, in both (Dunwell, Christmas & de Freitas, 2011).

Interactivity through direct engagement in terms of creating and sharing content is in its infancy, although the wider games development community has been modifying existing games software for years (e.g., the *Adventure Author* or *Revolution* modifications from *Neverwinter Nights*). The practice of modifying software ('modding')—previously the preserve of computer scientists and programmers—has become increasingly open to those with lower programming skills, in particular with the emergence of software development kits which are easier to use than programming languages and are often available for free over the Internet (e.g., the Unreal engine). The practice of modding games presents a potential scope for self-authoring the production of personalized immersive and interactive learning spaces to support specific learner communities. However, it also raises copyright questions around any systematic reuse of game content and assets (Protopsaltis et al., 2010).

Although a relatively recent phenomenon, 'modding' is part of a wider movement in which individuals take control over the tools and development of content. It is also part of a wider move towards *collective intelligence* (Turner & Wolpert, 2004), *crowd sourcing* (Good & Su, 2011) and *content co-creation* (Gibson, 2012) that could have quite an impact upon education and new learning—not just in terms of delivery of content but, critically, on how educational content is produced and deployed (Jung, Song & Cho, 2012). In particular, the *co-creation of content* is becoming a significant part of how individuals reach and communicate with wider societies and communities online—for example, through virtual worlds, games, social software tools and e-publishing. In the learning context, this is part of the wider move towards open access and open educational resources.

As part of this wider trend, learner-authored content may provide for a completely novel approach to learning through exploration, investing the learner with a sense of empowerment that may also work particularly well with underserved learners (de Freitas, Savill-Smith & Attewell, 2006). Other authoring tools are becoming available to support experiential or exploratory styles of learning (Mehm et al., 2012); one early example of this trend was *Game Maker*—a drag-and-drop tool created by Mark Overmars at Utrecht University—that has since been used as a teaching tool for both game design and elementary programming principles (Ford, 2009). Recent research has focused upon how game authoring can support narrative development (Robertson & Good, 2005) and promote literacy and creativity (Robertson & Howells, 2008; Howells & Robertson, 2012). Computer animations encourage critical thinking and may also be used as assessment tools. These tools can also be used to facilitate role plays, discussion and problem solving and include programming languages such as *Scratch*, game engines such as *Blender* and *Unity 3D* and authoring platforms such as *Thinking Worlds*.

Ultimately, interactivity operates on a sliding scale between no interactivity with learning content at one side of the scale, to authoring one's own content and tools at the other. If we consider the subject areas of our current curricula it seems logical to suggest that different levels of interactivity will align with particular kinds of learning (e.g., higher order cognition) and different capabilities. At the start, learners are novices; therefore, the need for *guidance* more than control of interactions will be prioritized. As they progress to expert status, far less or no guidance may be necessary and they can begin to play an e-mentoring role for others in the group or community. Changing roles requires different interactions and degrees of control over interaction with others.

LEVELS OF FIDELITY

One of the main debates in the field of simulation research, a debate that moved into the field of games for learning, centres upon the *level of fidelity* required in training simulations. One component that has been well researched and that can assist game design is the understanding of how high the levels of fidelity need to be for particular learning experiences. Taken from film studies, how the immersive training world is represented has, of course, an impact upon the pedagogic strategies used and the effectiveness of the learning activities undertaken. In the past, for example, with the use of overhead projectors, how realistically the data was presented to the learner was less of a consideration than *what* was presented. However, with the use of video and film footage, and in particular with the use of immersive learning tools, *how the information and activities are presented* can be as important as *what is presented*. This also goes back to our earlier discussion about physical and virtual spaces and how the two interact, promoting greater opportunities for the learner to interact with other 'actors' or participants in the activities.

Broadly, *fidelity* refers to the verisimilitude of the environment and to verisimilitude of the activities and experience designed in the environment. The issue of fidelity of the environment, according to the learning outcome or practice, is in some ways a confusing one with respect to serious games and virtual worlds. This is because of a mismatch between the levels of realism and verisimilitude that the average person expects and the level of verisimilitude required to convey the learning outcome. Increasingly, commercial games (e.g., *Call of Duty*, *Far Cry III*) are raising the standard of verisimilitude that can be produced in an entertainment game, but the 'uncanny valley' principle seems to predict a trailing-off point where negative transfer can be created because of over-realism or fidelity that is too high (Mori, 1970; Mashahiro Mori's work was with robots but a similar problem has been noted in film animations and with virtual characters; see Schneider, Wang & Yang, 2007). Essentially, if a simulation is too photo-realistic, the small flaws can become the focus of attention and start to jar. The apparent lack of any need to suspend belief means that inconsistencies—with real-world physics or optics—when they are encountered can destroy the key sense of the immersion into and engagement with the simulation.

Recently, in one emergency response training game for example, where 3D verisimilitude is less important than audio fidelity, there has been an attempt to move away from raising fidelity, and this development has been led to 'zero fidelity games' (Toups et al., 2011). However, this bucks the prevailing trend. The move towards higher-fidelity games in commercial titles is being followed to an extent in educational games and simulations, with increasingly high levels of verisimilitude to real-life situations (Issenberg et al., 2005). In our multiplayer online game evaluation of *Code of Everand*, for example, we were surprised at the high numbers of underage game players who were playing *Call of Duty* (Dunwell et al., 2012), but besides our concerns, such titles drive up expectations about the quality and fidelity of educational games. (See Case Study 4: The *Code of Everand* Game.)

Box 3.2   The *Code of Everand* Game

The *Code of Everand* game was commissioned as part of the UK Department for Transport's Think! campaign to reduce numbers of children killed or seriously injured on the road (Dunwell et al., 2012). Studies have found that information about safe road crossing is available but the behaviour towards road crossing changes as children get older due to higher risk taking and peer influence. Because of these factors best practices are not always maintained, leading to death and injuries on the road.

The use of a multiplayer online game was selected for a number of reasons, including to facilitate children using their existing knowledge of road crossing, making safe road crossing 'top of mind', making safe road crossing more interesting and emphasizing participatory media rather than 'messaging', as in television campaigns. A massively multiplayer online role play game (MMORPG) was chosen because the commissioners of the game wanted children to be engaged for longer durations of time than occur in a typical television advertisement. MMORPGs like *World of Warcraft*, developed by Blizzard Entertainment, attract around ten million subscribers (as of October 2012) and bring together a persistent online world for supporting social groups with quests and activities. *Code of Everand* provided a fantasy land crisscrossed by magical spirit channels with strange monsters. Players took on the roles of pathfinders who would find safe crossing points in the virtual world in order to safely traverse the channels (see Figures 3.2 and 3.3.)

The game was developed by Area/Code (now Zynga) in New York City and was aimed at 9- to 13–year-olds. Sixty-two thousand children in the United Kingdom in the 9–15 age range played the game for an average of 31 minutes. Half of the children played the game in a single session. The game was regarded as a unique way of engaging the target audience of 9–13 years with a focus on boys because in 2006, 65% of all 9- to 11-year-olds killed or seriously injured were boys.

The game allows the children to rehearse best practices with road crossing—for example, looking left and right before crossing—as well as teaching skills around more complicated route planning and selection of safest crossing points. Through *analogical learning transfer* the children can improve their skills and keep road crossing 'top of mind'.

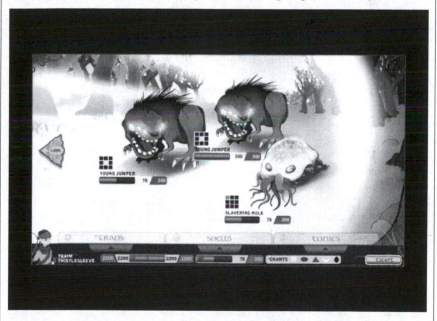

Figure 3.2 Monsters in *Code of Everand*. Reproduced with the kind permission of Area/Code Entertainment; artist: Doug Ra.

Continued

Box 3.2: Continued

Figure 3.3   Spirit channels in *Code of Everand*. Reproduced with the kind permission of Area/Code Entertainment; artist: Doug Ra.

Educational games have been shown in a number of studies to change behaviour. In *Squire's Quest!*, for example, studies showed behavioural change with respect to childhood obesity, where an incentive to rehearsing skills was used rather than informational approaches (Baranowski et al., 2003; Cullen et al., 2005). Similarly, the study on the game *Re:Mission*, found behavioural change with children taking chemotherapy; the game supported behavioural change with better medication adherence which would provide long-term benefits and save lives (Kato et al., 2008). Awareness-raising of issues such as relationships and sex education (RSE) are addressed in the *Prepare* game commissioned by the Health Innovation and Education Cluster for West Midlands (South). A cluster-randomized controlled trial undertaken in local schools ($n = 504$) found positive results in favour of the game-based approach when compared to existing methods based on surveys of self-reported measures of psycho-social preparedness for avoiding coercion or coercive behaviour.

The methods used in the *Code of Everand* evaluation combined a mixed-method approach including a national survey ($n = 1,108$), player survey ($n = 1,038$), qualitative focus sessions with players and game engine data analysis. The full results are in the report (Dunwell et al., 2012). The main findings confirmed that serious games are engaging and well received by children; according to their self-reporting only 12% found the game boring.

One of the most striking findings from the study showed that *Call of Duty* was the most popular game played by the 9- to 15-year-olds; 53% of boys and 12% of girls were playing this game, which is rated PEGI-18, indicating that children are playing adult games more generally than age-specific games such as *Club Penguin*. *Code of Everand* was primarily played at home, with 80% of logins from there. Over the year of the study there were 106,547 players logging in to the game and 541,310 unique visits to the game's website. Of the 99,683 unique players, 88.13% were from the United Kingdom.

The national survey indicated that children play a wide variety of games. While a majority of children play action and adventure games (73% and 75%, respectively), other game types such as puzzles (66%), role playing games (56%) and simulation games (56%) were also widely played. So while a lower-fidelity game such as *Code of Everand* has the potential to engage for a median of 31 minutes, sustaining play for longer periods is demanding for a title which is not in the gaming 'mainstream' of high-fidelity console games. Of the UK players, users fell into three groups: low play time (0–30 minutes; $n = 47,895$; 48.4%), moderate play time (30–60 minutes; $n = 20,646$; 20.9%) and high play time (60 minutes or more; $n = 30,391$; 30.7%).

According to the player survey findings, 'Finishing quests was one of the most strongly agreed with positive activities within the game, emphasizing the importance the quest structure might play in guiding and directing players towards goals. More than 60% of players agreed that they liked the graphics, story and multiplayer aspects of the game.' (Dunwell et al., 2012: 93).

Overall the game was successful: of the 16% of those who heard about the game 3% went on to play it. However, as the national survey indicated, the expectations of children for games like the $200 million game *Call of Duty* implies that higher levels of fidelity, interactivity and in-game communications are required if a serious game is to engage players for longer time periods: 'To *reach* a large audience may not require a level of investment equal to *Call of Duty* (a $200m game), but to *sustain* engagement, particularly given the attention span of children, appears a far more demanding task' (Dunwell et al., 2012: 93).

Box 3.3 *The PR:EPARe Game*

PR:EPARe (Positive Relationships: Eliminating Coercion and Pressure in Adolescent Relationships) is an educational game developed by a cross-disciplinary team of UK researchers from Coventry University's Studies in Adolescent Sexual Health research group and applied researchers

Continued

Box 3.3   *Continued*

and developers from the university's Serious Games Institute. The game was used to promote a blended learning solution for teaching about RSE amongst school students between the ages of 13 and 14, the most appropriate age for a game intervention in this area (Brown, Bayley & Newby, 2012).

Based on a game show format, the game involves two levels. First there is group participation (as a class) on a quick-fire question and answer level; here several scenarios around coercive behaviour are presented by the game show hosts (see Figure 3.4). The second level of the game involves role playing of the students, who take on a first-person role within the game playing through a scenario as either the coercer or the coerced person (see Figure 3.5). During play, the teacher can pause the game to discuss particular issues or highlight particular points. Teacher and students can also add the editable text boxes to promote the best verbal responses to coercive situations.

The study involved undertaking a cluster-randomized controlled trial with year 9 students ($n = 504$) in three secondary schools in Coventry and Warwickshire. Classes were randomized into a control group (without game play) and a game play group (full results can be found in Arnab et al., forthcoming). The students completed baseline measures of the change objectives, which were reassessed in a later follow up analyses of variants. ANOVA was undertaken to identify which change objectives were affected

Figure 3.4   The *PR:EPARe* game takes the format of a game show. Reproduced with the kind permission of the Serious Games Institute, Coventry University.

Figure 3.5 A scenario in the *PR:EPARe* game. Reproduced with the kind permission of the Serious Games Institute, Coventry University.

by the game play group (Brown et al., 2012). The findings recognized that the game brought psychological preparedness for 9 out of the 16 measures.

The teachers leading the classes were given a facilitator's handbook and game. The five teachers all organized the classes slightly differently. They noted the engagement of the students, and researchers noted how the students grasped the complexity of the sexual coercion scenarios. In one scenario, for example, a boy texts a girl and asks her what colour underwear she is wearing; then the quizmaster asks, Is this coercion? The answer is 'maybe'—this created quite a lot of debate and mixed responses to the question in the classes. Notably, the students displayed a real understanding of the different perspectives of the characters in the game. Overall the children really enjoyed the game play.

While the results of the full study will aim to tease out the indicators of behavioural change, clearly awareness raising was notable and engagement in the difficult-to-teach subject area RSE, where students are often embarrassed, shows real potential for using this mechanism as a blended learning tool in classrooms. The game type and style could work very well for other types of learning such as ethics, religious education or citizenship, where higher cognitive learning and more grey areas and complexity are in evidence.

The confusion of teachers over which games to select for which specific learning skills, has led to game design approaches that focus upon particular skills and tasks and that can be easily deployed into formal learning contexts (de Freitas & Oliver, 2006). To serve these markets, the emergence of mobile games, mini-games and Flash games has evolved. This approach borrows from the early simulation trainers and in particular from associative learning approaches, with an emphasis upon simple skills, repetition of tasks and incremental difficulty. These kinds of games are often task-centred in nature and short in duration, and are sometimes referred to as drill-and-practice games as they rely upon repetition and associative approaches to training (Gagné, 1970), and often the activities will become increasingly difficult. There are many examples of this approach to game-based learning; for example, from math skills in *Max Trax*, key skills in *Key Skills Trainer* and basic skills in the British Broadcasting Corporation's *Skillswise* and *Webwise* to more complex surgical skills used in trainers and simulations such as *MIST-VR* and *GI-Mentor* (Graafland, Schraagen & Schijven, 2012; Kolga et al., 2008). More recently educational mobile games apps are gaining popularity, particularly for their ease of access; games such as *Immune Attack* and *Math Blaster* can be used to brush up on skills as and when convenient and thus add an informal element to formal learning.

These smaller games and web resources are most effective at targeting specific skills, in contrast to 'microworlds' where more open-ended experimentation works well. These games are more limited in scope, but may be easier to test and use in practice because they are more targeted and require fewer ICT skills on the part of the tutor and learner. These kinds of games are often developed in Flash and can often be accessed directly over the web. Use is generally with Flash Media Player, which can be downloaded relatively easily. Ease of access and use are making these games relatively popular, but they cannot be modified (as animations) and are limited in application.

The use of mobile technology and pervasive gaming is also relatively recent (Bjork et al., 2002; Kukulska-Hulme & Traxler, 2005). Some academic pilot projects have tried to evaluate these games. One study (Jegers & Wiberg, 2006) of a leisure game in Sweden, *Supafly*, that uses a soap opera format explored three aspects of pervasive gaming: mobile place–independent game play, integration between the physical and the virtual worlds and social interaction between players. Interestingly, the study found that the game was not used on the move but either at home or work, the link between the virtual and physical was not clear to the player and players also stayed within established social groups rather than making new friendships. Several other game-based learning applications using mobile devices are being piloted. In addition to *Savannah* (Facer et al., 2004), which used mobile devices to map virtual spaces onto real spaces, other mobile games such as *Urban Tapestries* and *MobileGame* aim to map physical spaces onto the virtual.

The *Urban Tapestries* project allows users to author their own virtual annotations of physical locations through use of personal data assistants and mobile phones; the project allows collective memory of spaces to develop organically over time (Lane, 2003). *MobileGame* developed as part of the European Union–funded MOBIlearn project allows participants to 'experience immersion in a mixed reality environment' (Schwabe & Goth, 2005: 192). The game is used for orientation days at a university, and involves small teams of two to four people. The 'rally' is structured as a competitive and cooperative game in which each team tries to catch another. The approach centres upon the strength of gaming as a collaborative and team-building activity or set of activities, although it is not strictly a learning game *per se*.

Another type of game genre that has varying components of crossing between virtual and physical spaces is the 'mixed reality' or 'alternate reality' game. These include *I Love Bees*, developed in 2004 as a trailer for *Halo 2* and reaching 250,000 players (McGonigal, 2011). The main strength of 'mixed reality games' is that they allow for traversing between virtual, physical and online spaces (Petridis et al., 2011). For educational purposes this genre of games has the added benefit of being relatively low in cost. But there have not been many examples of this genre applied successfully for strictly educational purposes as yet.

Much of the simulations literature highlights the importance of *feedback*, and, in particular, 'after action reviews' or debriefing (Crookall, 1995). In education we tend to talk about summative and formative feedback, but the value of immediate feedback can be significant for corrective behaviour and deeper engagement within a subject area. This can allow learners to alter their performance more quickly, as they can more easily adapt to mistakes made and identify corrective behaviour; importantly in critical learning environments, this can lead to accelerated learning times (Delanghe, 2001), and it has been observed that the same consideration holds true for children's education (Vasilyeva, 2007).

Games with less visual realism can be very effective for cognitive assistance, a factor today with aging populations and the need to extend the quality of our lives. Marketed as a cognitive assistive tool, the commercial game *Brain Trainer* is based upon the cognitive research of Michael Merzenich, a neuroscientist and co-founder of Posit Science in San Francisco; it is being used with octogenarians to reverse cognitive aging. Another similar game is *Dr Kawashima's Brain Training: How Old Is Your Brain?*, which combines arithmetic puzzles such as Sudoku as well as other quizzes completed at high speed. Higher-order cognitive development is explored in the *Selene* game (Carter, Wilbanks & Reese, 2009). Puzzles are a particularly popular genre amongst female game players according to one recent study (de Freitas & Jarvis, 2009).

Fidelity can thus contribute to the varying levels of engagement and motivation in the game or environment, but can also be used to immerse the learner in activities and missions framed by narrative story lines and characters, providing a sense of control on the part of the game player. Crucially, the use of relatively low-fidelity graphics can also have powerful learning potential—for example, supporting cognitive assistance and higher cognitive learning through elements of immediate feedback. Fidelity here is to task not physics or visuals. Whether the imagery is animated and 2D or visually realistic and 3D in format, the fidelity of the tasks and exercises is paramount to the successful outcomes of the learning experience. Through feedback mechanisms built into the environment, learners know what mistakes they have made and where they went wrong and this allows them to reflect upon what has been learnt. Together the elements of game, experience and good multimedia design combine to make up an engaging learning experience that can motivate students through immersion and interactivity.

4 Learning as Exploration and Experience

This chapter considers *the theories of learning* that relate to and can inform *the methods of learning* that are currently most frequently deployed or co-ordinated in computer generated learning environments.

New learning—by which I mean new learning approaches, methods and technologies—involves the use of new tools, and as I have highlighted in the previous chapters, it involves social elements, exploration and a sense of play. However, it also requires and depends on the application of different learning methods and different teaching methods, so we need to explore the pedagogic strategies that best support the new approaches. The term *pedagogy* is of Greek origin and simply refers to the theories of learning. As I mentioned in the introduction to this volume, this was a component in the classical Greek model for education which involved *a system, teaching theory and learning theory.*

The system, which later formed the basis of the neo-classical 19th century model for education, involved the communication of a preferred curriculum of different disciplines or study subject areas by expert adult tutors or teachers to groups of young learners or students.

Teaching theory involves an understanding of the use of different methods of teaching and the relative merits of different approaches—for example, dialectic or Socratic. In both the ancient Greek and the 19th century models, what was called the *didactical* approach involved the recital and explanation of a disciplinary narrative, key facts or concepts and the interrogation of students by the teacher. Today we use a combination of these traditional teaching methods, but as I have pointed out, new forms of learning, such as social learning or learning in computer generated learning environments (CGLEs), are being complimented by new forms of teaching.

Pedagogy, or the theory of learning, on the other hand, is the vestigial tail of the classical Greek model that was somewhat forgotten in the traditional institution based model of the 19th and 20th centuries. This is really because the methods of learning were, up until recently, fixed to relatively uniform teaching methods and institutional requirements; consequently, there was less need to consider the development or consideration of diverse theories when the practices were so uniform. Today, however, there are new settings where learning is taking place and new methods, approaches and tools are being explored by teachers and learners alike. It is therefore helpful to be aware of some of the pedagogic considerations that relate to the methods of learning and teaching in current simulations, educational games and CGLEs. In other words, we need to explore some of the theoretical and scientific considerations that can help to inform our understanding of different forms of learning.

ALL PLAY AND GAMES

To understand the processes of learning through experience and open-ended exploration in our current cultural period, it is important to first revisit the relationship between play and learning. It is notable that defining *play* has historically been problematic. Over the centuries, the definition has undergone many descriptive changes, according to the dominant cultural theory of any given time.

Play was regarded in 'structuralist' terms up until the last forty years; here, the characteristic *elements* of play were considered as separate from one another. Just as play was considered 'outside of us', so too were games considered in distinct terms, definitive and *outside* of our interactions and social context. One example of this tendency is demonstrated by the work of Roger Caillois, who defined games as 'free, separate, uncertain, unproductive, governed by rules and make-believe' (1962: 6). This structuralist analysis of play still prevails in some quarters (see, e.g., Avedon & Sutton-Smith, 1971; Juul, 2003; Salen & Zimmerman, 2004), but to my mind it is problematic in the extent to which it separates any analysis of play from the context within which it takes place.

Ludwig Wittgenstein assesses the approach thus:

> We are inclined to think that there must be something in common to all the entities, which we commonly subname under a general term. We are inclined to think that there must be something in common to all games, say, and that this common property is the justification for applying the general term "game" to the various games . . . The idea of a common property of its particular instances connects up with other primitive, too simple, ideas of the structure of language (1972: 17).

However, just as all learning is contextualized, so too is game play part of its context and embedded into social practices. It is interesting to note that while the structuralist formulation of play primarily focussed upon the characteristic *elements of* play, the *post-structuralist* formulation of play focuses upon players and their interaction with the game and its environment, re-connecting play with its context(s). One example of this 'post-structuralist' approach is demonstrated in Marie-Laure Ryan's work on virtual reality and narrative, which gives an overview of the transition to post-structuralism using the following description:

> [It is proposed that we] replace the notion of literary representation with the concept of play. The concept "has two heuristic advantages: (1) play does not have to concern itself with what it might stand for, and (2) play does not have to picture anything outside of itself" (Iser, 327: 250, quoted in Ryan, 2001: 188).

This conception of play illustrates a substantially altered consideration of and engagement with the notion of play from the original structuralist definition. The new approach works better for us and parallels our modern understanding of play within virtual spaces (Benford et al., 1998).

When considering play as a contained activity within a virtual space—or in this case a metaphorical space—it is necessary to give emphasis to *the act of playing* as well as the environmental context within which play is taking place. Over the last 30 years, as structuralism led to deconstruction, the focus of interest in playful (ludic) metaphors has transferred from *ludus* to *paidia*; in simple terms, there has been a shift from the notion of the game as a rule-governed activity to that of play as a 'subversion of rules' (Ryan, 2001: 188). In even simpler terms, notes Ryan, "Children at play do not follow established rules but invent their own" (2001: 185).

In parallel with the importance of the player and how he or she 'reads' or plays the game, this conceptualization leads both theoretically and practically to greater preference being placed on the 'interactivity' of social play. Consistent with Ryan's interpretation, focus on the player, the tolerance of a degree of subversion of the rules—for example, exploratory play—the increased fidelity in the *diegetic* space within the world of play and greater scope for control and interactivity have started to deliver substantial developments in the uses of play.

Today this tendency has led to the evolution of increasingly more realistic games and simulations, demonstrating higher levels of fidelity coupled with greater levels of control and interactivity. Crucially, these new forms are dependent on the concept of play but we must be clear that although a person plays a first-person military shooter, the game elements are an addition to what is at its root, a training simulator. Playing, in this context, refers to the use of a simulation for exploratory or experiential learning rather than the playing of a game. Play, in this sense, means the practice and rehearsal of real-life activities without suffering real-life/physical penalties. I will address the issue of violence in computer games later on in this chapter, but only briefly, because the debate is not really pertinent to the design of simulations for *educational learning*. The point I wish to make here is that how we define play and learning has a direct bearing upon the way we design and develop CGLEs. At the same time, it *is* useful to have an understanding of the 21st-century notion of play and learning as overlapping concepts.

Perhaps even more radical still, some theorists are considering play and learning in an even closer way, even proposing a radical understanding of formative learning (and development) as *synonymous* with play. For example, John Byers (1998) turns to Gerald Edelman (1992) for an explanation about how learning from play may take place on a microneuronal level:

> Edelman describes, through elaboration of his theory of neuronal growth selection that perceptual categorization, memes, affect and more combine to form cortical maps, one after another. By becoming sequentially organized into useful adaptive patterns, the lionesses may, in their rough and tumble play example, be establishing new and dynamically interconnected maps each time they play. They are mutually developing cooperative non-dominating behavior which seems to have evolved as a unit. . . . These maps . . . remain present and available for modification throughout life, but certainly accumulate most rapidly in infancy and juvenile times. They are . . . also 'value laden' and could certainly form a major cartography of learning (Edelman, 1992, quoted in Byers, 1998: 255).

Through scientific advances in brain scanning and neuroscience, gradually we are building up a deeper understanding of how game play can support development and learning. Empirical evidence emerging from functional magnetic resonance imaging (fMRI), electroencephalogram (EEG), near infrared spectroscopy (NIRS) and from the use of other more lightweight brain- computer interfaces (BCIs) for recording brain activity (e.g. Neurosky, Emotiv), are opening up our understanding of what is happening during game play and learning (Ninaus et al., forthcoming). These studies will in time reveal not only the strengths of game play but also how play and games support motivation and engagement; the observation that they do has also been supported in other literature (e.g. Garris, Ahlers & Driskell, 2002). One study found that 'activation of reward-related mesolimbic neural circuits stems primarily from *participatory engagement* in game play (interactivity), rather than from the effects of vivid and *dynamic sensory stimulation*' (Cole, Yoo & Knutson et al., 2012; emphasis added).

In other studies, evidence for *presence* in virtual worlds was found. For example, Thomas Baumgartner and colleagues, in their electroencephalogram (EEG) studies (2006, 2008), found a positive link between the presence experienced in virtual worlds and cortical activation found in parietal brain areas and involved in spatial navigation. In another study Silvia Kober, Jürgen Kurzmann, and Christa Neuper (forthcoming) concluded that parietal brain areas may be important for *presence* experience as these brain structures are involved in producing an egocentric representation of space. Martin Klasen and colleagues found that flow theory was demonstrated by specific neural activation patterns; here each of the content factors, such as balance between ability and challenge, 'was characterized by specific and distinguishable brain activation patterns, encompassing reward-related midbrain structures, as well as cognitive and sensorimotor networks' (2012: 485).

In the area of perceptual skills, brain scans with users have shown a positive impact upon different perceptual measures such as motor skills (Green & Bavelier, 2003) and mental rotation performance (Boot et al., 2008), while executive control, such as working memory, was associated with game play activity (Basak et al., 2008). Genaro Rebolledo-Mendez and colleagues found self-generated data and attention levels could be correlated in their study, using a more lightweight BCI (2009b). These approaches to gathering data from users during game play and learning, however, have considerable challenges in terms of study design, accurate measurement of study findings against a baseline *and* measured output against true proxy for learning efficacy (Ninaus et al., forthcoming). In a recent review of the area, Manuel Ninaus and colleagues found that

> for EEG, a common assertion is that measurements can be related to attention and focus. fMRI and NIRS, by comparison, may offer more specific insight into performance in narrowly-defined cognitive tasks. Generalizing these assertions, however, is challenging, given the task-specificity of many studies, and complexity of the underlying physiological system. Therefore, baselines must be established on a per-activity basis (Ninaus et al., forthcoming).

Edelman's work, and indeed other neuroscientific and neuropsychological studies of learning and play, may provide a watershed for learning theory regarding not only how learning has become a 'scaffold' for thinking and behaving and how it is predicated upon the link between human processes within the environment but also through telling us more about how our imagined and simulated mental processes and activities (rehearsal and practice) work.

While brain scanning has been cumbersome in the past, particularly with fMRI scanners, new lightweight home devices like BCIs offer new potential to capture feedback from the brain dynamically and to use this data as part of immediate feedback in the game. The value of understanding brain activity *during* game play, and being able to use it as a feedback mechanism in-game, is that games in the future can be regulated and paced according to live data about user attention, motivation and skills levels—such as in the game *Focus Pocus*, in which levels of attention can be monitored from children with attention deficit hyperactivity disorder. While studies considering this approach are restricted, the possibilities of the BCI as a feedback device for games *is* a matter for new studies: for improving game play, mapping against human behaviour and supporting people with mental conditions and disabilities (Colman & Gnanayutham, 2012; Plass-Oude Bos et al., 2010; Scherer et al., 2012).

To add to these considerable advances in human computer interfaces, scientific work around the discovery of 'mirror neurons' has shown how a new class of visuomotor neuron is in evidence in the monkey's premotor cortex:

> These neurons respond both when a particular action is performed by the recorded monkey and when the same action, performed by another individual, is observed. Mirror neurons appear to form a cortical system matching observation and execution of goal-related motor actions. Experimental evidence suggests that a similar matching system also exists in humans. (Gallese & Goldman, 1998: 252).

The main reason for this faculty, posit the authors, could be as a mind reading facility, or perhaps it could be a sort of mental validation system. 'According to "simulation theory", other people's mental states are represented by adopting their perspective: by tracking or matching their states with resonant states of one's own' (Gallese & Goldman, 1998: 494). In related work, Vittorio Gallese describes these findings in relation to human empathy, considering the role of action and agency: 'Agency constitutes a key issue for the understanding of intersubjectivity and for explaining how individuals can interpret their social world' and considers mirror neurons as playing a role in language formation (Gallese, 2001: 34; see also Kohler et al., 2002). Perhaps the mirror neurons play the role of supporting the mapping process that Edelman has described as the 'cartography of learning'. Mirror neurons, then, may hold clues to aid understanding of the relationship between play and learning.

The new research findings emerging from neuroscientific and neuropsychological studies are giving us a better picture of how we are learning and how we learn in game play, but the full extent of this new science is just beginning to unfold, leading us into a new era of understanding not just about learning but about human behaviour, social interactions and, importantly, about how humans interact within their environments. Significantly here, we have identified how and why play might be so significant to how humans develop and learn and why more play-centred approaches to learning may explain accelerated learning, and the memory of the learning, long after the event. As we have seen from the evidence emerging from cognitive and physiological studies, this is because multisensory interactions with our environment and the sense of presence that is of *being there* engages us at a deeper egocentric level.

According to Edelman, the link between play and learning is forged by 'a cartography of learning' whereby through the 'rough and tumble' of play 'new and dynamically interconnected maps [are generated] each time they play' (Edelman, 1992, quoted in Byers 1998: 255). While these maps are being constantly modified throughout our lives, they are primarily generated during infancy, and probably during the 'sensitive period' (Byers, 1998: 210–211). But, significantly, Edelman believes that these maps themselves could be the 'major cartography of learning'. In game play research the term *map* is replaced by *templates*. For example,

> Behavioural modelling is favouring the hypothesis that avid video game players are better able to form templates for, or extract the relevant statistics of, the task at hand. This may suggest that the neural site of learning is in areas where information is integrated and actions are selected; yet changes in low-level sensory areas cannot be ruled out (Ninaus et al., forthcoming).

Our understanding of the links between play and learning is extending and the work in neuroscience, neurobiology and neuropsychology clearly has a lot more to teach us about our interactions within our environments, how play really operates in the infancy and juvenile periods *and* our understanding of the bio-neural mechanisms involved when we learn. But what is clear from the preliminary research, is that the interaction between learners and their environment seems to be as prominent a consideration as it is in the work of Jean Piaget and Lev Vygotsky.

EXPERIENCE AND EXPLORATION

Exploration of our environment through play and game play, free play and decision making are important aspects of how we learn, and approaches that support these aspects of learning are critical. Scientific research can inform how effective computer generated environments (CGEs) can be designed, developed and deployed in the near future, but we also need to confirm best practices in teaching and to provide tutors and teachers with the necessary support, models, frameworks and tool sets that they require today. With this consideration in mind, over the last ten years, a group of international researchers associated with game-based learning, serious games, simulations and technology enhanced learning, have been focusing upon delivering these tools for aiding teachers and teaching practitioners to deliver e-learning content. These tools, models and approaches include game design frameworks (Kiili et al., 2012; Moreno-Ger et al., 2008; Staalduinen & de Freitas, 2011); learning design frameworks and patterns (Sharpe & Beetham, 2007); e-learning models and frameworks (de Freitas & Jameson, 2012); the exploratory learning model (de Freitas & Neumann, 2009).

The observations relating to learning theory that emerged from a CGLE, the medical training simulator *Triage Trainer*, prompted this author and Tim Neumann to consider how we can adapt learning content to game design. In particular, the work informed the development of the *exploratory learning model* (de Freitas & Neumann, 2009), a variant of David Kolb's 'experiential learning' (Kolb, 1984), extending Kolb's model to include exploration.

As a *defining* concept, the pedagogic consideration of *exploration as both a type and method of learning* needs more emphasis. *Exploration* is as much about demarcating and controlling the environment as it is about interacting with the environment through social interactions, transactions and activities. These activities may be occurring in relatively open-ended contexts, such as researching or in specifically designed activities, like assessment-based portfolio assignments. But with that exploration and interrogation of the environment comes a greater scope for role play. Here, the use of structured but flexible narrative opens up applications for re-enactments online; for example: re-playing episodes in history, playing the roles of key figures in history and undertaking work-based learning for those in a particular profession, such as legal practitioners, clinical staff or emergency workers.

One way of considering the issue is with a notional model of exploratory learning—in this case, one which extends from Kolb's well-known 'experiential learning cycle' (1984) to include an additional consideration—that is, *exploration as a pedagogic tool* for helping tutors (as well as learners) to organize both physical and virtual learning experiences or activities.

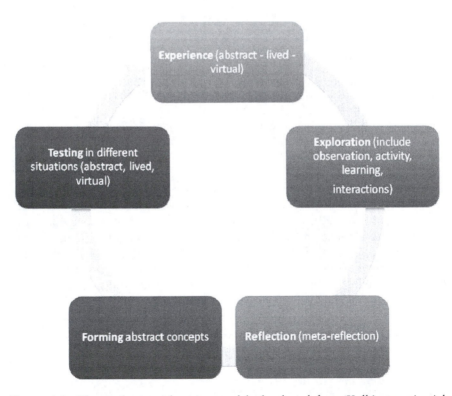

Figure 4.1   The exploratory learning model, developed from Kolb's experiential learning model. Reproduced with the kind permission of Sara de Freitas.

In Figure 4.1, we can see the extension of the experiential learning cycle model, to include exploration in the cycle of learning, as considered from a constructivist perspective. Although all aspects of learning are incurred during the learning process, the engagement of *exploration* foregrounds the interactivity of experiences in 3D and immersive environments, particularly in the sense of involving learner control. This, then, prompts us to consider the potential merits of the learner producing his or her own content.

While *experience* provides a point of connection at the interface between the learner and the environment, that experience is circumscribed by context. *Exploration* sets new boundaries within which the *context can become plural*—for example, conceptual, physical, hybrid, virtual or online. The learner can also play a more active role through experience of the physical and virtual spaces and also through the sets of interactions with other learners, as an integral aspect of the learning processes. In a sense here, *exploration is analogous with free play*, whereas other experiential interactions are time and rule bounded learning play. In computer generated learning environments, the *balance between exploration and structured experiential learning seems to be vital.*

Simulated experiences and environments designed for learning offer us the capability to structure learning, exploration and 'free play', whilst still offering a sense of control over those experiences and the environment. This is, perhaps more significant for cognitive development in very young children and its importance during the 'sensitive period' suggests exploratory and experiential learning simulations have at least one obvious niche to develop into. However, whether the 'explore and experience' approach is embraced and developed within any national or federal system depends on whether our education systems and institutions can adjust to reflect the plurality of the many valid and effective learning methods and tools that are now available to teachers and learners. Again, whether they do or not, it will not in my opinion affect the increasing commercial development or the societal consumption of learning tools or methods that work.

Exploratory learning, in relation to CGEs, offers scope for development and progress through a cyclic process of experiencing, exploring, reflecting, abstracting and testing. Here, then, the line between thinking, living, learning and playing is less bounded. If learning was *just* about experiencing something, then there would be no question of worrying about learning transfer between the simulated learning environment or game and the real world. But learning transfer is not just about replication of processes and responses in predictable ways; it is also about reflecting on, contextualizing and adapting responses drawn from lived or simulated behaviour to different or new circumstances—for example, developing team building skills in team sports or activities and transferring the acquired skills, to the workplace environment. Although 'generic' or transferable skills are considered pejoratively or as soft skills, in fact they are still useful skills, particularly today. This is because generic and transferable skills such as learning to learn, leadership, creativity or analytical ability are so valuable in working environments or sectors where rapid or routine changes are occurring. As a general rule, *specialized* skills that can only be used in rarefied circumstances have less practical value for translation into pragmatic contexts. This is why there is a general move to try to define which skills are most relevant to 21st century careers. In Europe, for example, the result has been a shift towards a more general baccalaureate system.

A summation of our experiences becomes less about defining moments in our lives and more about developing our own distinctive approach to problems—for example, based upon a combination of past experience, the application of skills, negotiation of problems and team working to solve problems. Our individual 'cartography of learning' develops from our explorations of physical, virtual and online spaces. This mental map gives us a conceptual framework with which to *make sense of experiences*, be they learning or work-based. This in turn helps to support the forward development of our skills and responses to the environment, to construct understandings relevant to our contexts, and at the same time allows us to reflect upon shared views, to negotiate decisions and to plan interactions within our environments.

Approaches to learning, if learning is understood as *sets of experiences and activities*, thus need to find new ways to map against the human and informational processes—as experienced by the individual learner. One aspect of this mapping is the collection of data about human behaviour. Rather than do this artificially, we can collect data through natural interactions and behaviour within CGEs, such as in multiplayer educational games. Using this approach, behaviour and interactions can be logged and analyzed (supplemented by using artificial intelligence techniques) over time, and the resultant map can be used to inform and develop an increasingly tailored and personalized learning model for the individual.

Creating inter-relationships between our activities in the virtual world and the physical world has benefits for learning, for example, the rehearsal of skills in virtual environments that can be applied in the physical world, while learner control, exerted by learners over their avatars, gives an added sense of control that can empower students (Kiili et al., 2012). Rehearsing skills through role play in virtual environments can, for example, be used to teach citizenship in a more stimulating way or to familiarize oneself with complex systems (Zielke et al., 2009), thereby *bringing to life* key theoretical concepts in practical circumstances (Carter, Wilbanks & Reese, 2009).

As noted in the experiential and exploratory models, the stage of *reflection* is crucial for facilitating higher-order cognition. In CGEs, reflection aids transfer between lived experiences in virtual *and* physical contexts. The role of reflection in learning *with CGEs*, therefore, is just as central to the effectiveness of learning. Reflection here may involve solitary consideration, broader discussion, general debriefing, summative or formative personalized or group feedback and discussions. However, the role of the tutor—in providing effective constructive critique of views and the forming of consensus within learning groups—is a critical component for this step in the learning process. Even in purely online learning, some tutorial feedback or interaction is desirable.

The emphasis upon reflective practice builds on the work of John Dewey's concept of practical inquiry, with three situations: pre-reflection, reflection and post-reflection (Dewey 1991; Garrison, Anderson & Archer, 2000). Reflection is still central throughout the learning process and the role of meta-reflection is particularly important to support the main challenge—that is, effecting learning transfer between virtual, online and physical contexts. The formation of abstract concepts, can thus be supported either within or outside of the learning session and these can then be tested in a range of different contexts such as in the workplace, in other physical locations or through building upon sets of related learning experiences that make use of physical, virtual and online interactions and activities, thereby building up a constructive understanding of the processes in play.

Exploration provides a new conceptual tool for learning in the CGE, one that can extend some of the pedagogic elements that are well understood in face-to-face teaching: including exemplification, illustration, building empathy with characters to reinforce understanding, feedback, scaffolding learning, reflection and meta-reflection.

PEDAGOGICAL ETHICS: THE ETHICS OF LEARNING

There are other ways of thinking about learning theory besides those I have touched on in the sections above. One such way that may be particularly relevant to the consideration of *new learning* and CGLEs is the consideration of the ethical issues that pertain to the theories of learning. This consideration is not just an academic preserve, and we can think of the ethical component of learning theory in terms of the societal concerns that we have for education and for learning in general. Here, *what we learn*—the content of the curriculum, discipline, lesson or educational texts and material—is as important, as *how we learn*.

One example of this would be the consideration of faith-based and secular approaches to education and the content of educational material. Interestingly, we can see that ethics plays a part in the assessment of both approaches. On one side of the debate, those who advocate faith-based approaches or materials perceive that secular approaches lack the moral components that civilized societies wish to instil in their young. On the other side of the debate, the proponents of secular approaches worry that faith-based schools may promote sectarianism and that they lead to societal divisions and confrontation.

I don't mean to imply here that any particular educational approach is right or wrong, in that sense of ethics. What we mean by *ethics*, in pedagogy, is really: the consideration of *the implications of what we learn*—the content of our learning materials—and *the implications of learnt behaviours* which may be perceived as desirable or undesirable, useful or harmful in the wider adult society.

When I refer to New Learning I do not mean to advocate the engineering of a revolution that sweeps away the traditions of the past. I am very fond of some of these traditions and particularly the idea that we put some societal effort into the management and delivery of education and the production of learning content. However, one of the ethical issues that is, in a general sense, relevant to the consideration of computer generated learning environments and simulations is the commercialization of learning content.

There is an economic logic to the increasing commercial development of CGLEs, social learning platforms and education simulations or games. In terms of sales, learning games could, the logic goes, rival the best-selling leisure titles in the computer games market. Logic also suggests that if the commercial content development market stays outside the system, then it can sell its products to individual learners, as long as they prove effective, more profitably than it can through discounted group licenses for classes or to each institution as part of the public system. This may seem like an academic point but in fact, one possibility here is that the commercialization of the production of educational materials, tools and platforms, could lead to the commercialization of learning in general, with an education market dominated, not by public bodies and institutions, but by brands and products.

One factor here will be the degree to which digital platforms, products, CGLEs and simulations *can* deliver accelerated learning processes and outcomes. My own opinion is that commercial developers will focus on the potential benefits of the automation of key learning processes and opportunities combined with rapid-repeat automated testing, to give their products the competitive edge that will help them develop a growing education market and succeed in it.

Another factor, however, will be the development of home schooling, remote access to classes and hybrid learning—that is, the use of commercial products and platforms to enhance and augment traditional institution-based learning. As I mentioned earlier, the question of whether it is a 'good thing' or a 'bad thing', if children or students access their classes from home, is not answerable in absolute terms. And here is where our consideration of ethics comes in. The child who is being physically bullied might well benefit from not being in the classroom. Conversely, the child who bullies might be suspended but can still receive an education from home—using remote access to classes—while other children are protected from the risk of harm. Either way, there are ethical considerations that arise out of our approaches to learning and learners that have to be weighed, when we assess the application of different learning theories.

We might also consider here, in ethical terms, the possibility of learnt behaviours that might *not* be desirable—in wider societal terms—when we look at CGLEs and simulations or indeed at new learning approaches. For example, at what point does empowerment of the learner tip over into a lack of respect for the experience and qualification of the tutor? Equally, how careful must we be about letting our children get used to the notion of actions without consequences?

This last question brings me back to the promise I made earlier to address the general perception that the most popular video games are all violent. This perception is one that I have encountered on many occasions, and is often raised by those who feel that this 'fact' about leisure games argues against the use of computer generated learning environments or simulations for educational purposes. Video games, of course are really computer programs or applications—that, is they are software. So when we talk about the most popular software, we also need to think of word processing packages, mail applications and operating systems. We can see that 'violence' doesn't really feature in the design of effective word processing software or social media application quite so easily, and we need to carry that logic and understanding over to CGLEs and learning simulations or games. One of the reasons why I advocate the involvement of public education systems and institutions in the development of digital learning content, is because I feel that this would help to ensure that future educational content is designed with citizenship values in mind that would, for example, discourage the violent behaviours—if that is deemed to be an important educational function by parents and policy makers. However, I am certainly not saying that *adults* should *not* be allowed to experience fictional films, games, books, paintings, museums or plays that feature violence. Rather, it's important to understand that the developers of CGLEs and professional training simulations are well aware that they are producing learning content for educational purposes and are not therefore trying to create violent fictions. The two markets are quite different and, in my experience, one of the defining characteristics of computer generated educational simulations or professional training simulations is that the incorporation of a reflection of real-world ethics is usually a feature of the design.

Conclusions
New Learning in the Digital Age

In the previous chapters, we considered the contexts of learning and how, in certain learning contexts, the roles of the learner and the tutor are changing and how new learning approaches are characterized by the foregrounding and empowerment of *the learner*. At the same time, I have tried to highlight the potential benefits to be gained from allowing more creativity on the part of teachers and tutors *and* from the contribution of learners to the development of tools and content. Additionally, I have tried to set out some of the key design principles—as they are currently understood—involved in the design of effective, intuitive and engaging simulations and computer generated learning environments (CGLEs). Lastly, I have tried to give the reader a working sense of how the concept of learning theory informs our approaches to learning and education, and how theoretical, neurological and ethical considerations apply to new learning and CGLEs.

The 19th century model of education used the book, the classroom, the lesson, the teacher and curricular disciplines to organize learning practices, but today these are giving way to multimedia learning content, the Internet, CGLEs, social learning and learning activities, casual stochastic learning and cross-disciplinarity. Our education system, much of which was developed during the 19th century, had its focus upon literacy and numeracy and on the mediation and acquisition of knowledge sets that were held to support the values of the day and the needs of growing industrial societies. Today in the post-industrial world, the drive for skills is still there, but in this age they have to support the growth of informational societies. As a result, our systems need to adapt to this change and provide skills and understandings that are rather more flexible, human process-centred and service orientated.

In the introduction to this book I noted that if we are to see the wider use of new learning methods in education—and in particular, the systemic uptake of computer generated learning environments, simulations and games—we needed to explore the merits of such an innovation.

I have not set out to be a champion of the use of computer generated learning environments or simulations *per se,* but I wish to advocate what I believe is the self-evident wisdom of utilizing all the most effective learning methods and tools that are now available to us. With more of an awareness of—and open-mindedness to—the diversity of effective new approaches and tools, we gain the benefit of multiple strategies from which we can gain different kinds of learning and different kinds of learner. In other words, we gain the benefit of choice.

I believe we are living through a long revolution that started in the 18th and 19th centuries with industrialization and which has continued through the digital or information innovations of the 20th century. The conceptual underpinning of this long revolution is a simple notion, and that is *automation*. We have achieved the automation of human labour; we have achieved the automation of information processing—that is, some of the elements of human thought; and in our age, we are now working on the automation of learning and education.

One conclusion here, then, is that perhaps the most important benefit to be gained from New Learning and CGLEs, is not just the facilitation of *new learning* approaches but that the potential gain is nothing less than the achievement of significantly accelerated human learning patterns. The development of the potential for the automation of academic testing and examination is, of course, one factor here that can accelerate the rate of learning progress, and it is important to understand the benefits of the *rapid repeatability* of learning simulations and simulated tests for the 'test and progress' model of educational accreditation. However, the increasing accessibility of educational content and learning opportunities plays a part here, too.

In this book, I wanted to look at the challenges facing engineered or systemic transitions in education and particularly the challenges facing institutional adaptations to new learning approaches and tools. Today, the question of how learning strategies and infrastructures can adapt to support new learning is being considered by most educational institutions. And the debates around open access have started to undercut the idea that institutions of learning—schools, colleges or universities—can just carry on as before, unaffected by the developments of digital information sciences and technologies.

The emergence of CGLEs, learning simulations and learning games offers a challenge for the political and institutional control and delivery of learning content, and the *commercial* drive for content production and content delivery has implications for the long-term future of public institutions. However, whilst the dominant orthodoxies are being challenged by the efficacy and economics of CGLEs and *new learning* approaches, the traditional institutions of learning still, at the moment, have the opportunity to be involved in the development of learning content, learning platforms and learning tools.

Indeed, as I have tried to highlight, the co-construction—by tutors and learners—of new digital tools and learning platforms can help to support new approaches to learning and at the same time places control back into learners' and tutors' hands—thereby expanding the opportunities for the creative design of learning content within the institutional wing of the education system. I believe it is a grave mistake to forget the intrinsic motivations of our teachers, tutors and learners because *their* place and continuing relationship in the new approaches to learning, in the new learning platforms and computer generated learning environments is guaranteed.

I have no doubt that teachers will have an equally important role in the new learning approaches that we see in CGLEs and training simulations; they may even have an enhanced and more enjoyable role in which, just like the learner, exploration and greater environmental variety in the teaching/learning experience are important intrinsic considerations. I have tried to emphasize that good teachers and structured tuition are vital to effective learning in CGLEs, social learning platforms and professional training simulations. We can automate testing and we can automate the provision of learning simulations for remote or repeated practice sessions. We cannot automate a 'duty of care' familiarity with individual students or a computer generated teacher who could cope with the nuances of educational discourse and tuition. The requirement in CGLEs and simulations for the co-ordination of group learning experiences and the role of complex human concepts in learning—ethics, social customs, manners, social interactions and negotiations—means that our teachers will continue to be central to the learning process. However, whether the best or the majority of teachers will be working for state institutions or commercial companies in future is another matter.

The commercial development of digital learning platforms, content, and tools is now a fact, and I have tried to be even handed in presenting that fact. Institutions and state systems can be a part of the development of new digital learning platforms, content and tools and *can* compete in an increasingly competitive education market. Equally, the commercial development of effective learning tools is a positive development, and so I have noted the contribution of the commercial sector and how that contribution is becoming increasingly important *to learners*. Crucially, the digital education market potential is huge; therefore, the commercial development of markets and commercial competition will surely continue to grow.

Rising student populations on every continent and a global economic downturn have put more financial strain on our educational systems, further pushing some education policy towards faster uptake of new learning strategies and practices. Consequently, the remote learning and open access approach—to commercial and publicly owned educational resources—is set to be used far more widely than it has been.

The development of remote online learning, CGLEs and new approaches suited to new digital platforms and tools is reshaping the delivery of learning, but the debate on the political and institutional systems of education is just beginning. The way that content is delivered is an important component of this debate, as is commercial competition, but ultimately the necessity for these institutions to adapt quickly to the challenges of learner empowerment and preference is clear.

I have presented some of the research and theory that we have in relation to the *validation* of different approaches to learning. Here we can use different strategies to ensure our approaches are appropriate and effective. On the most basic human level, we can look to preference, but thereafter we can benefit from an understanding of our neurological make-up and of the human memory to inform the effective design of learning experiences. Knowing how we remember things or what learning strategies facilitate human memory processes is useful to the design of more effective learning strategies and to the design of learning tools and content. At the same, knowing that not all individuals perceive and conceptualize the world in the same way and that different groups require different learning strategies or benefit from particular strategies must inform our systems and our consideration of a diversity of approaches. Consequently, neurological testing of learners in different contexts is one way of looking at the validation of learning theory or practice—that is, by comparing neurological activity in different learners and for different types of learning.

However, our traditional education model comes with its own strategy for testing learning theories and practices, and that is the accreditation mode of education. *Accredited formal learning* is still central to our social and political educational policy and strategy. However, testing new approaches or learning platforms within the state sector of education is difficult. This is partly because there are ethical issues involved in societal data gathering, but mostly it is because the new tools and approaches are not yet accredited themselves. One strategy for the state sector to validate new approaches, then, is to find a routine way to license trials of new methods, platforms or tools. It seems logical that such trials should not involve the disruption of learners' preparations for key qualifications.

Alternatively, the commercial development of future CGLEs can be aligned with the modules and testing criteria of the existing state accreditation systems. In that case, validation within the state accreditation system would only be for augmented approaches rather than for any one platform or approach. However, home schooling, remote access and independent learning academies are on the rise, and voluntary participation in validation trials for new commercial learning platforms may be more feasible in future.

The efficacy of computer generated learning environments and simulations in general has been validated. And as long as the respective design principles—some of which I have outlined in this book—are properly considered, the efficacy of these tools will improve. Like our learners, though, our new methods, tools and approaches need to be plugged into a routine 'test and progress' system.

Today we have the scientific understanding of how learning in computer generated environments (CGEs) can be more effective than traditional methods; we have developed the pedagogic basis for good design and we are working towards replicable learning patterns and designs for different learning contexts.

While this book suggests adopting exploratory learning, this is in many ways an addendum to the recognition that the learning experience is the basic unit of new learning. Experiential learning, as advocated by John Dewey, David Kolb and others in the constructivist tradition is part of a wider understanding of a need to reorganize the emphases in the theories used to understand our current practices. Experience and exploration are thus in some ways, at least, the key change agents for new learning and certainly provide the most effective tools for delivering it.

The role played by CGEs in education is growing, not least because it is a method for making learning content more engaging. But the extent to which it is adopted depends upon a better understanding of what learning is and how it is understood. For example, while scientific evidence exists to show the efficacy of game-based approaches, a general systemic and institutional resistance to accepting this finding has been striking. But if we don't start to engage with the science and we don't make any effort to use these tools, both to engage learners and to facilitate learning, then we will be depriving students of arguably one of the most powerful learning tools available.

I have written this book in the hope that it will help give all who read it a guide to learning theories and practices and to education in general as well as a better understanding of the developments of new approaches and new learning technologies. For policy makers, educationalists and our institutions of learning I have tried to set out the challenges that new learning approaches and platforms and commercial competition pose to our state systems. I have also, I hope, highlighted that there is still plenty of time for our systems and institutions to adapt organically to the new learning tools and a changing landscape—as long as there is a willingness to do so. For developers and designers of computer generated learning environments, simulations or educational games, I wanted to present a framework for understanding learning. The contexts of learning, an understanding of the intrinsic and social motivations of the learner, the roles of the teacher and learner, the content we learn from or with and the theories of learning are all key considerations in the design criteria of effective computer generated learning platforms, environments and simulations. Additionally, there is research available to developers, and this too can be helpful in the pursuit of effective design. For parents and learners, I also wanted to give a report 'from the front', as it were, to let them know what they can expect from the development of digital learning approaches in the near future. For these readers, I wanted to highlight that the diversity of digital approaches, tools and platforms will increasingly mean that parents and learners will have *choices*.

In conclusion, I want to advocate the enthusiastic exploration of *new learning*—that is, new learning theories, tools and methods—not to spite our ancestors' efforts but in the best traditions of their example: if there are better ways of doing things, more effective ways or more economical ways, we should do as we ask our children to do, we should learn and adapt so that we can take advantage of the benefits we can gain from new approaches. In this case, what is at stake is the enhancement of perhaps the most precious human faculty of them all: the capacity to learn.

Appendix A
Glossary of Terms

Term	Description
Avatar	An avatar is an interactive representation of a player in a games-based or three-dimensional interactive graphical environment.
Educational games	Games for learning are often imaginary (e.g. fantasy) interactive and immersive environments in which role play, skills rehearsal and other learning (e.g., collaborative or problem-based) may take place individually or in teams. Related terms include: *serious games, game-based learning, meaningful games*.
Exploratory learning	Learning through exploring environments, *realia*, lived and virtual experiences with tutorial and peer-based support. This notion of learning is based upon the idea that learning patterns can be helpfully transferred to dissimilar situations through meta-reflection. Unlike Kolb's 'experiential learning' this process is not always circular (although it may be), and does not rely upon physical experiences. Rather, the approach acknowledges the cognitive processes that help individuals to use their imagination and creativity to draw out lessons from *social interactions and environmental interactions*. Exploratory learning can be supported through different media, and through multimedia, interactions and textual engagement (de Freitas & Neumann, 2009).
Four dimensional framework	The four dimensional framework developed by de Freitas and Oliver (2006) is designed to aid tutors selecting and using games in their practice. The framework includes context, learner specification, pedagogy and representation as four key aspects for selecting the correct game for use in learning practice.
Game console	A game console is an electronic machine for playing dedicated video games. Game consoles may need a separate output device such as television or computer monitor. The main input device is a games controller (e.g., a hand controller or joystick).

Term	Description
Game engine	Each computer, video game or interactive application with synchronous graphics has a game engine. The game engine is the central software component, providing the underlying technologies. The engine greatly simplifies the task of games development and often allows the game to be used on different platforms (e.g., different game consoles and PC operating systems).
Gamification	Gamification is the use of game metaphor, elements or approaches in non-game contexts, usually to engage users.
Immersive worlds	*Immersive worlds* is used in this report to mean simulations, games and other interactive, often 3D virtual spaces or crossover spaces (e.g., between the virtual and physical worlds).
Microworlds	These are worlds created with objects and artefacts to allow learners to explore a given imaginary or mock realistic domain or environment in an open-ended way.
Modding	Modifying software in order to allow use in a different context or for different ends to that originally intended, or to further develop the software. Popular game 'mods' include *Revolution* from *Neverwinter Nights*.
Massively multiplayer online role play games (MMORPGs)	Multiplayer online role play games, such as *World of Warcraft*, have a subscriber base of 10.2 million (as of the first quarter of 2012) and use the web to support online game play communities. These games are engaging and have led to new forms of digital activity and new groups of avid Internet users. Role play games such as *World of Warcraft* or *Call of Duty* include players taking on the identity or identities of avatars in the game. *World of Warcraft*, for example, has different roles: orcs, warriors and members of the alliance. These entertainment games are very popular and include game clans which work together and the use of social software for supporting communications.
Massive open online course	A massive open online course is a type of online course that is designed for large audiences and delivered via the web for free. Inspired by the open educational resources movement, it provides a different model for distance learning. Recent examples include Coursera, edX and Udacity.
New learning	Not to be confused with the synonymous term meaning Renaissance humanism, *new learning* is used in this book to refer to the move towards experiential, active and immersive learning (Simons et al., 2000).
Pervasive gaming	Pervasive gaming uses mobile phones and other handheld devices and electronic media such as personal digital assistants, tablets and the Internet to allow users to play the game in different locations and at different times—so the game is always available to the player.

Term	Description
Serious games	Serious games are so called because they integrate gaming elements within non-entertainment contexts such as for learning or training, awareness raising or business engagement. The name also refers to a movement of researchers and developers who are working towards developing games specifically aimed at non-entertainment audiences.
Simulations	Simulations are non-linear synthetic training environments that allow learners to rehearse different scenarios, tasks, problems or activities in advance of real-life interactions or to update skills.
Social interactive learning	*Social interactive learning* is a term the used in this book to mean learning primarily driven by social interactions and within social communities.

Appendix B

List of Selected Educational Games

This list is compiled from resources on the web and extracts from Sara de Freitas's *Serious Virtual Worlds* report for the Joint Information Systems Committee. For the full report, see http://www.jisc.ac.uk/media/documents/programmes/elearninginnovation/gamingreport_v3.pdf.

Serious Game Title and Link	Description
America's Army: http://www.americasarmy.com	*America's Army* is a 3D online game based upon training for the Army. The game was developed by the United US Army and Department of Defense experts to 'provide civilians with an inside perspective and a virtual role in today's premiere land force'; it has been used effectively as a recruitment tool. Developed with a significant budget, *America's Army* has high levels of fidelity and game playability. Since *America's Army* was launched in July 2002, it has become very popular and there have been nine million downloads to date (at the end of 2012), placing it among the top five most popular online computer games.
Civilization: http://www.civilization.com	*Civilization* is a strategy game which is based upon a single-player turn-based format. The game is a role play game, and the player takes on the role of the ruler of a civilization, starting with only one unit and intending to build up to an empire which can compete with other civilizations (including Roman, Aztec and Incan civilizations). The game tests the player with tasks of exploration, warfare and diplomacy and presents the player with decisions about new city location, investment of resources and war tactics. The game was launched in 1991 for MicroProse and developed by Sid Meier, who developed the game with ideas based upon a board game also called *Civilization*, manufactured in the United Kingdom in 1980 by Hartland Trefoil (later by Gibson Games), and in the United States in 1981 by Avalon Hill. The game has had many sequels, including, most recently, *Civilization IV*.

Serious Game Title and Link	Description
Code of Everand: http://areacodeinc.com/projects/code-of-everand/	*Code of Everand* was a popular multiplayer online game developed by Area/Code for the UK Department for Transport. The game was played by around 100,000 children, mainly based in the United Kingdom, and aimed to raise awareness about road crossing behaviour. The game was animated in style and had an appeal to children 9–15 years of age. The multiplayer game combined adventure elements with collection of points and values to engage the player (Dunwell, Christmas & de Freitas, 2012).
Floodsim: http://www.playgen.com	*FloodSim* is a web-based game developed with the aim of raising awareness of issues surrounding flooding policy and citizen engagement in the United Kingdom. The game was commissioned by Aviva, an insurance company, and was developed by Playgen, a London-based company. It has been played by a large number of users (n = 25,000) in a relatively short period of time (four weeks) during autumn 2008. *FloodSim* allows the player to take on the role of a flood policy strategist employed to implement a selection of strategies for addressing the risk of flooding over the course of three years based on a pre-defined budget. The game was evaluated positively by the Serious Games Institute, which found that the game was effective for raising awareness of the issues and for targeting its audience (Rebolledo-Mendez et al., 2009a).
Food Force: http://www.wfp.org/stories/online-game-food-force-puts-players-front-lines-hunger	*Food Force* is a Facebook game developed for the World Food Programme by KONAMI Digital Entertainment. The game aims to raise awareness about the food programme. This multiplayer social game puts the player in charge of the world's largest humanitarian aid agency to make decisions and has been played by an estimated ten million people. The game is part of the Game for Change movement, and raises funding while entertaining players (Wong et al., 2007).
Global Conflicts series: http://www.globalconflicts.eu/	*Global Conflicts* is an award winning educational game series developed by Serious Games Interactive, a Danish company. The games focus upon learning around citizenship, geography and media studies courses. The series promotes learning about different global conflicts, giving emphasis to the key themes of climate change, globalization, democracy, human rights, terrorism and poverty. The series has been developed with teachers in mind and in line with curriculum requirements, making it easy to use in classroom teaching (Zielke et al., 2009).

Serious Game Title and Link	Description
Immune Attack: http://www.fas.org/immune-attack/	Released in 2008, *Immune Attack* was developed for the Federation of American Scientists by Escape Hatch Entertainment. Early game development was undertaken with US National Science Foundation funding by Brown University and the University of Southern California. The single player game teaches immunology to students (Kelly et al., 2007).
Levee Patroller: http://cps.tbm.tudelft.nl/site/content/levee-patroller.	*Levee Patroller* is an early example of a successful serious game, and is still used to train patrollers of the levee system in the Netherlands. It is a 3D immersive game developed on the Unreal 2 games engine and is now maintained and offered by a commercial company, Delft GeoSystems BV (Harteveld et al., 2010).
Math Blaster: http://www.mathblaster.com/	The *Blaster* series has been in use since the late 1980s and is a veteran of educational gaming. The series was developed by Davidson and Associates but is now owned by Knowledge Adventure (Rice, 2007).
Re:Mission: http://www.re-mission.net/	*Re:Mission* is a well-known serious game developed by the US-based HopeLab to change behaviour around medication adherence in children with cancer. The game is an animated multilevel game in which the player takes on the role of Roxxi, a nanobot, who helps to destroy cancerous cells. The work of Pamela Kato on the game and evaluation helped to prove the efficacy of game based approaches for changing behaviour (Kato et al., 2008).
Revolution: http://www.educationarcade.org/node/357	*Revolution* is a multiplayer game based on events during the American Revolution and located in the town of Williamsburg, Virginia, and is set in 1775, before the violent rebellion there. The game puts students in the place of one of seven characters including a lawyer, a patriotic blacksmith and an African American house slave. This allows students to experience the daily social, economic and political lives of the town's inhabitants. The game can still be downloaded from the Education Arcade website and is a modification of *Neverwinter Nights* (Jenkins et al., 2009).
River City: http://muve.gse.harvard.edu/rivercityproject/	Based on Active Worlds Inc. technology, the River City research project was funded by the US National Science Foundation. It is an interactive computer simulation allowing science students to learn scientific inquiry and 21st-century skills. The game utilizes inquiry-based learning methods and has an animated look and feel (Ketelhut, 2007).

Serious Game Title and Link	Description
Selene: A Lunar Science Gamehttp://selene.cet.edu/	*Selene* is a single player Flash-based game for learning about lunar geology, and is aimed at students nine years old and above. The game was developed as part of the NASA-sponsored Classroom of the Future at the Center for Educational Technologies (http://www.cet.edu) at Wheeling Jesuit University (http://www.wju.edu) and continued to receive funding under the National Science Foundation and the CyGaMEs project. Ian Bogost contributed to the game design.
SimCity (known as *SimCity Classic*): http://www.simcity.ea.com/play/simcity_classic.php	Released in 1989, *SimCity* is a city-building simulation game. Designed by Will Wright, SimCity was a Maxis product. Since its inception it has been made available on different platforms and consoles. Simcity has many sequels, including *SimCity 2000* (1994), *SimCity 3000* (1999) and (1999) and *SimCity 4* (2003). The game cannot be won or lost, and departs from the usual genres of games, creating its own sub-category of a simulation game. The players can mark land as commercial, residential or industrial and accordingly change tax rates and add energy grids and transportation networks. Players can also be confronted with disasters such as flooding, fires, earthquakes and even attacks by monsters.
Total War series: http://www.totalwar.com	*Total War* is a strategy game series developed by the Creative Assembly. The series of games mix turn-based strategy and the management of resources, and also involve real-time tactical control of battles similar to *Civilization*. The first game of the series, *Shogun: Total War* was released in 2000; the most recent game, in 2011, was *Total War: Shogun 2*. Published by Activision, Sega and Electronic Arts, the series has been very successful over the last ten years, bringing innovations in mass battle scenes and blending real-world historical detail with multiplayer capabilities.
Triage Trainer: http://www.trusim.com/?page=Home	*Triage Trainer* was a game developed by Trusim (a Division of Blitz Games) on their proprietary games engine. It was one of two games developed (with *Patient Rescue*) and built upon their earlier work done on the *Interactive Trauma Trainer*. It was a very high-fidelity game aimed at emergency responders and medical staff to train for best practices in triage. The game is now considered one of the 'first generation' of serious games. Studies using the game demonstrated that game-based approaches were more effective than traditional techniques (e.g., Knight et al., 2010).

Serious Game Title and Link	Description
Quest Atlantis	*Quest Atlantis* is a 3D multiuser learning environment for educating children 9–15 years of age, and utilizes a narrative programming tool kit to engage children in inquiry based learning. While the game is no longer available online, over the course of five years 65,000 children played in the learning environment, undertaking quests, developing virtual characters and interacting with other students. Sasha Barab was the principal investigator of this US National Science Foundation–funded project (Barab et al., 2005, 2010).
World without Oil: www.worldwithoutoil. org/metacontact.htm	*World without Oil* is an alternate reality (or mixed reality) game created to raise awareness and support dialogue around what would happen if the world ran out of oil resources. Developed by San Jose, California, game writer and designer Ken Eklund, the game was played over a short period in 2007. Combining elements of an alternate reality game with a serious game, it used Twitter, blogs and websites to trigger debate and discussion around the important issue of oil shortages and their impact upon the world economy. The game aimed to use collective intelligence, creating a record that would have value for educators, policy makers and everyday people in order to help anticipate the future and minimize negative outcomes.

Appendix C

List of Virtual World Categories

Reproduced from Sara de Freitas's Serious Virtual Worlds report for the Joint Information Systems Committee. For the full report, see http://www.jisc.ac.uk/media/documents/publications/seriousvirtualworldsv1.pdf.

Category of Virtual World	Examples	Learning potential
Role play worlds	*World of Warcraft, Everquest, Guild Wars*	There has been little sustained research into the learning or educational benefits of MMORPGS. The scope for learning may be in role play approaches perhaps focusing upon professional development. Potential for learning in vicarious ways. Team-working skills, leadership skills, communications.
Social worlds	*Second Life, Open-Sim, CyWorld, ActiveWorlds* For children: *Habbo Hotel, Club Penguin*	Social worlds tend to be immersive worlds without specific quests. They are primarily social and focus upon community building activities and social communications between friends and colleagues. Social worlds for children and young adults are often animated and in 2D/2.5D. Children use these environments for communicating with other friends or sharing content. The success of these environments has led to a proliferation of formats and worlds. Some virtual worlds for children have tie-ins with toys or films (e.g., *Barbie-Girls World*), and are marketed as part of the franchise. Social learning tasks or assignments could be placed within social world settings.

Category of Virtual World	Examples	Learning potential
Working worlds	*Open* Wonderland, previously *Project Wonderland*	These worlds focus upon corporate communications and business support facilities. Open Wonderland is a 100% Java open source tool kit which initially brought together interactive video conferencing with capabilities for voice and document sharing. Increasingly businesses are global concerns and often staff are location independent workers without access to offices; this makes the use of 3D-rich environments for collaboration appealing and cost saving. For learning there have been projects that linked global learners together for online lectures and mixed teaching cohorts (some based in classes and others linked by video conferencing facility). The project was originally funded by Sun Microsystems until its acquisition, when it became a community-supported open source project.
Training worlds	*America's Army, OLIVE*	These worlds are specifically for training. They are focused upon particular professions and aim to provide training that may not be possible in real-life situations, are life threatening or have many possible scenarios or outcomes. While to date these have often focused upon military training, increasingly medical education and training are making use of the tools.
Mirror worlds	*Google Earth*	Mirror worlds are quite literally worlds or 3D visualizations that mirror the physical world. *Google Earth* is the most well known of these. Increasingly through mash-ups, mirror worlds can be embedded into other applications. The bringing together of different applications is facilitated by interoperability—and this presents interesting options for education and training, especially where a blend of real and virtual spaces may be beneficial, such as field trips and multimedia production.

Appendix D
List of Virtual Worlds

List updated from Sara de Freitas's Serious Virtual Worlds report for the Joint Information Systems Committee. For the full report, see http://www.jisc.ac.uk/media/documents/programmes/elearninginnovation/gamingreport_v3.pdf.

No.	Virtual World	Links: (All accessed 20 January 2013)	Description
1	Active Worlds	http://www.activeworlds.com	Active Worlds hosts a universe of over 1,000 3D virtual worlds. Active Worlds' most popular world is AlphaWorld. Access to the worlds is free and facilities there include shopping, chat and playing online games.
2	Active Worlds Educational Universe	http://www.activeworlds.com/edu/awedu.asp	Active Worlds Educational Universe is an entire Active Worlds universe allocated for educational activities. The aim is to make the Active Worlds technology available to educational institutions for a lower cost.
3	Citypixel	http://www.citypixel.com	Citypixel is an animation-based virtual world. Users can lease flats, play games and chat with neighbours. It is more of a social world and is free to join. There are currently 26,541 city residents.
4	Club Penguin	http://www.clubpenguin.com	Part of the Walt Disney Company, Club Penguin was set up in 2005. It is a virtual world aimed at children, and is used for playing games, interacting and playing.
5	Cyworld	http://www.cyworld.com	Cyworld is a South Korean social online community. It encourages a buddy system, and the exchange and storage of photographs, and has bulletin boards. The social world usership peaked at 19

No.	Virtual World	Links: (All accessed 20 January 2013)	Description
			million in 2006, when as many as 90% of South Koreans in their 20s were registered users of the world.
6	DubitPlatform	http://www. dubitplatform.com/	The Game Application Markup Language platform comes with a specialist tool kit which aims to be easy to use and for creative people and requires less development know-how than other platforms. The platform is used by various clients, such as the Cartoon Network, which commissioned *MiniMatch*, which attracted over 5 million players in the first week and supported over 12,000 concurrent players.
7	Entropia Universe	http://www. entropiauniverse. com	Mindark's *Entropia Universe* is a continuation of Project Entropia. It allows for money made in the virtual world to be easily converted back into real money. The social world also allows for businesses and entertainment. It is free to download and doesn't use subscription charges.
8	Gaia Online	http://www. gaiaonline.com	*Gaia Online* is a social world for teens. Here users play games, create their own space and profiles, chat and explore. It currently has over 26 million registered users and has around 7 million unique visitors per month. There are shops and online forums, and videos to watch.
9	Google Earth	http://earth.google. com	*Google Earth* is a mirror world. It combines powerful Google searching functionality with satellite images, including maps and 3D visualizations of buildings and cities. Searchable via postcode, the resource is being used for a range of purposes from finding directions to research and education.
10	Habbo	http://www.habbo. com	*Habbo* is a Finnish social networking site for teens. It was launched as *Habbo Hotel* in 2000 in Finland and since then has become popular internationally. It is animated rather than 3D and includes chat rooms and discussion forums. Each user is a 'habbo' and can customize his or her avatar. As of August 2011, over 230 million avatars had been registered and there were on average 10 million unique visitors per month.

No.	Virtual World	Links: (All accessed 20 January 2013)	Description
11	*Hipihi*	http://www.hipihi.com/index_english.html	*Hipihi* is a Chinese virtual social 3D world created by its residents. Graphically it is very attractive and in terms of functionality is closest to *Second Life*. The user demographic is slightly more female than male.
12	*IMVU*	http://www.imvu.com	Palo Alto, California, based *IMVU* offers 3D chat, customizable avatars and a 3D environment. In beta testing, this more social-orientated software has a free sign up and 3D messaging. The world also includes virtual currency and the opportunity to create and sell products.
13	*Kaneva*	http://www.kaneva.com	*Kaneva* combines social networking with a virtual world. A social world, *Kaneva* allows for avatar customization, social chat and sharing of interactive content. In 2010 *Kaneva* released its 3D Applications and 3D App Game Developer programs, shifting emphasis to smaller-scale 3D application development. It had five million registered users in June 2010.
14	*Media Grid: Immersive Education*	http://immersiveeducation.org	*Immersive Education* is a Media Grid initiative which combines 3D graphics, games and simulation technology, voice chat and rich digital media for supporting collaborative learning online. Made available to university students, the world is now being piloted with school children and corporate training. It aims to create a more immersive experience in support of learning objectives and curriculum, using a computational grid development platform designed for networked applications that use digital media.
15	*Moove*	http://www.moove.com	The German *Moove* was founded in 1994. It currently has over 1.5 million members worldwide. *Moove* is another social world community based upon avatars and social interactions. The system is accessible via the Brandworld Tools released in 2005.
16	*The musiclounge/vSide*	https://www.vside.com/app/start	Billed as the 3D Facebook, this online 3D social space for teens was created by Doppelganger. Online parties and the use of cartoon-like avatars and forums are designed in a stylish way to attract teens.

No.	Virtual World	Links: (All accessed 20 January 2013)	Description
17	NASA World Wind	http://worldwind. arc.nasa.gov	Originally released in 2004 by NASA, *World Wind* (1.4) is a free, Java, open source mirror world. The geobrowser overlays NASA satellite imagery, aerial photos and publicly available geographic information system data onto a 3D model of the earth, and allows users to zoom in from satellite pictures.
18	OLIVE	http://www.saic. com/products/simu-lation/olive/	*Online Interactive Virtual Environment platform* has been used for training purposes. It is a private world, and can be accessed through licensing payment structures. It has been used for military, medical and professional purposes. It is currently owned by SAIC.
19	Open Croquet Project	http://www.openc-roquet.org	*Croquet* is an open source software development community supporting the creation of virtual worlds. Based upon Squeak architecture, it is used to support resource sharing, collaboration and communications between its users.
20	Open Source Metaverse Project	http://metaverse. sourceforge.net	The *Open Source Metaverse* project provides an open source platform similar to *Second Life* and *There.com*. The serve engine can be installed locally so users can create their own metaverse (analogous with the Apache web server for web content). It is modular, flexible and extensible.
21	Open Simulator	http:// opensimulator.org	The **OpenSimulator** project is a virtual worlds server for creating 3D virtual environments. It has been described as a reverse-engineered *Second Life*, and allows users to run their own *Second Life* island on their own computer without opening up firewalls. It can be run as a standalone application or as a collaborative world like *Second Life*. It is written in C# and is modular, allowing developers to extend functionality via plug-in modules. The next step is to allow users to move objects between *OpenSim* and *Second Life*.
22	OpenQwaq	http://code.google. com/p/openqwaq	OpenQwaq is an application based upon Squeak open source implementation of Smalltalk and the Croquet Project. The main developers include Alan Kay, David Smith, Andreas Raab and David Reed. OpenQwaq is aimed at supporting virtual

No.	Virtual World	Links: (All accessed 20 January 2013)	Description
			collaborative solutions for enterprises. It offers document sharing, programme management and virtual operations centres, as well as corporate training capabilities.
23	Open Wonderland (formerly Project Wonderland)	http:// openwonderland. org	Based upon Sun Microsystem's Darkstar technology, *Open Wonderland* is a Java virtual worlds tool kit for creating collaborative experiences. The application allows for document sharing and games. The project is open source, and has particular strengths with supporting virtual meetings and voice chat.
24	PlayStation Home	http:// uk.playstation.com/	Also known as *Home*, *Playstation Home* is a virtual 3D social gaming platform developed by Sony Computer Entertainment. Home launched in 2008, and allows users to create a customized avatar, shop for new products, play games and network. It had 23 million members in August 2011.
25	Protosphere	http://www. protonmedia.com	Produced by Protonmedia for business uses, the platform offers the usual functionality of avatars, social networking and a 3D interface
26	Second Life	http://www. secondlife.com	*Second Life* is a 3D virtual world launched in 2003. The emphasis here is on creating your own avatars and content, but the Linden dollar is the main currency. With over 13 million residents at its peak, *Second Life* is one of the more popular virtual worlds, possibly because the barrier to joining the community is so low in terms of computer specification and its free membership. But recently high associated costs have driven users in large numbers to the open source *OpenSim*.
27	There.com	http://www.there. com/	Also offering free membership, *There. com* provides text chat, instant messaging and customizable avatars. Again it is a social world and 'therebucks' are the virtual currency used. The technology is the basis of the *OLIVE* platform now owned by SAIC.

No.	Virtual World	Links: (All accessed 20 January 2013)	Description
28	*Tixeo*	http://www.tixeo. com	*Tixeo* is a live 3D meeting tool aimed at enterprise. The products include 3D meetings and a 3D workstation. Available to demo for free.
29	*Whyville*	http://www. whyville.net	*Whyville* is an educational Internet site aimed at children 8 to 16 years old. It aims to engage users in learning covering a broad range of subjects such as art, business, geography and science. *Whyville* has more than seven million players, and its users engage in virtual world simulation based games and role play. The project has been praised for its safety and is sponsored by governmental, non-profit and corporate organizations.
30	*Webkinz*		*Webkinz* is a virtual children's world. It relies on stuffed toy animals that can be bought and contain a code printed on it. This code allows access to the *Webkinz World* website, where the user can own a virtual version of the toy for online multiplayer play. In 2006 Webkinz had one million online accounts.
31	*VastPark platform*	http://www. vastpark.org/	*VastPark* is an open source platform for developing virtual worlds, built on the .NET Framework. Its strongest point is its efficient architecture, built with a view towards the future of communication platforms. However, despite its architecture it is not as popular as some other virtual worlds.

Notes

NOTES TO CHAPTER 1

1. Stanford Encyclopedia of Philosophy, s.v. "Social Institutions". Accessed 30 August 2012 at http://plato.stanford.edu/entries/social-institutions/ .
2. International Association for K–12 Online Learning, "Fast Facts about Online Learning," retrieved 20 February 2012 at http://www.inacol.org/press/docs/nacol_fast_facts.pdf.
3. J. M. Bridgeland, J. J. DiIulio Jr. & K. B. Morison, *The Silent Epidemic: Perspectives of High School Dropouts*, quoted in International Association for K–12 Online Learning, 'Fast Facts about Online Learning'.

References

Aarseth, E., Smedstad, S. & Sunnana, L. (2003). A multi-dimensional typology of games. M. Copier and J. Raessens (eds). *Level up: Digital games research conference proceedings*. Utrecht. University of Utrecht: 48–53.

Aldrich, C. (2009). *Learning online with games, simulations, and virtual worlds: Strategies for online instruction* (Vol. 11). Jossey-Bass.

Allison, C., Campbell, A., Davies , C.J. , Dow, L., Kennedy, S., McCaffery, J.P., Miller, A.H.D., Oliver, I.A. & Perera, G I U S 2012, 'Growing the use of Virtual Worlds in education: an OpenSim perspective'. M. Gardner, F. Garnier & C.D. Kloos (eds), in: Proceedings of the 2nd European Immersive Education Summit: EiED 2012. E-iED, Universidad Carlos III de Madrid, Departamento de Ingeniería Telemática, Madrid, Spain, pp. 1–13, 2nd European Immersive Education Summit, Paris, France, 26–27 November.

Allison, S.E., Walde, L.von, Shockley, T., O'Gabard, G. (2006). The development of self in the era of the internet and role-playing games. *The American Journal of Psychiatry*, 163, 381–385.

Amory, A., Naicher, K., Vincent, J. & Adams, C. (1999). The use of computer games as an educational tool: Identification of appropriate game types and game elements. *British Journal of Educational Technology*, 30(4): 311–321.

Arnab, S., Brown, K., Clarke, S., Dunwell, I., Lim, T., Suttie, N., Louchart, S., Hendrix, M., de Freitas, S. (forthcoming) Supporting Relationship and Sex Education in the Classroom with a Serious Game: PRE:PARe. *Computers and Education*.

Avedon, E. M. & Sutton-Smith, B. (1971). *The study of games*. Huntington. New York. Krieger.

Barab, S., Thomas, M. Dodge, T., Carteaux, R. and Tuzun, H. (2005). Making learning fun: Quest Atlantis, a game without guns. *Educational Technology Research and Development*, 53(1): 86–107.

Barab, S.A., Gresalfi, M.S., & Ingram-Goble, A. (2010). Transformational play: Using games to position person, content, and context. *Educational Researcher*, 39(7), 525–536.

Baranowski, T., Baranowski, J., Cullen, K. W., Marsh, T., Islam, N., Zakeri, I., Honess-Morreale, L. & Demoor, C. (2003). Squire's Quest! Dietary outcome evaluation of a multimedia game. *American Journal of Preventive Medicine*, 24, 52–61.

Bardzell, S. & Odem, W. (2008) The Experience of Embodied Space in Virtual Worlds. An Ethnography of a Second Life Community. *Space and Culture*, 11(3): 239–259.

Baron-Cohen, S. (1987), Autism and symbolic play. *British Journal of Developmental Psychology*, 5: 139–148.

Barrett, T. & Moore, S. (2011) *New Approaches to Problem-based Learning: Revitalising Your Practice in Higher Education.* New York & Abingdon: Routledge.

Barry Issenberg, S., McGaghie, W. C., Petrusa, E. R., Lee Gordon, D., & Scalese, R. J. (2005). Features and uses of high-fidelity medical simulations that lead to effective learning: A BEME systematic review. *Medical teacher*, 27(1), 10–28.

Barton, K. and Maharg, P. (2006) E-simulations in the wild : interdisciplinary research, design and implementation of simulation environments in legal education. In: Games and simulations online learning. *Information Science Publishing*, Hershey, USA, pp. 115–148 .

Barton, K. & McKellar, P. (2011) From masters to games-master: managing disequilibrium and scaffolding in simulation-based learning. In de Freitas, S. & Maharg, P. (Eds) (2011), *Digital Games and Learning.* London & New York. Continuum Press, pp. 226–249.

Basak, C., Boot, W.R., Voss, M.W., Kramer, A.F. (2008) 'Can Training in a Real-Time Strategy Video Game Attenuate Cognitive Decline in Older Adults?' *Psychology and Aging*, Vol. 23, No. 4, pp.765—777.

Baumgartner, T., Speck, D., Wettstein, D., Masnari, O., Beeli, G., & Jäncke, L. (2008) 'Feeling present in arousing virtual reality worlds: prefrontal brain regions differentially orchestrate presence experience in adults and children', *Frontiers in Human Neuroscience*, Vol. 2, pp.1–2.

Baumgartner, T., Valko, L., Esslen, M., & Jäncke, L. (2006) 'Neural correlate of spatial presence in an arousing and noninteractive virtual reality: an EEG and psychophysiology study', *Cyberpsychology & Behavior*, Vol. 9, No. 1, pp. 30–45.

Becker, K. & Parker, J. (2012) *The Guide to Computer Simulations and Games.* Indianapolis: John Wiley & Sons.

Bekoff, M. and Byers, J. (1998). (eds.). *Animal play. Evolutionary, comparative and ecological perspectives:* 243–259. Cambridge. Cambridge University Press.

Benford, S., Greenhalgh, C., Reynard, G., Brown, C. & Koleva, B. (1998). Understanding and constructing shared spaces with mixed-reality boundaries. *ACM transactions on computer-human interaction*, 5(3): 185–223. September.

Bentham, J. (1987) *Utilitarianism and Other Essays.* New York & London: Penguin Books.

Benyon, D. (2010) *Designing Interactive Systems: A Comprehensive Guide to HCI and Interaction Design.* Harlow. Essex. Pearson Educational Limited.

Berners Lee, T. (2000) *Weaving the Web: The Past, Present and Future of the World Wide Web by its Inventor.* London & New York: Texere Publishing Ltd.

Bessiere, K., Seay, F., Kiesler, S. (2007). The Ideal Elf: Identity Exploration in World of Warcraft. *Cyberpsychology and Behavior*, 10: 530–535.

Brewer, J. B., Zhao, Z., Desmond, J. E., Glover, G. H. & Gabrieli, J. D. E. (1998). Making Memories: Brain Activity that Predicts How Well Visual Experience Will Be Remembered. *Science*, 281 (5380), 1185–1187.

Bjork, S., Holopainen, J., Ljungstrand, P. and Mandryk, R. (2002). Ubiquitous Games. *Personal and Ubiquitous Computing* 6: 358–361.

Blinka, L. (2008). The Relationship of Players to Their Avatars in MMORPGs: Differences between Adolescents, Emerging Adults and Adults. *Cyberpsychology: Journal of Psychosocial Research on Cyberspace*, 2(1).

Boot, W. R., Kramer, A. F., Simons, D. J., Fabiani, M., Gratton, G. (2008) 'The effects of video game playing on attention, memory, and executive control', *Acta Psychologica*, Vol. 129, No. 3, pp.387–398.

Bos, D. P. O., Reuderink, B., van de Laar, B., Gürkök, H., Mühl, C., Poel, M., & Heylen, D. (2010). *Brain-computer interfacing and games. In Brain-Computer Interfaces* (pp. 149–178). Springer London.

Boud, D. and Feletti, G. (Eds.) (1991). *The Challenge of Problem Based Learning.* New York: St. Martin's Press.

Brannick, M. T., Salas, E. & Prince, C. (2009) *Team Performance, Assessment and Measurement: Theory, Methods and Applications*. New Jersey. Lawrence Erlbaum.

Brown, S. (1998). Play as an organizing principle: clinical evidence and personal observations. M. Bekoff and J. Byers (eds.). Animal play. *Evolutionary, comparative and ecological perspectives*: 243–259. Cambridge. Cambridge University Press.

Brown, K.E., Bayley, J., & Newby, K. (2012). Serious Game for Relationships and Sex Education: Application of an Intervention Mapping approach to development. In S. Arnab, I Dunwell & K. Debattista (eds.) *Serious Games for Healthcare: Applications and Implications. IGI Global*; Hershey, PA.

Buljac-Samardzic, M., Dekker-van Doorn, C. M., Van Wijngaarden, J. D., & Van Wijk, K. P. (2010). Interventions to improve team effectiveness: a systematic review. *Health Policy*, 94(3), 183–195.

Burch, N. (1982) Narrative/Diegesis—Thresholds, Limits. *Screen* (1982) 23 (2): 16–33.

Burghardt, G. M. (1998). The evolutionary origins of play revisited: lessons from turtles. M. Bekoff and J. Byers (eds.). Animal play. *Evolutionary, comparative and ecological perspectives*: 1–26. Cambridge. Cambridge University Press.

Byers, J. A. (1998). Biological effects of locomotor play: getting into shape or something more specific? In M. Bekoff and J. A. Byers (eds). Animal Play. *Evolutionary cooperative and ecological perspectives*. Cambridge. Cambridge University Press, pp. 205–220.

Caillois, R (1962). *Man, play and games*. London: Thames and Hudson.

Carter, B., Wilbanks, L., & Reese, D. D. (2009). Enhancing science education through instructional games that prepare students for knowledge acquisition. In I. W. Gibson, R. Weber, K. McFerrin, R. Carlsen, & D. A. Willis (Eds.), *Proceedings of Society for Information Technology and Teacher Education International Conference* 2009 (pp. 1410–1417). AACE: Chesapeake, VA.

Castells, M. (1996) *The Information Age: Economy, Society and Culture*. Volume I. The Rise of the Network Society. Oxford: Blackwell.

Castells, M. (1997) *The Information Age: Economy, Society and Culture*. Volume II. The Power of Identity. Oxford: Blackwell, 1997.

Castells, M. (1998) *The Information Age: Economy, Society and Culture*. Volume III. End of Millennium. Oxford: Blackwell.

Choi, B., & Baek, Y. (2011). Exploring factors of media characteristic influencing flow in learning through virtual worlds. *Computers & Education*, 57(4), 2382–2394.

Chudacoff, H. (2007) *Children at Play: An American History*. New York & London. New York University Press.

Coffield, F., Moseley, D., Hall, E. & Ecclestone, K. (2004) *Learning styles and pedagogy in post-16 learning: a systematic and critical review*. London: Learning and Skills Research Centre.

Cole, S.W., Yoo, D.J. & Knutson, B. (2012) Interactivity and Reward-Related Neural Activation during a Serious Videogame. *PLoS ONE* 7(3): e33909.

Collier, K.G. (1980). Peer-group learning in higher education: The development of higher order skills in *Studies in Higher Education* 5(1): 55–62.

Collis, B & Moonen, J. (2001). *Flexible Learning in a Digital Age: Experiences and Expectations*. London: Kogan Paul.

Colman, J. & Gnanayutham, P. (2012). Assistive technologies for brain-injured gamers. In: *Information Technology & Computer Science 8th Annual International Conference*, 21—24, May 2012, Athens, Greece.

Conole, G., de Laat, M., Dillon, T. & Darby, J. (2008). Disruptive technologies, pedagogical innovation: Whats new? Findings from an in-depth study of students use and perception of technology. *Computers & Education*, 50 (2): 511–524.

Kalantzis, M., & Cope, B. (2000). A multiliteracies pedagogy: A pedagogical supplement. *Multiliteracies: Literacy learning and the design of social futures*, 239–248.

Copier, M and Raessens, J (eds) (2003). *Level up: digital games research conference proceedings*. Utrecht: University of Utrecht, 48–53.

Coughlan, S. (2012). GCSEs replaced by 'English Bac' in key subjects. BBC News online on 17th September 2012. Last retrieved online on 28th December 2012 at: http://www.bbc.co.uk/news/education-19626663.

Crookall, D. (1995). *Debriefing: The key to learning from simulations/games*. Thousand Oaks. California. Sage Publications.

Csikszentmihalyi, M. (1992). *Flow. The psychology of happiness*. London. Rider.

Csikszentmihalyi, M. & Hunter, J. (2003) 'Happiness in Everyday Life: The Uses of Experience Sampling', in *Journal of Happiness Studies* 4: 186–199.

Cullen, K. W., Watson, K., Baranowski, T., Baranowski, J. H. & Zakeri, I. (2005). Squire's Quest: intervention changes occurred at lunch and snack meals. *Appetite*, 45, 148–51.

Deardorff, A. S., Moore, J. A., Borges, N. J., & Parmelee, D. X. (2010). Assessing First Year Medical Student Attitudes of Effectiveness of Team-Based Learning™. *Med Sci Educ*, 2, 67–72.

de Freitas, S. (2005) The paradox of choice and personalization in S. de Freitas & C. Yapp (eds) *Personalizing Learning in the 21st Century*. Stafford. Network Educational Press: 13–16.

de Freitas, S. (2006). Learning in Immersive Worlds. Bristol. Joint Information Systems Committee. See: www.jisc.ac.uk_eli_outcomes.html.

de Freitas, S. (forthcoming). *Freedom and Information: How Information is Changing in the Digital Age*. London and New York: Routledge.

de Freitas, S. & Jameson, J. (2012) *The e-Learning Reader*. London & New York: Continuum Press.

de Freitas, S., & Jarvis, S. (2009). Towards a development approach for serious games. Games-based learning advancements for multi-sensory human computer interfaces: Techniques and effective practices. *IGI Global*. Hershey, PA.

de Freitas, S. & Liarokapis, F. (2011) Serious Games: A New Paradigm for Education? In *Serious Games and Edutainment Applications*, Ma, M. et al. (eds.), 9–23, Springer: London UK

de Freitas, S. & Maharg, P. (Eds) (2011), *Digital Games and Learning*. London & New York. Continuum Press.

de Freitas, S. & Neumann, T. (2009). The use of 'exploratory learning' for supporting immersive learning in virtual environments. *Computers and Education*, 52(2): 343–352.

de Freitas, S. & Oliver, M. (2005). Does e-learning policy drive change in higher education? *Journal of Higher Education Policy and Management*, 27, (1): 81–95.

de Freitas, S. & Oliver, M. (2006) How can exploratory learning with games and simulations within the curriculum be most effectively evaluated? *Computers and Education*, 46 (2006) 249–264.

de Freitas, S., Oliver, M., Mee, A., & Mayes, T. (2008). The practitioner perspective on the modelling of pedagogy and practice. *Journal of Computer Assisted Learning*, 24(1), 26–38.

de Freitas, S., Rebolledo-Mendez, G., Liarokapis, F. Magoulas, G. & Poulovassilis A. (2010). Learning as immersive experiences: using the four dimensional framework for designing and evaluating immersive learning experiences in a virtual world. *British Journal of Educational Technology*, 41(1): 69–85.

de Freitas, S. & Routledge, H. (In press) Designing Leadership and Soft Skills in Educational Games: The e-Leadership and Soft Skills Educational Games Design Model (ELESS). *British Journal of Educational Technology*.

de Freitas, S., Savill-Smith, C. & Attewell, J. (2006). Computer games and simulations for adult learning: case studies from practice. London. Learning and Skills Research Centre.

de Freitas, S. & Yapp, C. (eds.) (2005). *Personalizing learning in the 21ˢᵗ century*. Stafford. Network Educational Press.

Delanghe, F. (2001). Validating small arms simulation. *Military Training and Simulation News*, 6: 31–34.

Department for Education web pages on the introduction of the English Baccalaurate (2012). See Department for Education Web site, last retrieved online on 28ᵗʰ December 2012 at: http://www.education.gov.uk/schools/teachingandlearning/qualifications/englishbac/a0075975/the-english-baccalaureate.

Dervin, B. (1983). *An overview of sense-making research: Concepts, methods, and results to date*. The Author.

Deterding, S., Sicart, M., Nacke, L., O'Hara, K. & Dixon, D. (2011). Gamification: using game-design elements in non-gaming contexts. In *Proceedings of the 2011 annual conference extended abstracts on Human factors in computing systems* (CHI EA '11). ACM, New York, NY, USA, 2425–2428.

Dewey, J. (1997). *Experience and education*. New York. Touchstone.

Dewey, J. (1991). *How we think*. Prometheus Books.

DeKoven, B. (2002). *The well-played game*. Lincoln, NE. Writers Club Press.

Dickey, M. D. (2011). Murder on Grimm Island: The design of a Game-Based Learning Environment. In S. de Freitas & P. Maharg (Eds) *Digital Games and Learning*. New York and London: Continuum Press: 129–151.

Druin, A. (2002). The Role of Children in the Design of New Technology. *Behaviour and Information Technology*, 21(1) 1–25.

Druin, A & Solomon, C. (1996) *Designing Multimedia Environments for Children: Computers, Creativity and Kids*. Hoboken: New Jersey. John Wiley & Sons.

Dunwell, I., Christmas, S & de Freitas, S. (2012) Code of Everand: Evaluation of the Game. London: Department of Transport. Last accessed online on 23rd March 2013 at: http://assets.dft.gov.uk/publications/think-research/code-of-everand-2011.pdf.

Dunwell, I., de Freitas, S., Jarvis, S. (2011) Four-dimensional consideration of feedback in serious games. In *Digital Games and Learning*, de Freitas, S. and Maharg, P., Eds., Continuum Publishing: 42–62.

Edelman, G. (1992). *Bright air, brilliant fire. On the matter of the mind*. London. Penguin.

Egenfeldt-Nielsen, S. (2005). *Beyond Edutainment: Exploring the Educational Potential of Computer Games*. IT-University Copenhagen.

European Commission Eurostat, (2012). Last retrieved online on 28ᵗʰ December 2012 at: http://epp.eurostat.ec.europa.eu/statistics_explained/index.php/Unemployment_statistics.

Facer, K., Joiner, R., Stanton, D., Reid, J., Hull, R. and Kirk, D. (2004), Savannah: mobile gaming and learning? *Journal of Computer Assisted Learning*, 20: 399–409.

Faria, A. J. (2001) The Changing Nature of Business Simulation/ Gaming Research: A Brief History. *Simulation & Gaming*, 32: 97–110.

Ford J. L. Junior (2009). Getting Started with Game Maker. Course Technology: Boston, MA, US: Cengage Learning.

Foucault, M. (1980). Edited by C. Gordon. Translated by C. Gordon, L. Marshall, J. Mepham, K. Soper. Power/Knowledge: Selected Interviews and Other Writings 1972–1977. Bury St Edmunds, Suffolk: The Harvester Press.

Francis, R. (2006a). Towards a pedagogy for game-based learning. Paper presented at JISC Online conference: Innovating with e-Learning 2006. 30th March. Available in Innovating e-Learning Practice—The proceedings of the

JISC Online Conference: Innovating e-Learning 2006. Cheltenham. Direct Learn Services Ltd. Last retrieved online on 11th June 2013 at: www.jisc.ac.uk/elp_conference06.html.

Francis, R. (2006b). *Revolution: Learning about history through situated role-play in a virtual environment.* Paper presented at the American Educational Research Association Conference, San Francisco, United States. April 2006.

Fransson, A. (1977), *On Qualitative Differences In Learning: IV—Effects of Intrinsic Motivation and Extrinsic Test Anxiety On Process and Outcome.* British Journal of Educational Psychology, 47: 244–257.

Frazer, J. G. (1991). *The golden bough: The classic study in magic and religion.* London and Basingstoke. Macmillan.

Fullerton, T. (2005). The play's the thing: Practicing play as community foundation and design technique. Proceedings of the International DiGRA Conference, June 16th—20th, 2005, Vancouver, British Columbia, Canada.

Gagné, R. M. (1970) *The conditions of learning.* (2nd ed.). Oxford: Holt, Rinehart & Winston.

Gallese V. (2001) The 'shared manifold' hypothesis. From mirror neurons to empathy. *Journal of Consciousness Studies*, Volume 8, Numbers 5–7, pp. 33–50(18).

Gallese, V. & Goldman, A., (1998) *Mirror neurons and the simulation theory of mind-reading, Trends in Cognitive Sciences*, Volume 2, Issue 12, Pages 493–501.

Gardner, P. (2005) Classroom Teachers and Educational Change, 1876–1996, in *The RoutledgeFalmer Reader in History of Education.* Ed. G. McCulloch. Oxford & New York: Routledge, pp 214–229.

Garris, R., Ahlers, R., & Driskell, J. E. (2002). Games, motivation, and learning: A research and practice model. *Simulation and gaming,* 33(4): 441–467.

Garrison, D. R., Anderson, T., & Archer, W. (2000). Critical inquiry in a text-based environment: computer conferencing in higher education. *The Internet and Higher Education,* 2(2–3), pp. 87–105.

Gee, J-P. (2003). *What Video Games Have to Teach Us About Learning and Literacy.* Basingstoke: Palgrave Macmillan.

Gennette, G. & Lewin, J. (1990) *Narrative Discourse Revisited.* New York, Cornell University Press.

Gerver, R. (2010) *Creating Tomorrow's Schools Today: Education—Our Children—Their Futures.* London & New York: Continuum Press.

Giang, M. T., Kafai, Y. B., Fields, D. A., & Searle, K. A. (2012). Social Interactions in Virtual Worlds: Patterns and Profiles of Tween Relationship Play. In *Computer Games and New Media Cultures* (pp. 543–555). Springer Netherlands.

Gibson, R. (2012). Encouraging Customer Co-creation Online: Why Money Doesn't Matter. *Design Management Review,* 23(1), 58–62.

Good, B. M. & Su, A. I. (2011) Games with a Scientific Purpose. In *Genome Biology,* 12: 135.

Graafland, M., Schraagen, J. M., & Schijven, M. P. (2012). Systematic review of serious games for medical education and surgical skills training. *British Journal of Surgery,* 99(10), 1322–1330.

Gray, P. (2011) The Decline of Play and the Rise of Psychopathology in Children and Adolescents. *American Journal of Play,* 3(4): 443–463.

Green, C.S. & Bavelier, D. (2003) 'Action video game modifies visual selective attention', *Nature,* Vol. 423, No. 6939, pp.534–537.

Green, C.S., Li, R., Bavelier, D. (2010) 'Perceptual Learning During Action Video Game Playing', *Topics in Cognitive Science,* Vol. 2, No. 2, pp.202–216.

Greene, J. A., Bolick, C. M., & Robertson, J. (2010). Fostering historical knowledge and thinking skills using hypermedia learning environments: The role of self-regulated learning. *Computers & Education,* 54(1), 230–243.

Greeno, J.G., Collins, A.M. & Resnick, L. (1996) Cognition and Learning. In D.C. Berliner & R.C. Calfee (Eds) *Handbook of Educational Psychology*, NY: Simon & Schuster Macmillan, 15–46.

Griffiths, M. (1999). Violent video games and aggression: a review of the literature. *Aggression and Violent Behaviour*, 4(2): 203–212.

Guha, M., Druin, A., Chipman, G., Fails, J., Simms, S. & Farber, A. (2004). Mixing ideas: a new technique for working with young children as design partners. In *Proceedings of the 2004 conference on Interaction design and children: building a community* (IDC '04). ACM, New York, NY, USA, 35–42 .

Harteveld, C. (2011) *Triadic Game Design: Balancing Reality, Meaning and Play*. London, Dordrecht, Heidelberg, New York: Springer.

Harteveld, C. (2012) *Making Sense of Virtual Risks: A Quasi-Experimental Investigation into Game-Based Training*. Doctoral Thesis. Delft University.

Harteveld, C., Guimarães, R., Mayer, I. S., & Bidarra, R. (2010). Balancing play, meaning and reality: The design philosophy of Levee Patroller. *Simulation & Gaming*, 41(3), 316–340.

Hays, R. T. (2005). The effectiveness of instructional games: A literature review and discussion (No. NAWCTSD-TR-2005-004). NAVAL AIR WARFARE CENTER TRAINING SYSTEMS DIV ORLANDO FL. Herz, J. C. (2001). Gaming the system; what higher education can learn from multiplayer online worlds. *Educause, Publications from the Forum for the Futureof Higher Education*. Last accessed 7th August 2006. URL: http://www.educause.edu/ir/library/pdf/ffpiu019.pdf.

Hill, C. (1991) *The World Turned Upside: Radical Ideas During the English Revolution*. London & New York: Penguin.

Hofferth, S. L., & Sandberg, J. F. (2001). Changes in American children's time, 1981–1997. Advances in Life Course Research, 6, 193–229, Jai Press (Imprint of Elsevier), Netherlands. .Hopkins, I. M., Gower, M. W., Perez, T. A., Smith, D. S., Amthor, F. R., Wimsatt, F. C. & Biasini, F. J. (2011) Avatar Assistant: Improving Social Skills in Students with an ASD Through a Computer-Based Intervention. Journal of Autism and Developmental Disorders 41(11): 1543–1555.

Horton, W. (2012) e-Learning by Design. San Francisco: John Wiley & Sons.

Howells, C., & Robertson, J. (2012). 9 Children as Game Designers. *Virtual Literacies: Interactive Spaces for Children and Young People*, 84, 142.

Huizinga, J (1980). *Homo ludens: a study of the play element in culture*. London: Routledge and Kegan Paul.

Iacovides, I., Aczel, J., Scanlon, E. & Woods, W. (2012) Investigating the relationships between informal learning and player involvement in digital games. In *Learning, Media and Technology* 37, (3): 321–327.

Inal, Y. & Bagiltay, K. (2007). Flow experiences of children in an interactive social game environment. *British Journal of Educational Technology*, 38(3): 455–464.

International Software Federation of Europe (2010). Video Gamers in Europe. ISFE Consumer Survey. Interactive Software Federation of Europe. Last retrieved online on 30th January 2013 at: http://www.isfe.eu/sites/isfe.eu/files/video_gamers_in_europe_2010.pdf.

Jarvis, S. & de Freitas, S. (2009). Evaluation of an Immersive Learning Programme to support Triage Training. *Proc. of the 1st IEEE International Conference in Games and Virtual Worlds for Serious Applications*, IEEE Computer Society, Coventry, UK, 23–24 March, 117–122

Jegers, K., & Wiberg, M. (2006). Pervasive gaming in the everyday world. *Pervasive Computing*, IEEE, 5(1), 78–85.

Jenkins, H., Camper, B., Chisholm, A., Grigsby, N., Klopfer, E., Osterweil, S. & Guan, T. C. (2009). *From serious games to serious gaming*. Edited by U. Ritterfeld, M. Cody & P. Vorderer. Serious Games: Mechanisms and Effects. Routledge, New York, 448–468.

Johansen, J. K. (2009). *The impact of OpenCourseWare on paid enrollment in distance learning courses* (Doctoral dissertation, Brigham Young University).

Jones, K. (1985) *Designing Your Own Simulations*. New York. Methuen Press.

Jung, J., Song, J. & Cho, Y. (2012). A Case Study on the Knowledge Construction of Learners through Participative Designing and Developing in a Game Making. In T. Amiel & B. Wilson (Eds.), *Proceedings of World Conference on Educational Multimedia, Hypermedia and Telecommunications 2012* (pp. 2004–2012). Chesapeake, VA: AACE.

Juul, J. (2003). The Game, the Player, the World: Looking for a Heart of Gameness. M. Copier and J. Raessens (eds). *Level up: Digital games research conference proceedings*. Utrecht. University of Utrecht: 30–45.

Kato, P. M., Cole, S. W., Bradlyn, A. S. & Pollock, B. H. (2008). A Video Game Improves Behavioral Outcomes in Adolescents and Young Adults With Cancer: A Randomized Trial. *Pediatrics*, 122, 305–317.

Kay, J. (2001). *Learner control. User Modeling and User-Adapted Interaction*, 11(1), 111–127.

Kelly, H., Howell, K., Glinert, E., Holding, L., Swain, C., Burrowbridge, A., & Roper, M. (2007). How to build serious games. *Communications of the ACM*, 50(7), 44–49.

Ketelhut, D. J. (2007). The impact of student self-efficacy on scientific inquiry skills: An exploratory investigation in River City, a multi-user virtual environment. *Journal of Science Education and Technology*, 16(1), 99–111.

Ketelhut, D. J., Nelson, B. C., Clarke, J., & Dede, C. (2010). A multi-user virtual environment for building and assessing higher order inquiry skills in science. *British Journal of Educational Technology*, 41(1), 56–68.

Kiili, K. (2005). Digital game-based learning: Towards an experiential gaming model. *The Internet and higher education*, 8(1), 13–24.

Kiili, K., de Freitas, S., Arnab, S., & Lainema, T. (2012). The Design Principles for Flow Experience in Educational Games. *Procedia Computer Science*, 15, 78–91.

Kitchen, A. (1999) The Changing Profile of Entrants to Mathematics at A Level and to Mathematical Subjects in *Higher Education in British Educational Research Journal* 25(1): 57–74.

Klasen, M., Weber, R., Kircher, T. T. J., Mathiak, K. A. & Mathiak, K. (2012) Neural contributions to flow experience during video game playing. *Social Cognitive and Affective Neuroscience* 7 (4): 485–495.

Knight, J., Carly, S., Tregunna, B., Jarvis, S., Smithies, R., de Freitas, S., Mackway-Jones, K. & Dunwell, I. (2010). Serious gaming technology in major incident triage training: A pragmatic controlled trial. *Resuscitation Journal* 81(9): 1174–9.

Kober, S. E., Kurzmann, J., & Neuper, C. (2012) 'Cortical correlate of spatial presence in 2D and 3D interactive virtual reality: An EEG study', *International Journal of Psychophysiology*, in press.

Kohler, E., Keysers, C., Umiltà, M. A., Fogassi, L., Gallese, V. & Rizzolatti, G. (2002) Hearing Sounds, Understanding Actions: Action Representation in Mirror Neurons. *Science* 297 (5582): 846–848.

Kolb, D. A. (1984). *Experiential Learning*. Englewood Cliffs.

Kolga, S. M., Hedman, L., Enochsson, L., Kjellin, A., & Felländer-Tsai, L. (2008). Transfer of systematic computer game training in surgical novices on performance in virtual reality image guided surgical simulators. *Studies in health technology and informatics*, 132, 210.

Krentz, A. (2004). Play and education in Plato's Republic. In Proceedings of the 20th World Congress of Philosophy, Philosophy of education, 1–7. Boston,

Massachusetts (August 10–16, 1998). See: http://www.bu.edu/wcp/Papers/Educ/EducKren.htm. Last accessed 11th February 2004.

Kukulska-Hulme, A. & Traxler, J. (2005) *Mobile learning: A Handbook for Educators and Trainers*. New York & London: Routledge.

Kuss, D.J. & Griffiths, M.D. (2012) Internet gaming addiction: A systematic review of empirical research. *International Journal of Mental Health and Addiction*, 10, 278–296.

Lane, G. (2003). Urban Tapestries: Wireless networking, public authoring and social knowledge. *Personal Ubiquitous Comput.* 7, 3–4 (July 2003), 169–175.

Laurillard, D. (2002). *Rethinking University Teaching: A conversational framework for the effective use of learning technologies* (2nd edition). London. Routledge Falmer.

Lave, J., & Wenger, E. (1991). *Situated learning: Legitimate peripheral participation*. Cambridge university press.

Liarokapis, F., Macan, L., Malone, G., Rebolledo-Mendez, G. & de Freitas, S. (2009). A Pervasive Augmented Reality Serious Game, *Proc. of the 1st IEEE International Conference in Games and Virtual Worlds for Serious Applications*, IEEE Computer Society, Coventry, UK, 23–24 March, 148–155.

Linden Lab. (2004). Second Life Officially Opens Digital World to College Students for Exploration and Study of Design and Social Communities. Retrieved October 1, 2008 from http://lindenlab.com/pressroom/releases/04_09_20 .

Linden Lab. (2008). Markus, T. A. (1993) *Buildings and Power: Freedom and Control in the Origin of Modern Building Types*. New York & London: Routledge.

Marsh, J. (2010), Young children's play in online virtual worlds. *Journal of Early Childhood Research* 8 (1): 23–39.

Mathiak, K. & Weber, R. (2006) Toward brain correlates of natural behavior: fMRI during violent video games. *Human Brain Mapping*, 27(12): 948–956.

Mayes, T., de Freitas, S. (2004). Review of e-learning theories, frameworks and models. JISC e-learning models study report. London. The Joint Information Systems Committee. See: http://www.jisc.ac.uk/elp_outcomes.html.

Mayes, T. & de Freitas, S. (2007). Learning and e-Learning: The role of theory. In H. Beetham & R. Sharpe (eds) *Rethinking pedagogy in the digital age*. London. Routledge, pp. 13–25.

McGonigal, J. (2011). *Reality is broken: Why games make us better and how they can change the world*. London: Penguin Press.

Mehm, F., Reuter, C., Göbel, S., & Steinmetz, R. (2012). Future Trends in Game Authoring Tools. Entertainment Computing—ICEC 2012. Lecture Notes in *Computer Science* Volume 7522, 2012, pp 536–541. Springer .

Meyer, J. H. & Land, R. (2005) Threshold concepts and troublesome knowledge (2): Epistemological considerations and a conceptual framework for teaching and learning. *Higher Education*, 49(3): 373–388

Milolidakis, G., Kimble, C., & Grenier, C. (2011). A Practice-Based Analysis of Social Interaction in a Massively Multiplayer Online Gaming Environment. In M. Cruz-Cunha, V. Varvalho, & P. Tavares (Eds.), Business, Technological, and Social Dimensions of Computer Games: Multidisciplinary Developments (pp. 32–48). Hershey, PA: Information Science Reference.

Mill, J-S. (1998) *John Stuart Mill: On Liberty*. Oxford: Oxford University Press.

Moggridge, B. (2010) *Designing Media*. Massachusetts: Massachusetts Institute of Technology Press.

Moreno-Ger, P., Burgos, D., Sierra, J. L., & Fernández-Manjón, B. (2008). Educational Game Design for Online Education. *Computers in Human Behavior*, 24(6), 2530–2540.

Mori, M. (1970). The uncanny valley. *Energy*, 7(4), 33–35.

National Advisory Committee on Creative and Cultural Education. (1999). All our futures: creativity, culture and education. London.

Negroponte, N. (1995) *Being Digital*. London: Hodder & Stoughton.

Nielsen, J. (2000) *Designing Web Usability: The Practice of Simplicity*. Indiana. New Riders Publishing.

Ninaus, M., Dunwell, I., de Freitas, S., Ott, M., Lim, T., Souchart, S. & Bellotti, F., (forthcoming) Assessing the efficacy of using neurophysiological methods for monitoring brain activity in serious games and virtual environments. A review of the literature. *International Journal of Technology Enhanced Learning*.

Oblinger, D. G. & Oblinger, J. L. (2005). Educating the Net Generation. *Educause*. Last retrieved online, 31st July 2006 at: http://www.educause.edu/content.asp?PAGE_ID=5989andbhcp=1

Ondrejka, C. (2004). Escaping the gilded cage: User created content and building the metaverse. *New York Law School Law Review*, 49, 81.

Ondrejka, C. (2008) "Education Unleashed: Participatory Culture, Education, and Innovation in Second Life." *The Ecology of Games: Connecting Youth, Games, and Learning*. Edited by Katie Salen. The John D. and Catherine T. MacArthur Foundation Series on Digital Media and Learning. Cambridge, MA: The MIT Press, 2008. 229–252 .

Ortega, R. (2003). Play, activity and thought. In D. Lytle (ed.) *Play and educational theory and practice*, 99–115. Westport. Connecticut. Greenwood Publishing.

Overmars, M. (2004) Teaching Computer Science through Game Design. *Computer*, 37(4): 81–83.

Paraskeva, F., Mysirlaki, S., & Papagianni, A. (2010). Multiplayer online games as educational tools: Facing new challenges in learning. *Computers & Education*, 54(2), 498–505.

Patall, E. A., Cooper, H.; Robinson, J. C. (2008) The effects of choice on intrinsic motivation and related outcomes: A meta-analysis of research findings. *Psychological Bulletin*, Vol 134(2): 270–300.

Pelletier, C. (2005) 'Studying games in school: a framework for media education', refereed paper published by the Digital Games Research Association, last accessed online on 11th June 2013 at: http://core.kmi.open.ac.uk/display/83099..

Pelletier, C. (2009) Games and Learning: What's the Connection? *International Journal of Learning and Media*, 1 (1): 83–101.

Peters, V. A. M. and Vissers, G. A. N. (2004). A Simple Classification Model for Debriefing Simulation Games. *Simulation and Gaming*, 35(1): 70–84 (2004).

Petridis, P., Dunwell, I., Arnab, S., de Freitas, S. (2011) Building Social Communities around Alternate Reality Games, *Proceedings of the 2011 Third International Conference on Games and Virtual Worlds for Serious Applications*. Pages 76–83. IEEE Computer Society Washington, DC, USA .

Piaget, J. (2007a). *The child's conception of the world*. Rowman & Littlefield Pub Incorporated.

Piaget, J (1999). *Play, dreams and imitation in childhood*. London: Routledge.

Piaget, J. (2007b). *The psychology of intelligence*. London & New York: Routledge.

Plato (1992). *The Republic*. London: Everyman.

Protopsaltis, A. Panzoli, D., Dunwell, I. & de Freitas, S. (2010). Repurposing Serious Games in Health Care Education, XII Mediterranean Conference on Medical and Biological Engineering and Computing, (MEDICON 2010), Chalkidiki, Greece, May 27–30, Springer, Heidelberg, *IFMBE Proceedings*, 29, pp. 963–966

Quinn, C. (2005) *Engaging Learning: Designing e-Learning Simulation Games*. San Francisco: Jon Wiley & Sons.

Rebolledo-Mendez, G., Dunwell, I., Martvnez-Miron, E.A., Vargas-Cerdan, M.D., de Freitas, S., Liarokapis, F. & Garcia-Gaona, A.R., (2009a) 'Assessing the Usability of a Brain-Computer Interface (BCI) that Detects Attention Levels in an Assessment Exercise', *Proceedings of the 13th International Conference on Human-Computer Interaction, Springer Lecture Notes In Computer Science*, San Diego, California, USA, 19–24 July.

Rebolledo-Mendez, G., Avramides, K., de Freitas, S. & Memarzia, K. (2009b). Societal impact of a Serious Game on raising public awareness: the case of FloodSim, in *Proceedings of the 2009 ACM SIGGRAPH Symposium on Video Games*. New Orleans, Louisiana, pp. 15–22.

Rice, J. (2007). Assessing higher order thinking in video games. *Journal of Technology and Teacher Education*, 15(1), 87–100.

Robertson, J., & Good, J. (2005). Children's narrative development through computer game authoring. *TechTrends*, 49(5), 43–59.

Robertson, J., & Howells, C. (2008). Computer game design: Opportunities for successful learning. *Computers & Education*, 50(2), 559–578.

Robinson, K. (2001). *Out of our minds. Learning to be creative.* Oxford. Capstone Publishing.

Rodgers, S. (2010) *Level Up: The Guide to Great Video Game Design.* Chichester, West Sussex: John Wiley & Sons.

Royal Society of Arts. (1999). *Opening Minds: education for the 21st century.* London.

Ruberg, B. (2006). Big reality: A chat with 'Big Game' designer Frank Lantz. Gamasutra, August 10th. Last retrieved online on 16th August 2006 at: http://gamasutra.com/features/20060810/ruberg_01.shtml.

Russell, T. L. (1999). No Significant Difference Phenomenon. *Educational Technology & Society*, 2, 3.

Ryan, M. L. (2001). *Narrative as virtual reality. Immersion and interactivity in literature and electronic media.* Baltimore and London. John Hopkins University Press.

Salen, K., Torres, R., Wolozin, L., Rufo-Tepper, R., & Shapiro, A. (2011). Quest to learn: Developing the school for digital kids. *The John D. and Catherine T. MacArthur Foundation Reports on Digital Media and Learning.* Cambridge, MA: The MIT Press.

Salen, K. & Zimmerman, E. (2004) *Rules of Play: Game Design Fundamentals.* Massachusetts, US: MIT Press.

San Chee, Y., Loke, S. K., & Tan, E. M. (2011). Learning as Becoming: Values, Identity, and Performance in the Enaction of Citizenship Education through Game Play. In R. Ferdig (Ed.), *Discoveries in Gaming and Computer-Mediated Simulations: New Interdisciplinary Applications* (pp. 128–146). Hershey, PA: Information Science Reference.

Sandal, M. J. (2009) *Justice: Whats's the Right Thing To Do?* London & New York: Penguin.

Savin-Baden, M. & Wilkie, K. (2006) *Problem-Based Learning Online.* Maidenhead: Open University.

Schell, J. (2008). *The Art of Game Design: A Book of Lenses.* Burlington, MA: Elsevier.

Scherer, R., Proll, M., Allison, B., & Muller-Putz, G. R. (2012, March). New input modalities for modern game design and virtual embodiment. In *Virtual Reality Workshops (VR), 2012 IEEE* (pp. 163–164). IEEE. Costa Mesa, CA, US.

Schmidt, H., Arend, A., Kokx, I. & Boon. L. (1994) Peer versus staff tutoring in problem-based learning, *Instructional Science*, 22 (4): 279–285.

Schneider, E., Wang, Y., & Yang, S. (2007, September). Exploring the uncanny valley with Japanese video game characters. In *Proceedings of DiGRA 2007 Conference*, pp. 546–549. Tokyo, Japan. SMU Press.

Schwabe, G., & Goth, C. (2005, November). Navigating and interacting indoors with a mobile learning game. In *Proceedings of the IEEE International Workshop on Wireless and Mobile Technologies in Education*. WMTE 2005. (pp. 8-pp). IEEE Computer Society Washington, DC, USA.Scott, R. (2001) Institutions and Organisations, London: Sage.

Selleck, R. J. (1972) *English Primary Education and the Progressives*. London: Routledge Kegan Paul.

Sharpe, R. & Beetham, H. (2007) *Rethinking Pedagogy for a Digital Age*. London & New York: Routledge.

Sharpe, R., Beetham, H. & de Freitas, S. (Eds) (2010), *Rethinking learning in the Digital Age*, London & New York: Routledge.

Shedroff, N. (2001) *Experience Design*. Indiana. New Riders Press.

Shute, V. J., & Torres, R. (2012). Where streams converge: Using evidence-centered design to assess Quest to Learn. In M. Mayrath, J. Clarke-Midura, & D. H. Robinson (Eds.). *Technology-based assessments for 21st Century skills: Theoretical and practical implications from modern research* (pp. 91–124). Charlotte, NC: Information Age Publishing.

Simon, B. (1991) *Education and the Social Order, 1940–1990*. London: Lawrence and Wishart.

Simons, R. J., Van der Linden, J., & Duffy, T. (2002). New learning: Three ways to learn in a new balance. In *New learning* (pp. 1–20). Springer Netherlands.

Singer, D. G., Singer, J. L., D'Agoustino, H. & DeLong, R. (2009) 'Children's Pastimes and Play in Sixteen Nations: Is Free-Play Declining?' in *American Journal of Play* 1: 283–312.

Slater, M & Wilbur, S. (1997) A Framework for Immersive Virtual Environments (FIVE)- Speculations on the role of presence in virtual environments. *Presence: Teleoperators and Virtual Environments* 6:66, 603–616.

Smith, R. (2010). The Long History of Gaming in Military Training. *Simulation & Gaming*, 41: 6–19.

Smithers, A., & Robinson, P. (2004). Teacher turnover, wastage and destinations. DfES Publications. Last retrieved online on 6th January 2013 at: https://nationalstrategies.standards.dcsf.gov.uk/publications/eOrderingDownload/RR553.pdf.

Staalduinen, J. P. v. & de Freitas, S. (2011). A game-based learning framework: Linking game design and learning outcomes. In: *Learning to Play: Exploring the Future of Education with Video Games*. M. S. Khyne (Ed.). New York, Peter Lang: 29–54.

Stam, R., Burgoyne, R. & Flitterman-Lewis, S. (1992) *New Vocabularies in Film Semiotics: Structuralism, Post-Structuralism and Beyond*. London & New York: Routledge.

Stephenson, N. (1994). *Snowcrash*. London. Penguin.

Szulborski, D. (2005). *This is not a game: A guide to alternate reality gaming*. New Fiction Publishing.

Ten Cate, O. & Durning, S. (2007) Peer teaching in medical education: twelve reasons to move from theory to practice, *Medical Teacher*, 29(6): 591–599.

Toups, Z. O., Kerne, A., Hamilton, W. A., & Shahzad, N. (2011, May). Zero-fidelity simulation of fire emergency response: improving team coordination learning. In *Proceedings of the SIGCHI Conference on Human Factors in Computing Systems* pp. 1959–1968. ACM New York, US.

Trilling, B. & Fadel, C. (2009) *21st century skills: learning for life in our times*. San Francisco, CA: Jossey-Bass.

Turner, V. (1987). 'Betwixt and between: The liminal period in rites of passage'. In L. Carus Mahdi, A. Foster & M. Little (eds). *Betwixt and Between: patterns of masculine and feminine initiation.* La Salle, Illinois: Open Court, pp. 3–19.

Turner, K. & Wolpert, D. H. (2004) *Collectives and the Design of Complex Systems.* New York: Springer.

Twenge, J. M. (2006) *Generation Me: Why Today's Young Americans Are More Confident, Assertive, Entitled—And More Miserable* Than Ever Before. New York: Simon and Schuster.

Twenge, J. M. & Foster, J. D. (2010) 'Birth Cohort Increases in Narcissistic Personality Traits Among American College Students, 1982–2006' in *Social Psychological and Personality Science* I: 99–106.

Twinning, P. (2007). *The schome-NAGTY Teen Second Life Pilot. Final Report.* Coventry: Becta.

Van Gennep, (1960). *The rites of passage.* Chicago. University of Chicago Press.

Van Looy, J., Courtoisa, C., De Vochta, M. & De Mareza, L. (2012) Player Identification in Online Games: Validation of a Scale for Measuring Identification in MMOGs. *Media Psychology,* 15 (2): 197–221.

Van Rooij, A.J.; Schoenmakers, T.M.; van den Eijnden, R.J.; van de Mheen, D. (2012) Videogame Addiction Test (VAT): Validity and psychometric characteristics. *Journal of Cyberpsychology, Behavior and Social Networking,* 15(9): 507–511.

Vasilyeva, E. (2007, March). Towards personalized feedback in educational computer games for children. In *Proceedings of the sixth conference on IASTED International Conference Web-Based Education-Volume 2* (pp. 597–602). Calgary, Canada: ACTA Press.

Veen, W. (2006). '2020 Visions Wim Veen's projections'. Paper presented at Online Educa in Berlin 2005.Last retrieved on 16th March 2006 at: http://www.global-learning.de/g-learn/downloads/veen_visions2020.pdf.

Veen, W. and Vrakking, B. (2006). *Homo Zappiens: Reshaping learning in the digital age.* London. Network Continuum Press.

Vygotsky, L. S. (1962) *Thought and Language.* Cambridge, Massachusetts: MIT Press.

Vygotsky, L. S. (1978) *Mind in Society: The Development of Higher Psychological Processes.* Edited by M. Cole, V. John-Steiner, S. Scribner & E. Souberman. London, England & Cambridge, Massachusetts: Harvard University Press.

Walsh, T. (2011) *Unlocking the Gates: How and Why Leading Universities Are Opening Up Access to Their Courses.* Princeton. Princeton University Press.

Warburton, S. (2009). Second Life in higher education: Assessing the potential for and the barriers to deploying virtual worlds in learning and teaching. *British Journal of Educational Technology,* 40(3), 414–426.

Warren, S. J., Dondlinger, M. J., McLeod, J., & Bigenho, C. (2012). Opening< i> The Door</i>: An evaluation of the efficacy of a problem-based learning game. *Computers & Education,* 58(1), 397–412.

Webster, F. (1995) *Theories of the Information Society.* London & New York: Routledge.

Wenger, E. (1998). *Communities of Practice: Learning, Meaning and Identity.* Cambridge. Cambridge University Press.

Wetsch, L. R. (2008) The "New" Virtual Consumer: Exploring the Experiences of New Users. *Journal of Virtual Worlds Research,* 1(2). Last retrieved online on 23rd October 2012 at: https://journals.tdl.org/jvwr/article/viewPDFInterstitial/361/273.

Whitmore, K. F. & Laurich, L. (2010) *What Happens in the Arcade Shouldn't Stay in the Arcade: Lessons for Classroom Design Language Arts,* 88 (1): 21–31

Willans, T. (2012). "Spatial Presence as a perceptual emotion: An expansion on cognitive feeling?" In *International Conference on Complex, Intelligent and Software Intensive Systems, 2012*. CISIS '12, 899–904. Palermo: IEEE.

Wittgenstein, L (1972). *The blue and brown books: preliminary studies for the 'philosophical investigations'*. Oxford: Basil Blackwell.

Woltering, V., Herrler, A., Spitzer, K., & Spreckelsen, C. (2009). Blended learning positively affects students' satisfaction and the role of the tutor in the problem-based learning process: results of a mixed-method evaluation. *Advances in health sciences education*, 14(5), 725–738.

Wong, W. L., Shen, C., Nocera, L., Carriazo, E., Tang, F., Bugga, S. & Ritterfeld, U. (2007, June). Serious video game effectiveness. In *Proceedings of the international conference on Advances in computer entertainment technology* (pp. 49–55). New York, USA: ACM.

Wood, D., Bruner, J. S., & Ross, G. (1976). The role of tutoring in problem solving. *Journal of Child Psychology and Psychiatry*, 17, 89–100.

Yee, N. (2003). Learning leadership skills. The Daedalus Project. Retrieved online, 27th July 2006 at: http://nickyee.com/daedalus/archives/000338.php.

Young, R. J. C. (1996) *Torn Halves: Political Conflict in Literary and Cultural Theory*. Manchester & New York: Manchester University Press.

Yukl, G. (1989) Managerial Leadership: A Review of Theory and Research. *Journal of Management*, 15 (2): 251–289.

Zagalo, N., Morgado, L., & Boa-Ventura, A. (2012). *Virtual Worlds and Metaverse Platforms: New Communication and Identity Paradigms*. Hersey, PA, US: Information Science Reference.

Zielke, M. A., Evans, M. J., Dufour, F., Christopher, T. V., Donahue, J. K., Johnson, P. & Flores, R. (2009). Serious games for immersive cultural training: Creating a living world. *Computer Graphics and Applications, IEEE*, 29(2), 49–60.

Index